THE

Life, Experience, and Correspondence

OF

WILLIAM BOWCOCK,

THE

LINCOLNSHIRE DRILLMAN;

Late Deacon of the Particular Baptist Church, assembling for Divine worship at Ebenezer Chapel, Liquorpond Street, Boston.

Written by Himself,

AND

PUBLISHED AFTER HIS DECEASE BY THE REQUEST OF A NUMEROUS CIRCLE OF CHRISTIAN FRIENDS.

LONDON:
PUBLISHED BY HOULSTON AND STONEMAN,
PATERNOSTER ROW.
G. J. & R. BANKS, 14, BERMONDSEY NEW ROAD.
———
1851.

ADVERTISEMENT.

The object which has prompted the publisher in presenting the following sheets to the public, is not filthy lucre, for a pecuniary loss is anticipated, and will be cheerfully met, in the hope of Zion's Deliverer being honoured, and some of the emancipated ones encouraged, instructed, and edified.

William Bowcock, or, as he was denominated, the Drill-Man, by which occupation he accumulated some considerable property, departed this life, May 4th, 1848, after enduring with Christian resignation and a good hope through grace, for nearly two years, that distressing malady, a cancer, one of the most painful and afflicting diseases to which the human frame is subject; and it also appears one of those diseases which defy the skill of medical men to check. Its ravages are fearful wherever it becomes seated. What a walking hospital the individual soon appears who is under its fearful dominion! What a gloom is cast over the future prospects of this world! Happy, thrice happy, is that individual who lives in communion with the God of grace, that when nature's breasts are dried up, he may find indeed that God is his all-sufficient one; he who gives out blessings richly, freely, abundantly, perpetually.

To witness the sufferings of the departed was heartrending. The feelings of some, who esteemed him as a brother, were so overcome as to deter them from visiting him, as they wished. God verified the truth of his word to him, "I will never leave you, I will never forsake you." Under paroxysms of grief, the Lord graciously broke in on his mind, frequently constraining him to exclaim it was good for him to be afflicted. The testimony he bore was soul-establishing, when tears were rolling down his disfigured countenance, through bodily anguish, expressions dropping from his lips of gratitude to God, for having blessed him with knowledge of faith in, and love to Jesus; for having led him into spiritual acquaintance with those heavenly mysteries which are soul-establishing, heart-cheering, devil-dethroning, world-overcoming, and God-glorifying. It was in the doings and dying of Jesus he sacredly enjoyed a sense of sins forgiven and heaven secured; this made visits to him profitable.

To behold him suffer was harrowing to natural feelings, but it was often a seminary of instruction, and a house of banquet. Gladly would I have avoided the scenery of woe, and gathered my repast in a more congenial path; but this was the road heaven ordained me to travel, and here he tutored me to reflect again and again on the love of that wonderful HIM who hated sin infinitely, immutably, and unceasingly; yet he took it on himself voluntarily, in all its guilt, filth, and degradation. Jesus did not merely look on our soul malady, and condemned condition; but he was made that which his holy soul abhorred, even sin, which he hated more than punishment. How soon we become weary of looking at a great sufferer, and gladly avoid the sight of an object in misery. Jesus was a man of like passions with ourselves, but free from any irregularity, for his were holy passions. He feared sufferings, hated iniquity, but loved his sinning brethren, and was resolved on saving. He endured voluntarily what he feared, and took on him what he hated Sin on him was the cause of all the dolorous woes, tears, and fears that he endured. He, as the Father's beloved, loving, and obedient son, feared the hidings of his father's face, and dreaded the infliction of his father's curse, for in these two consisted the principal part of the misery he endured in delivering his church from the curse of the law. It is in this mystery which the gospel exhibits, that the believer contemplates sufferings without being affrighted, and divine justice without being terrified; it is here we see divine rights vindicated, fault punished, and the faulty pardoned. Here Jehovah appears the friend of the vicious, and the foe of vice; here a pardon is enjoyed that elucidates the love of Christ, as matchless, causeless, measureless. Many waters could neither drown it, quench it, or cool it. In Christ's saving acts we behold his majesty, merit, mercy, and kindness.

O the undying praises which are due to this adorable Saviour! What ceaseless hallelujahs are the myriads of home-gone wearied travellers pouring out at his footstool, amongst whom is our departed brother; who, before he quitted this militant state, was sacredly prepared to unite with the church above, and blow in the ascription of praise, "Unto him that hath loved us and washed us from our sins in his own blood, and hath made us kings and priests unto God and his father, to him be glory and dominion for ever, and ever, Amen." What an unspeakable favour to be made a chorister in this supernatural choir! Truly, the repulsive language of the psalmist was the heartfelt sensibility of the departed, "Not unto us, O Lord, not unto us;" also the adversative particle, and the ascriptive declaration was what his heart responded to, "*But* unto thy name give glory, for thy mercy and for thy truth's sake."

May the Great Head of the Church, and the Saviour of his body, bless the perusal of these pages to the humble followers in his train, the substance of which was written by one who was thrust into the world, into menial servitude, at a very early age, without even having had the advantage of attending a village school. The Lord very mercifully led him, fed him, and instructed him, and has made it evident in the case of the departed, that none teach like the Lord, and truly it may be said, the Lord hath done great things for him, who being dead now speaketh, to the honour of Zion's deliverer. May it be useful to many of Zion's travellers, is the prayer of   THE PUBLISHER.

PREFACE.

Soon after it pleased the Lord to call me by his grace, and give me a feeling sense of my depravity and ruined condition, assisting me at the same time to cry unto him for mercy in the dear Redeemer's name, I began to write my thoughts and exercises of mind, sometimes in rhyme and sometimes in prose, folding up my scraps of paper when full, putting them carefully by, occasionally writing two or three pages at once, and then not so much in six months.

This course I pursued for many years, corresponding also with friends on religious subjects, retaining a copy for reference.

As some christian friends and correspondents expressed great pleasure in perusing over these papers, I have collected them together, transcribing them with some little alterations in this volume.

It will be seen that I am no grammarian, for schooling my parents were not able to afford me; but this affords me no grief, for natural attainments are not intended to be exhibited by my pen, but my desire is to set forth the rich reigning grace of God towards me the vilest of the vile, declaring what he hath done for my soul, in quickening, comforting, supporting, guiding, and preserving me these forty years in the wilderness. The Lord hath, in mercy to my poor soul, brought me off from all self-righteous dependencies, and enabled me to trust alone in the finished work of the glorious God-man for pardon and endless life. In a word, it is the Spirit of God in regeneration; the grace and good will of God manifested to his people in calling, teaching, and leading them, both in and by his word and providence; and the truth of God as made known in his holy word concerning his nature and perfections, his purposes and promises which he hath, in infinite mercy, made me acquainted with; these are the subjects I wish to set forth and promote among my christian friends for their edification.

Whosoever may peruse this manuscript, will have an opportunity of observing how gradually and graciously the Lord Jesus led me to see and mourn over my own awful condition as a law breaker, justly exposed to its awful denunciations, and to receive his truth in the love of it; uniting me with his Church; being baptised in his dear name; also the various exercises of my mind, the many ups and downs, the changes I have experienced in situations and circumstances; the connection in which I have stood with different societies of professing christians, the controversies I have had with different ministers and others, together with my meditatations, prayers, confessions, and thanksgivings; sometimes rejoicing in the Lord, at other seasons mourning his absence, occasionally full of joyful hope, expecting to be brought safely through all dangers and toils of the way; and through the riches of sovereign grace, possess the heavenly inheritance; and anon cast down under a sense of fresh contracted guilt, darkness and barrenness, and at this period to have no hope of seeing the blessed face of the once slaughtered Lamb; but through the reigning grace of my sin hating God, my present joys and future prospects of bliss are founded on the vicarious sufferings and perfected obedience of Jesus, the Son of God, which he accomplished according to covenant engagement, settled in ancient love on the behalf of elect sinners, before the world was made. May the precious blessing of the triune God of Israel attend the perusal of the following pages for his name sake, and thy soul's eternal welfare.

Dear reader, farewell.

W. BOWCOCK, DRILL-MAN.

THE LIFE, EXPERIENCE, AND CORRESPONDENCE

OF

WILLIAM BOWCOCK.

I was born January 6th, 1790, at Pinchbeck, in Lincolnshire. My parents, though industrious, were very poor, and could not afford their children any education; but my affectionate mother taught me and another brother and sister to read; being fond of books from my childhood, I took great delight in learning to read. My parents attended the preaching of the gospel, and my mind was impressed, in some measure, with eternal things. When about seven years of age, (about four years before my father died) my condition as a lost sinner appeared evident; that Jesus Christ came here to save such poor sinners as me excited my attention, and when hearing from the pulpit of the amazing love of God to poor sinners, in sending his dear Son into this world to save such vile and wretched sinners, and to inflict on him that punishment which was due to poor sinners like me; it often greatly affected me.

At the age of eleven years I went out to farmers' service, twelve miles from home. The family were profane, and here, alas, these early symptoms of godliness were nipped in the bud. Cursing and swearing was always in my ears; the worship of God disregarded; sin and wickedness abounded; the fear of God was not before their eyes. About the third sabbath after entering my place, I was full of uneasiness; to the barn my feet led me for retirement; the door I closed, and began to reflect on my altered position. Home now attracted my heart, that the house of God might be attended again; but here, alas, my new abode, Kirton End, there is none to go to. While pensive and sad in the barn, my new companions sought and found me sorrowing; their efforts were put forth to cheer me, saying I was mammy-sick; my poor soul became entangled, and I became a willing slave to sin.

Here I received the intelligence of my father's death, which produced some serious thoughts again; but like the early dew, they soon vanished. Not long after this the Lord laid his afflicting hand upon me and chastened me sore, but what was the feeling of my mind I do not now remember; but I recollect, to my shame, that after my recovery vain songs employed my lips, and like Lot's wife I looked back, and wished to be with my vain companions. After being at home with my widowed mother a considerable time, the parish was going to put me out a town apprentice, to be a drudge in a farm yard, without any remuneration until I had reached the age of twenty-one. This was a sore trial to my bereaved mother, but a widower, named R. Skerritt, who afterwards married my mother, took me for my food during winter. Here I can now see God indeed appeared for me in providence. In the spring of 1803 I went to service again, but among carnal people, at Swineshead; here the path of folly was pursued by me; but the next year I was removed to a dissenter's family in the same parish where I was born. Here was a door opened for me to attend the same meeting where my youthful feet had oft been in childhood to hear that venerable servant of the Lord, Isaac Woodward. The first time after so long an absence, I was so affected that I burst into tears, and was obliged to retire, not because the subject affected me, (for I do not remember what it was,) but it was a joy mingled with grief. Joy at seeing friends and relatives again in the house of God, uniting in his worship, and singing his worthy praises, which once was my delight; sorrow on reflecting how base my conduct had been.

Here I began to improve myself in reading and writing. During the winter evenings, myself and fellow servants united to buy candles and paper, our master gave us some instruction, and we used to write hymns and passages of scripture. At this time vice seemed amazingly checked; but alas, how soon are our feet turned away from rectitude; for the next year, 1805, my removal was into a large family where sin abounded, and alas, here I launched into sin deeper than ever, becoming a proficient in swearing. Ah, dear heart! a sight of my past conduct is truly grievous. Here I would remind my young reader how needful it is to keep good company, and parents should be careful as to the connexions their children form, for evil communications corrupt good manners.

But to proceed: the year 1806 ushered me into a new connexion at Postland. Here my master and mistress displayed great enmity to religion, but I had here to work much by myself, and many thoughts arose which produced great uneasiness, although the wicked habit of swearing continued. Frequently the terrors of hell took hold of me, so that the beasts and birds were enviable things to me; wishing at the same time that I had never been born. My perplexed mind was so full of dread that I trembled lest God should cut me down, and assign me my merited portion. Thus the Lord, who is rich in mercy, began to arouse my poor soul from that benighted and benumbed state into which I had sunk. Then was brought to my remembrance truths delivered in my ears years before, how that God sent his beloved Son to redeem poor sinners from the curse of the law, by his being made a curse for them. This caused me earnestly to wish that the Lord, in his providence, would deliver me from that place of sin and wickedness, and remove me to some religious family, that I might attend the means of grace, entreating him to enable me to seek after those things that accompany salvation, and that I might have an evidence, through his grace, that my sins were forgiven, which was of all things to me the most desirable; and blessed be the name of the Lord, he is ever more ready to hear than we are to pray. The following year, God, in his kind providence, directed my steps to Fleet, where I had great privileges, such as attending the means of grace both public and private, hearing and reading God's word, also free access to valuable books; and the Lord inclined my heart to receive the truth in the love of it.

The minister's name was Burgess, and the first text he preached on in my hearing was Psa. cxix. last verse, "I have gone astray like a lost sheep; Lord seek thy servant; for I do not forget thy commandments." It was truly applicable to my state, and I felt an increasing desire to attend the means of mercy, hoping the Lord would pardon my iniquity, and blot out my transgressions. The dear Redeemer, by his gracious teaching, caused the scales of ignorance to fall from my eyes; I had a sight and sense of my sin and misery, that I was constrained to say that of sinners I am chief, and that my heart was deceitful and desperately wicked; under the discovery I had of my vileness, my fears were that forgiveness would be for ever withholden from me. I could see no hope, and was ready to conclude the Lord will be favourable no more, his mercy is clean gone for ever. Under these sensibilities, I resolved to cease attending the house of God, but rather go and mingle with loose company, and get rid of my internal misery by mixing with the world. Oh, what a time of trouble and soul-darkness was this to me! but adored for ever be the name of the Lord, who prevented me by his grace, by his grace I say, and not my freewill, for I had scarcely resolved what to do than I was convicted that the only way to escape the wrath to come was to shun the road and society that leads there, for the wages of sin is death. Has not the Lord promised those that seek shall find? Does not Christ's blood cleanse from all sin? Is he not able to save to the uttermost? Under such thoughts as these, with many other scriptures, impressed on my poor tempest-tossed soul, instead of mingling with the wicked, I ventured once more to the house of God, with a who-can-tell? my heart uttering forth its longings for mercy.

"Wonders of grace to God belong,"

for I heard of him who is the chief among ten thousand, and felt him to be a suited Saviour to me in my forlorn condition. I heard that he was able to save to the uttermost all who had a desire to be saved by him, which was my case, and from that period down to the present I have been helped to hope in his precious name, and my prevailing desire has been to be interested in that glorious and complete salvation which Jesus the Lord hath wrought out for all his people. On a Lord's day the minister preached from Hab. ii. 3, "For the vision is yet for an appointed time, but at the end it shall speak, and not lie: though it tarry, wait for it; because it will surely come, it will not tarry." The Lord made it a time of refreshing to my soul. The dear man of God said that every one who was awakened to a sense of their lost estate, and was seeking to obtain mercy through Jesu's blood, that patiently waiting till the appointed time of the Lord, would issue in an answer to the desire of thy soul, even the forgiveness of all your sins, according to the riches of his grace. Truly my soul was put in a waiting posture; my hope blessedly fixed on the dear Lord Jesus for salvation and eternal life. The Lord opened my eyes to see how that his law extended to the secret thoughts of the heart. The internal depravity of my heart was discovered, and now the thoughts I had of some goodness being in the creature retired; the words of Jesus, recorded Matt. v 28, together with John's testimony, 1 Eph. iii. 15, and many similar scriptures, convinced me of my guiltiness to an extent that I had been unacquainted with before. I now feelingly declare my every act is dyed with sin; it cleaves to me, go where I may, or do what I will; reading my bible, prayer, confession, praise, or complaint; yea, my tears on account of sin are stained by sin. How we need washing in the blood of the sin-atoning lamb! These are humbling considerations. Where then is boasting? it is excluded.

Unclean and full of guilt and sin,
O Lord to thee I now begin
To lift my soul in humble prayer,
And thus salute thy gracious ear.
O condescend, thou God of love,
And see my lips begin to move
In humble prayer that thou would see,
And from my sins would set me free.
I humbly bow before thy throne,
And to my gracious God I own
How vile and sinful I have been.
Wilt thou forgive me every sin?
I plead not merit of my own,
For Lord thou know'st I am undone;
I've broken thy most holy laws,
And sinn'd against thy righteous cause.
What wicked oaths my lips have sworn!
How many sinful songs I've sung!
Went merry on the downward road,
That leads from happiness and God.
So hard was my deceitful heart,
That I could not from sin depart.
To vanity was prone and bent,
But still my mind was discontent.
Remorse about my conscience hung,
I knew that I was awfully wrong;
For when alone I often thought
That sin would bring me down to nought.

These thoughts did in such torrents flow,
That I knew not which way to go;
In bitterness of heart I sigh'd,
And sometimes to the Lord I cried.
That he in his good providence
Would from my station move me thence,
And fix me in some happy place,
Where I might hear and learn his grace.
And that he would dispose my heart
And make me choose the better part!
The Lord reveal'd his gracious will,
And my desires he did fulfil.
He brought me from that wretched place,
And fixed me where his gospel grace
Was preached, and then my heart inclined
To seek till I the Lord did find.
But O, my soul, adore his ways,
For ever praise the God of grace;
He all the work, from first to last,
Hath done, or else thou must be cast
In everlasting pain and shame,
Which was thy just desert for sin.
In sinful paths I persevered,
But God in mercy interfered;
Impressed my heart with my last end
I said my ways I will amend.
Instead of mending I grew worse,
And soon should brought on me the curse.
The more I strove to cease from sin,
The more defiled I was within.
But Jesus, blessed be his name,
From everlasting he's the same,
He saw me welt'ring in my blood,
And wand'ring further from my God.
But in the gospel he appears,
And said straightway dismiss thy fears
Ye that are labouring and oppressed
With all your sins, and can't find rest,
Come unto me, and you shall find
Refreshment for your weary mind.
Renounce thy own self-righteousness,
Put all thy trust in me for grace;
None ever trusted me in vain,
And still my promise is the same.
Come to the Lord by humble prayer,
Cast all thy confidence and care
On me. Fear not, I am the Lord,
And faithful to my holy word.
Thus did the joyful tidings sound
From Jesu's gospel all around;
But still my unbelieving heart
Was prone from Jesus to depart.
I saw myself so vile and base,
The worst of all the human race.
How can the Lord act righteously
To pardon such a wretch as me?
I scarcely could see any hope,
And now thought I, I must give up.
There's no salvation now for me,
I must go down to misery.
And as I did my follies mourn,
The Lord disposed my heart to turn.
Constant his earthly courts I trod,
My hopes hung hovering round his word;
Seeking for some kind promise there,
But still my mind was full of fear.
But Jesus did these fears remove,
And says, Poor sinner seek my love;
None that have sought can ever say
That they were empty sent away.
My power and love is still the same,
To bless my saints of meanest name.
Then, oh my soul come seek his face,
This kind encouragement embrace;
His promise is for ever sure,
And shall through endless years endure.
Christ is the ground of all my hope,
His promise bears my spirits up.
I'll seek salvation in his name,
Nor will he put my soul to shame.
My soul shall rest securely here,
In spite of every doubt and fear;
The time of life will soon be o'er,
When doubts and fears shall rise no more.
I do believe thy promise, Lord,
Help me to feed upon thy word;
Oh banish from me unbelief,
May I experience saving faith.
Oh fill my soul with heavenly love,
With light and comfort from above;
Make sinful thoughts from me depart,
Seal thy best image on my heart.
Whilst health and strength I do enjoy,
Let heavenly things my thoughts employ.
Still lead me through the paths of youth,
And guide me by the word of truth;
And if the Lord my soul hath lov'd,
O let me never be remov'd.
But may I still grow up in grace,
And walk in thy most holy ways;
From sin and Satan still defend,
Prepare me, Lord, for my last end;
And when my soul doth hence remov
Give me a mansion in thy love.
 April, 1809.

About this time my mind was greatly exercised respecting the doctrine of election, but like most free-willers, I tried to put away the doctrine, partly because my fears were that I was not elected, and that all my puny efforts would be unavailing in saving me, and partly because I thought if salvation was finished for all, then I might have a chance, so foolish and ignorant was I; but the word was powerfully felt, chosen in Christ before the foundation of the earth; that there is a remnant according to the election of grace. At this time I was, by the good providence of God, led to hear Mr. Crapps, of Spalding, whose testimony the Lord blessed to the establishment of my mind, and consolation of my heart. His text was Psa. cxxxviii. 8, "The Lord will perfect that which concerneth me: thy mercy, O Lord, endureth for ever: forsake not the works of thine own hands." The good man dilated on God's work in the heart of a poor sinner, showing it to be all of his grace, from first to last, that I was constrained to acknowledge salvation is all of grace. Electing love, ransoming blood, and invisible power appeared most conspicuous to my view, and cheerfully I exclaimed, all the praise is due to the God of grace. Plainly I saw, and now see, that none can open blind eyes but Christ; a dead man none can give life to but he who made all things. Jesus exclaimed, "No man can come to me except the Father which sent me draw him." Yea, the work of saving sinners I perceived from God's word is the Lord's, and who shall let or hinder? Isa. xliii. 13.

That there is an elect people is so manifest in the scriptures of truth, that a man must be wilfully perverse to deny the fact. When our dear Lord was warning his disciples of false prophets and teachers having gone out into the world, he says, "If it were possible, they would even deceive the very elect;" and when speaking of perilous times, he exclaims, "For the elect's sake these days shall be shortened." Peter addresses his epistle to the strangers scattered through the provinces, elect according to the foreknowledge of God. He also exhorts them to make their calling and election sure. Paul frequently speaks of the elect of God. With what holy triumph and exulting raptures does he speak when addressing the church at Rome!—"Who shall lay anything to the charge of God's elect? It is God that justifieth, who is he that condemneth? It is Christ that died, yea, rather that is risen again, and is at the right hand of God, who also maketh intercession for them." Then he challenges men and devils, with all their policy, cruelty, malice, and energy, to separate from the love of God, declaring we are more than conquerors, through him that hath loved us and washed us from our sins in his own blood. Such was the confidence of the great Apostle, and shall I, poor worm of the earth, deny or reject this great gospel truth? God forbid. Thus I mused on divine subjects for more than two years; sometimes like a reed shaken by the wind, at other times more settled in mind, but the question oft revolved in my mind, have I any comfortable hope that I am elected? This is an important question. My hopes are built alone on the perfect sacrifice which Jehovah Jesus presented when he offered himself a sacrifice, without spot, to God. On the atoning blood of the Lamb hangs my helpless soul. I know nothing short of Jesu's blood can cleanse my foul soul from pollution, and in him I put my trust; he is my only hope and chief joy. O my soul, cleave close to him, for it was Jesus alone, by his spirit and grace, that won thee over from the love of sin to love him. 'Twas thou, blessed Redeemer, that gave me new eyes, a new heart, and a new taste, to see, feel, and relish these supernatural mysteries of redeeming grace and dying love, so that I humbly say he chose me, or I had never chosen him; he loved me, or I had never loved him.

On the 10th of May, 1809, I attended a meeting of ministers held at Pinchbeck; the morning subject was Isa. xlix. 14—17. The minister spoke of the immutable love of God to his people. The afternoon was from Col. i. 19, showing the fulness of the Redeemer's love, grace, &c., as head over all things to the church. This was a blessed opportunity to my soul. On my return to Fleet, being then in servitude, I composed the following verses, on the association of ministers, held at Pinchbeck, 10th May, 1809.

Come, O my soul, and bless the Lord,
  For his almighty grace;
His power, his wisdom, and his love
  Endures from age to age.

Come, O my soul, adore his name,
  And speak his worthy praise,
Speak of the glorious Saviour's fame,
  As constant as thy days.

They spoke of God's eternal love,
  His sovereign power and grace,
Of Christ descending from above
  To save the human race.

He knows the people of his choice,
  With them are his delight;
Gives a foretaste of heavenly joys,
  And cheers their gloomy nights.

His church is graven on his hands,
  He can't forget his saints,
His eyes behold their several wants,
  He hears their sore complaints.

Christ is their head, how bright he
  shines!
  In him all fulness dwells;
His healing power, his love divine,
  And grace supplies them well.

See grace, and love, and mercy flow
  From God's eternal throne,
He guides and feeds his church below,
  And saves them through his Son.

Thrice happy is the church of God,
  How bright her glories shine;
Her garments washed in Jesu's blood
  Makes her appear divine.

O that I might enjoy a place
  Among the chosen seed,
With them partake of saving grace,
  And on my Saviour feed.

I long to know that I am thine,
  Beyond a doubtful case;
Witness dear Lord that thou art mine
  And thou shalt have the praise.

If through his sweet mercy my soul
  goes to heaven,
To Jesus alone all the glory be given,
My soul shall adore in sweet raptures
  of love,
And sing his loud praises with angels
  above.

At this period my mind was impressed with the ordinances of God's house, and I longed for the enjoyment of the privilege of uniting with the saints in church fellowship, and testifying to all around that I was a disciple of the meek and lowly Jesus. My mind was arrested with Jesu's words, "Whosoever is ashamed of me before men, of him will I be ashamed before my Father and before his holy angels; but whosoever confesseth me before men, him will I also confess before my Father and before his holy angels.

Under a conviction of these truths, in vain the sons of derision attempted to affect my mind. I was in soul earnest about personal salvation, and felt anxious to glorify Zion's deliverer. I was placed in providence where I regularly attended the general Baptist meeting house at Fleet. At this time I had embraced the sentiments called Calvinistic, believing that no man is capable of doing anything truly spiritual while he remains in an unregenerate state. Yet I loved many of the people with whom I worshipped, believing them to be God's saints; and God is my witness when I say I love all them that love the Lord Jesus Christ, and I resolved to make it manifest that the Lord Jesus had gained my affections and bound my hea.t fast, he having shed his love abroad in my heart by his Spirit. Having given up myself wholly to the Lord, it became my delight to obey his commands, uniting myself with his church, seeking further fellowship with him in his instituted ordinances; merit I was led to declaim, but the blessed salvation of the cross yielded me delight, and I felt it my privilege to serve the Lord Christ wholly, believing that whosoever is not fruitful in good works must be destitute of saving grace. I now embraced an opportunity of conversing with the minister on various subjects; our views differed much on some subjects, but on the whole he encouraged me, giving me some seasonable advice. I listened attentively, and thanked him for his kindness. Here let me give a word of advice to those who are sensible of their ruined state and are seeking after salvation, to converse with their minister and experienced Christians, unbosoming their minds on the subjects on which they wish to be instructed; private and social communion with saints on divine subjects, hath ofttimes refreshed me more than public preaching.

At this time a heavy gloom came over my mind, apprehending that some heavy calamity would overtake me, the following verses I penned:—

Should trouble come, and sore distress
  Bespeak my poverty,
I in a howling wilderness,
  And none to pity me—
If all my friends should turn my foes,
  And kindred drop and die;
My head would on thy breast repose,
  To soothe those sorrows dry.
Should sore afflictions press me down,
  And shake my feeble frame,
Support me still by thy right hand,
  My hope is in thy name.

Whene'er the Lord cause grief or pain
  It's always for our good.
Why should we murmur or complain
  No reason why we should.

It is a Father's chastening love
  And not an angry God;
O may I ever live to prove
  The sweetness of the rod.

Whilst his right hand my head sustains,
  I have no cause to fear;
Sweet pleasures mingle with the pains
  If Christ my Lord be there.

When Jesus dwelt in humble clay,
  Distress did him surround;
He had not where to lay his head,
  His sorrows did abound.

He bore what we could not endure,
  To save our souls from sin;
This thought should help our saddest hours,
  Make patience work within.

If this world's pleasures filled my heart,
  And troubles never come;
I should neglect the better part,
  And make this world my home.

Though pain and grief are not our choice,
  These are unwelcome guests.
Yet sure it is a warning voice,
  Seek ye my heavenly rest.

Throughout my life whate'er assails,
  Affliction or good health,
Whether I tread the hills or dales
  Of poverty or wealth—

I would devote myself to thee,
  And on thy care depend;
To thee in every trouble flee,
  My best, my only friend.

Be thou my guardian, dearest Lord,
  Throughout life's rugged road;
Lead by thy Spirit and thy word,
  Till I sit down with God.

Then I'll remember all the ways,
  The Lord hath led me through;
With love and joy adore his grace,
  And sing his praises too.

August, 1809.

Thus was my mind greatly exercised, sometimes hopeful, at other times sorrowful; anxious still to unite with his church, but my unworthiness distressed me

"If you tarry till you're better,
  You will never come at all."

Respecting the ordinance of believer's baptism by immersion, my mind was at a point concerning; the only wonder to me was, and is, how persons can remain blind to the subjects and mode. The example of Christ and the command of Christ, "He came straightway up out of the water," Matt. iii. 16; "Go ye into all the world, teach all nations, baptizing them in the name of the Father, and of the Son, and of the Holy Ghost, teaching them to observe all things, whatsoever I have commanded you." Why should John have selected Enon, where there was much water, if a bason full would answer the purpose? Paul commended the church at Corinth for keeping the ordinances as they were delivered, 1 Eph. xi. 2, but in this age the Baptists are spoken of derisively, for attending to God's positive commands.

My near relatives opposed me much, an uncle often burlesqued me, striving, if possible, to turn my young feet from keeping Christ's command. He was an avowed enemy to the Baptist cause, though a professor of the gospel. But thanks be to the Lord, who enabled me to weigh his arguments by the infallible standard, and all appeared lighter than down; and, taking God's word as my guide, I ventured, with great timidity and fear, to make application for membership, having had an interview with the minister, he advised me to give an account of the Lord's gracious dealings with me, which I did in writing. It was read over to the church, I was accepted as a candidate for baptism; a sense of my unworthiness of the privilege of uniting with his church pervaded my mind; but, blessed be the Lord, for he commendeth his love towards us in that while we were sinners, Christ died for us. Encouraged by the precious promises made to poor sinners, I ventured my eternal all into the hands of Jesus with a "Lord! save, or I perish."

A few days before I was baptised, I wrote a letter to my parents, informing them of the circumstance, and requesting their attendance; also, I requested them to shew my uncle the letter, as thereby they might perceive I was in earnest about my eternal well-being; and that my desire was to honour Christ by a cheerful subjection to his commands. The following is a copy of the letter sent to my parents:—

Fleet, October 16th, 1809.

DEAR FATHER AND MOTHER, &c.,

This comes with love to your souls, hoping it will find you all in health, as I am at present through mercy. I am about to inform you of a very important step which I am taking, and you will do well to give it a due consideration. The Lord hath opened the eyes of my understanding to see my lost, ruined state by sin, and hath enabled me by his grace to flee unto Jesus, and put my whole trust in him as my Saviour, my Redeemer, and my only hope, for without him I can do nothing, so weak, so helpless am I, that without him no spiritual act can be performed by me, but through Christ I can do all things. O what a privilege to have such an Almighty friend as the blessed Jesus, to whom I could repair in any time of need; he is my Prophet to teach, my Priest to atone, and my Prince to reign in and over me. Yea, he is the Captain of my salvation, I have enlisted under his banner; and through his grace, and in his name, I will set up my banner, and have turned my back upon the world, with all its maxims, charms, and concerns, to walk in the fear of the Lord, and in his ordinances; and amongst others I look upon Baptism to be an important one; I do not mean infant sprinkling, for that is not baptism, but an unscriptural ceremony, invented for secular purposes, by that Mother of Abominations, the Church of Rome.

We no where read in God's holy Word of an infant being baptized: but we have many instances of adult persons being baptized, and the New Testament is concise on the subject. I have confessed the precious Jesus to be my Captain, my King, and my all, feeling myself to be an insignificant subject of his; he has made it my delight to walk in his ways, for "Wisdom's ways are ways of pleasantness and all her paths are peace." And I hope to experience on the last Sabbath of this month the truth of the declaration; when I with several others, through the blessing of God hope to follow the Lord by being baptised in his name. I have written to apprise you of my intention. I hope you will let uncle and aunt S—— see this letter. Glad shall I be to see any of my young friends on the occasion. At nine o'clock, our worship commences; and if you think it worth your while to come and see, and hear, I hope the Lord may bless it to your soul. If you decline coming, my present step will preclude you from charging me with secrecy; through grace, I have not so learned Christ as to be ashamed of his cause. My Lord himself was immersed, and hath said, "He that confesseth me before men, him will I confess before my Father and his holy angels."

I am aware that I shall have to meet with much opposition, and not a little from near relatives; there is no doubt but my uncle will ridicule me, but what shall I say, surely the religion of Jesus opposes such a spirit; probably, my uncle will condemn me for not receiving his counsel when he conversed with me on the subject, and supplied me with a book to confute the doctrine of believers' immersion, the purport of which was, to prove infant sprinkling supplied the place of circumcision, and that it was a Scriptural ordinance, without bringing a single text of Scripture to prove it. Could the enemies to adult baptism supply one text to prove children were baptized by Christ or his apostles, that would suffice. I am convinced that if children were baptized, we should have some account given us of it in God's Word, for children are carefully mentioned in other cases when parties concurred. As for instance, when our adorable Emmanuel miraculously fed the multitude, they that were filled was about five thousand men; besides women and children. Matt. xiv. 20, 21. And again, it is said, they brought us on our way with our wives and children; Acts xxi. 5. No where do we read men, women and children were baptized; but in Acts viii. 12, we are informed that both men and women were baptized; and as to the mode, how evident it was by immersion, "They both went down into the water together, both Philip and the Eunuch;" Acts viii. 38. What go into the water to be sprinkled, would not the brink of the water have been sufficient, without going into it? "And when Jesus was baptized, he came up straightway out of the water;" Matt. iii. 16. How could that be, if he only went to the brink of Jordan, as you tell me? Let them rail as they will, the Scriptures are plain that believers were immersed in Jesu's name. Mother, do not say we have lost our son William, he is turned Baptist. Do you think I shall be excluded from the kingdom of God for departing from a practise so unscriptural as that which I was trained up in? My dear friends, so far is God from casting off his followers, that he hath said, "Them that honour me, I will honour." It is my honour to attend to the ordinances of the Great Head of the church. O that we may be stirred up to more diligence in seeking after those things that make for our endless peace! Remember there is balm in Gilead, there is a Physician there, able and willing to heal the most malignant disease of sin. Jesus takes no fee, and sends none away as incurable; for "his blood cleanseth from all sin." His invitation is, "O every one that thirsteth, come ye to the waters, and whosoever will, let him take of the water of life freely." But to conclude, I hope we shall not be separated in our affections, through a difference of opinion on these subjects, for if you and I have the happy privilege of calling God our Father, and Christ our Saviour, let us look forward to that blessed period when we shall meet with joy in our Father's house above, and all join in loud hallelujahs with the ransomed of the Lord, ascribing glory, honour, praise and blessing unto him that sitteth upon the throne, and to the Lamb for ever. I leave these things to your serious consideration, and remain,

Your affectionate son,   W. BOWCOCK.

This letter gave great offence to my uncle, but I am happy to say it did not break off all friendship between us, for since then, I have had much edifying conversation with him, which I shall have to notice in its proper place. My mother came sixteen miles to witness my subjection to God's ordinance, she had never witnessed the administration of the ordinance before, and expressed her satisfaction at what she saw and heard. For two years before I made application for membership, it is impossible to describe fully the exercises of my mind. I may say that sin and grace appeared to be like two mighty combatants within me, sighing for mastery; and alas! as I had then, so I still have to bemoan over an evil heart of unbelief, that is prone to depart from the living God. Sir, that cursed monster without, caused me to heave out many bitter sighs and cries to heaven for deliverance, saying in the bitterness of my soul, "O wretched man that I am, who shall deliver me from this body of sin and death." Rom. vii. 24. Notwithstanding these sensibilities, the Lord was pleased at seasons to favour me with joy and peace through believing, causing me to look unto him as my covenant God and Father in a precious Christ; God's promises at times, were made to me more precious than much fine gold, yea, sweeter also than the honey with the honeycomb, giving cheerful hopes of a blessed immortality.

Encouragement derived from the precious promises, composed a few days before the author was baptized, 1809.

Come, O my soul, adore the grace
Which brought me from those dangerous ways,
In which by sin thou fell.
That Saviour whom thou once defi'd,
Behold he loved thee, yea and died
To ransom thee from hell.

And now he calls thee to forsake
Thy sins, and on thy neck to take
  His yoke with sweet delight.
Come follow me, the Saviour cries;
Take up the cross, the shame despise;
  I'll make the burden light.

Now if you hear my sovereign voice,
Come make my holy ways your choice,
  And follow on to know,
Though tribulation and distress
May meet you in the way so fierce;
  Yet I will help you through.

Then, O my soul, fresh courage take,
Press forward still for Jesu's sake,
  Nor faint when troubles come;
Christ is thy friend, and will be still;
He'll guide thee safe to Zion's hill,
  Thrice happy happy home.

There shall we join the ransomed throng
Of saints and angels round the throne,
  To sing our Saviour's praise;
There shall we bask in beams of bliss,
And sing the Lord our righteousness,
  To everlasting days.

At length the day arrived in which I (with four others,) gave myself up unreservedly to the Lord of hosts, the God of Israel, in the solemn ordinance of baptism, and truly it was a happy day to my soul.

In the morning I arose with a thankful heart, praising his dear name who had done great things for me. I retired into the field, and there poured out my soul in ardent breathings to God, humbly imploring the Holy Comforter to assist me and my brethren to go through the solemnities of the day with a sweet sense of pardon and peace through the blood of the Lamb, and that his special blessing might rest upon the spectators.

At the hour appointed we assembled; with our pastor at our head we repaired to the water's edge, where our minister addressed a large assembly most appropriately. In the presence of all he implored God's blessing to rest on us, and that we might adorn the profession we were then publicly making. My soul was led out with him in earnest cry that it might be so. We then united in singing the 452nd hymn in Rippon's Selection: it was chosen by one of the candidates, and I found it soul-animating. We then, according to apostolic rule, both minister and candidates, went down into the water together, and he baptised us. The Lord caused me to say, from sensible manifestations, my cup runneth over.

I cannot reflect on these things without feeling the strongest emotions of gratitude and adoration unto him who pitied me in my condition, and snatched me as a brand from the burning.

> "My seeking thy face was all of thy grace,
> Thy mercy demands, and shall have all the praise."

Yes, blessed Jesus, it is thou that hath borne the heavy stroke of thy Father's vengeance, which was my due, and hath thereby effected my endless and honourable deliverance. Blessed be the name of Jehovah-Jesus for such matchless love.

Jesus having done such great things for a poor guilty youth like me, it is but my reasonable service and duty, yea, rather, let me say my great privilege to yield obedience to his holy commands; and all his disciples will assuredly find the truth of his word verified in their experience that in keeping his commandments there is great reward.

Oh that I might always enjoy a like sense of his cheering presence. But, alas, my corruptions, sin, and foolish thoughts pollute my joys, distress my soul, and occasion me to cry out unclean, unclean; were it not for the unchanging love and faithfulness of a covenant-keeping God, upon whom I am enabled to exercise faith, I should sit down in black despair at this moment, after twenty years profession. Blessed be his holy name, he will not desert the work of his own hands.

After the ordinance of baptism had been administered we attended public worship, and after singing and prayer, Mr. Burgess delivered an appropriate sermon on the occasion from Col. ii. 12, —" Buried with him in baptism, wherein ye are risen with him through the faith of the operation of God, who hath raised him from the dead." I found it instructing, encouraging, and truly edifying; for therein is the resurrection from the dead (which is the christian's source of hope and delight) plainly exhibited; also in this ordinance there is the emblem of a christian man's death unto sin, and resurrection to a newness of life; and our pastor plainly treated on the ordinance to our edification.

On the following sabbath we were received into full communion with the church; our minister alway addressing each member, laying his hand on them separately, and after thus addressing, gave us the right hand of fellowship. It was a time of love to my soul; the pardon of my sins, through a Ransomer's blood, was enjoyed sacredly. Would to God I was always in such a heavenly frame of mind; no worldly matters were allowed to intrude; sin was blessedly subdued; and I rejoiced in the favour of heaven " With joy unspeakable and full of glory." This was, I trust, an earnest and foretaste of that bliss which is hastening on, when I a wretch undone shall, through the merits of my dear Lord Jesus, sit down with the glorified saints to partake of the marriage supper of the Lamb, where we shall see his face in righteousness, live in the enjoyment of his smiles, and be employed in ceaseless praises with perfected songsters.

> "O glorious state! oh blest abode!
> We shall be near and like our God;
> Nor flesh nor sin no more control
> The sacred pleasures of the soul."

Such was my privileged state of mind in passing through the ordinance of baptism into a church state on the earth. Blessed be the Lord, many times since then he has favoured me in beholding this ordinance attended to; also sweetly hath the Lord led me into fellowship with himself at the table of commemoration, where my ruined condition has been viewed by the greatness of the loss Christ underwent for my recovery. Here I have reflected with profit on his ancient riches which he emptied himself of, and became poor, that we may be enriched; he became incarnate, voluntarily suffered, bled, and died to save rebellious worms from hell, which was my just desert. Come then, my soul, rejoice in thy privileges, and praise the Lord for such love and favour. Had not Jesus borne the curse due to me I must have sunk for ever. Had not Jesus revealed his great love to my soul I never had known it. My soul thankfully exclaims with that sweet singer in our British Israel,

> "Twas well, my soul, he died for thee,
> And shed his vital blood;
> Appeased stern justice on the tree,
> And then arose to God."

And there he ever liveth to make intercession for all who come to God by him. With such an Intercessor in view Paul exclaims to his believing brethren, "Let us draw near with a true heart in full assurance of faith, having our hearts sprinkled from an evil conscience, and our bodies washed with pure water." Heb. x. 22.

On one occasion my esteemed pastor preached from Col. iii. 11. On my return to my room I attempted some of my ideas to cast into rhyme, for it deserves not the name of poetry. In looking over them at this far distant period they refresh my mind, and bring to my remembrance former times, when the candle of the Lord shone upon my head, and his ordinances were most refreshing to my soul. How many barren seasons since then I have had to cry out, my leanness! my leanness!

VERSES ON "CHRIST ALL IN ALL:"
THE BELIEVER'S PORTION AND FELICITY.
(Col. iii. 11.)

Christ is all! oh glorious thought!
'Tis all we need, and all we want;
And all the comfort we possess
Springs from the fulness of his grace.

His grace is an unbounded store;
He fills the hungry, clothes the poor,
He loves the humble, contrite soul,
And makes the wounded spirit whole.

We broke the holy law of God,
And justice calls for sinner's blood;
All Adam's offerings guilty be,
And by the law are doomed to die.

In what a dreadful helpless case
Adam was plunged with all his race;
No power nor will to serve the Lord,
But still rebelled against his word.

Oh, wretched sinners! we are curst,
And we must own the sentence just;
The blessed Jesus took our part,
And pity moved his tender heart.

He laid his radiant glory by;
He came to dwell below the sky;
Fulfilled the law which we had broke,
Then for our sins was offered up.

To save us from the wrath of God
He offered up his precious blood:
See what a glorious sacrifice
To raise our souls above the skies.

Come now ye saints, and love the Lord
Who saves you by his holy word;
Redeems you from the dreadful fall,
And thus becomes your all in all.

Now let us join to praise his name;
Be this our comfort, joy and aim;
Sing and proclaim his wondrous grace
Who taught our souls to seek his face.

Jesus hath undertook our cause;
For us fulfilled the holy laws;
And wrought a robe of righteousness
For all who love and seek his face.

Though we are weak yet Christ is strong;
He is our portion and our song;
He'll guide us through life's rugged road,
And bring his followers home to God.

Come, then, poor guilty sinners, come,
In Jesu's arms there yet is room;
He'll feed your souls with heav'nly grace
And clothe you with his righteousness.

'Tis in this robe his church shall shine,
'Tis this that covers all her shame:
Our own is ragged righteousness,
But Jesu's robe is heaven's best dress.

Soon shall the important day arise;
Soon shall we mount the upper skies;
O may we in that robe appear,
Then shall we shine most brilliant there.

Pardon our sins, most dearest Lord;
We plead the merits of Christ's blood:
To thee we look, on thee we call,
'Tis Jesus is our all in all.
1809.

Soon after my association with the Church, I was called upon to exercise my gifts at the prayer meetings; unexpectedly our pastor called upon me to engage, and as I had never opened my mouth publicly to call on God, I trembled greatly and feared exceedingly; my heart was up unto God for help, and I made an attempt; thanks to the name of the Lord, I was not a stranger at a throne of grace; and he who had heard my cries in private, was now present to assist me in public; and God made it a refreshing time to me.

The hymn I gave out was 521 Dr. Rippon's selection, composed on the 9th verse of the 119th Psalm, "Wherewithal shall a young man cleanse his way?" By taking heed thereto according to thy word; it appeared most applicable to me.

I will just give the reader an account of my ignorance respecting the nature of God and the subject of prayer; the Lord may make it helpful to some poor ignorant broken-hearted sinner like myself, into whose hands my scribble may fall. The experience of the Lord's saints have been helpful to me, and the Lord can make helpful what I write to others; but this I leave to him, who worketh all things after the council of his own will. So truly ignorant was I on my first awakening, that I wondered how God, who dwelt in heaven so far distant as I was told, could see and hear what a feeble voice like mine uttered. It was declared to me that he filled heaven and earth: then my mind was exercised about the how, because not seeing or feeling him, opposed the idea according to my conception; for what substance can he be, neither for me to see or feel him? I was so foolish and brutish. That I was accountable to God, and guilty before him, I keenly felt; and O how I wished it were my privilege to pray, but how to ask I knew not! In trying, my breath seemed spent in the air. When the scriptures which said—"Come unto me all ye that labour and are heavy laden, and I will give you rest," were read by me, the perplexing thought was, "Where is Jesus Christ, that I may go to him and confess my sin?" And, although I often heard and read that we must approach unto him by faith, yet it was so perplexing to me to know how it was to be done; and much time and many sighs were heaved from my bosom before I could at all conceive of what faith was. But amidst all my confusion, that scripture aided me greatly, which saith, "He that cometh to God must believe that he is, and that he is the rewarder of all them that diligently seek him." The Lord, in a gradual way, brought me to see that faith is a full persuasion of the truth of God's word, produced by the operations of the Holy Ghost, with an attachment to the things of God revealed by the word: it is the gift of grace. I think it was more than a year after my soul was distressed on the account of sin, before I dare formally try to pray; for I could not tell if I had faith or not; and I read those words with a tender conscience, "Whatsoever is not of faith, is sin."

I have oft thought since that those desires were my best prayers; if there is such a thing as *best* proceeding from a heart like mine. My soul was now wearied under the burden of my sin and guilt; I longed sorely for deliverance. At this time, being engaged in rolling a piece of fallow ground, I stopped the mare, went behind the roller, kneeled down, and poured out my soul in some faint broken cries to the Lord Most High, that I might be washed from all sins in the precious blood of Christ; the Lord relieved my soul on the spot. I was as one who was cured of a deadly disease; I was as a condemned malefactor, who had received a pardon from his Prince; words cannot express the relief I found. In about another hour after, I had recourse to the same practice; and with a heart of thankfulness, I blessed and praised his name, for hearing my cries and relieving my soul. Then I came to an understanding of David's words, "When I kept silence, my bones waxed old through my roaring all the day long." I acknowledged my sin, and my iniquity have I not hid. I said, I will confess my transgressions unto the Lord, and thou forgavest the inquity of my sin. "Bless the Lord, O my soul!" great peace of mind have I oft enjoyed at the throne of grace, since that never-to-be-forgotten period; and I hope ever to enjoy the privilege of access to my Father's throne, through the propitiatory sacrifice which Christ offered when he offered himself without spot to God. Many, yea very many times, hath God refreshed my soul in those meetings, where saints assemble for social prayer. I can say, with thankfulness, it has been good for me to draw nigh to God, while I have heard others call such meetings legal, needless, and useless; to me they have been renewing and invigorating times. Thus, the Lord, who is rich in mercy, taught me, a guilty plough-boy, to call on his name: he heard me, and brought me up out of an horrible pit and out of the miry clay, and set my feet on a rock, and established my goings; putting a new song in my mouth, even praise unto our God.

Here I would record the goodness and mercy of God towards me, in providentially preserving me in most imminent dangers; the first instance was when but young, and which circumstance I well remember. On passing over a single plank bridge, leading over the Hammond-Beck, out of my father's yard, into Pinchbeck-Fen, I fell in; my mother coming in at the time, heard a splashing in the water, and looking instantly into the drain, she saw me struggling, she sprang to my assistance and rescued me. My parents had lost their first-born at the age of five years in a similar way, about half a mile from where I had met with a watery grave, but for the Lord's interposition.

At the age of eleven, I was thrown by a mare which I was riding, my head was dashed against a stone—was taken up apparently lifeless, but the Lord preserved me from the death which appeared inevitable.

Another remarkable deliverance from death was when about fifteen years of age; it was in winter, and at the village of Postland, where I lived as farmer's boy. I was driving three horses drawing manure on the land, we had to pass through a very bad gate-sted, up to the horses knees in soft dirt—a frost had hardened the top. By the horses stepping on it, it broke; they plunged—I lost all management of them, they came too much to the near side—pressed me between the gate-post and cart, either the shaft or the wheel, (for I was so alarmed as not to know which) pushed me into the dyke; I fell on the ice, which gave way; as I was falling backwards among the ice, the cart was coming rapidly, one wheel beside the gate-stead in the dyke where I lay, which, if providence had not prevented, would have covered me in a watery grave; but the wheel caught the tunnel end, and the hinder part of the cart the gate-post, and there it stuck so fast that the horses could not stir it, so I escaped. All the thoughts I had in my mind at the time was, that my end was come; and that it would be denominated a sad accident; not a thought about my eternal state crossed my mind.

These events transpired while I was in a carnal state. Had my poor soul been summoned by either of these dispensations to the judgment bar, I must have went justly where my sins had fitted me for, to the regions of endless misery! but he, who is infinitely, wise, ordered it otherwise. Oft since the Lord has called me by his grace, have I been led to say with one of old, "preserved in Jesus Christ and called;" and with holy David, "my times are in thy hands:" and again, "surely goodness and mercy hath followed me all my days." Since I have fled to Jesus for life and salvation, I experienced a remarkable deliverance from a perilous position in which I was placed. At this time my lot was cast among a family of Dissenters, members of the same church with me. In hay time, I was going for a load of hay with a pole waggon, two horses a breast and one in front; on my way I saw a boy coming with a wheelbarrow containing a dead sheep; my horses appeared to take no notice of the vehicle or its contents, until we almost came abreast of each other, when the first horse sprang from the middle of the road on the borders of a river; she ran a considerable distance, pulling the whole with her until we came to the Clow bridge, and then the whole was overturned into the river. The first horse's gears caught the bridge and kept it from the river; there was a woman in the waggon, who mercifully escaped unhurt. I was riding on the near side horse, and my left leg was pressed down under her side with my foot in the stirrup, (it was usual to have a saddle for the waggoner to ride on) almost to the bottom of the river, and some time elapsed before I could extricate myself from this perilous situation, so that I have here to record the Lord's mercy in delivering me from so great danger.

I felt overpowered with a sense of God's goodness at the time, and with adoring gratitude I praised him for his delivering mercy.

In various straits and difficulties, when there was no eye to pity, nor hand to help, then Jehovah stretched out his powerful arm to save. May the repeated instances of his kindness become inducements to love and trust him. He took me, and pitied me, guided and guarded me from my infant hour, and brought me up to manhood. He has enlightened my understanding, given me to feel the evil of sin, and to see the preciousness of Jesus, blessed me by the riches of his grace, put his fear in my heart. He that hath done such great things for me hath pledged himself to do more, yea, he hath declared he will perfect his own work. Blessed be God who giveth everlasting consolations, and a good hope through grace.

In the year 1811, I received an invitation to spend an evening with a few christian friends at Long Sutton, to commemorate a member's birthday. Previous to my going I penned the following verses:—

ON A FRIEND'S BIRTH-DAY, NAMED S. HILL.

Once more, my dear friends, we together are come,
But let us remember, this is not our home;
We're followers of Jesus, we're pilgrims still,
And trust we are travelling to fair Zion's hill.

Together we're come, a few moments to spend,
To keep the birth-day of our Sister and Friend;
But let us not keep it with vain idle mirth,
Lest we are cut off, in folly, by death.

But now, as at all times, with prayer and praise,
With thanks, and with joy, Ebenezer we'll raise;
To him, that first taught us to trust in his word;
And hope for salvation through Jesus's blood.

We all are poor sinners and cleave to this earth,
We wander'd from God, from the day of our birth;
But Jesus beheld the sad state we were in,
He lov'd us, and came to redeem us from sin.

He left the bright realms of his ancient abode;
Came down to this earth, taking on him our load,
Of sorrow and sin, putting it far away,
To save us poor captives as satan's foul prey.

Fear not then, believer, but trust in his name;
Remember the errand on which Jesus came;
To save us from dying, (his grace we receive,)
He finished salvation for them that believe.

Now, Jesus, salvation doth freely impart,
Let each of us closely examine our heart;
For all our pretended religion is vain,
Except we've an interest in him that was slain.

Written, June 23, 1811.

This year it pleased God in his all-wise providence to call away by death my respected master, Mr. Negus, in whose family I had formerly lived three years. The following verses I composed, with the passages of scripture annexed, and sent to the bereaved widow, which, she affirmed, proved very consoling to her under the trial.

ADDRESSED TO Mrs. PHŒBE NEGUS, ON THE DEATH OF HER HUSBAND,

Who departed this life, October 21st, 1811, aged 39 years.

Now, will you permit me, my dear Christian friend,
To write to you for this happy end; (*a*)
To comfort your down cast disconsolate soul!
Though death hath thee wounded, yet Christ makes thee whole.

The loss of a husband, so loving and kind,
A father so tender, is grievous you find;
We sympathize with thee in this heavy loss,
And the Christian, 'tis written, must take up his cross. (*b*)

But, why so dejected and given to grief? (*c*)
Apply thou to Jesus, he'll give thee relief:
His grace is sufficient, thy wants he'll supply, (*d*)
For he hears the young ravens and pities their cry. (*e*)

(*a*) Psalm xlii. 5.—"Why art thou cast down, O my soul? and why art disquieted in me? hope thou in God: for I shall yet praise him for the help of his countenance."

(*b*) Luke ix. 24.—"Whosoever doth not bear his cross, and come after me, cannot be my disciple."

(*c*) 2 Corinthians xii. 9.—"My grace is sufficient for thee: for my strength is made perfect in weakness."

(*d*) Philip iv. 19.—"My God shall supply all your need, according to his riches in glory, by Christ Jesus."

(*e*) Psalm cxlvii. 9—11.—"He giveth to the beast his food, and to the young ravens that cry."

If the fowls of the air, and the beasts of the field, (*f*)
Thus partake of his care, what proof doth this yield ;
How much more his people, for whom Jesus died ?
Though their grace he will prove, for their faith must be tried. (*g*)

Think not that thy Saviour deals hardly with thee,
For this is his will to his people we see :
To wean our affections from created good,
And take up our portion in Christ who is God. (*h*)

Then take up thy Bible, the Christian's delight,
'Twill aid and instruct thee, by day and by night :
Then read thou, with comfort, unto thy life's end,
That Christ is thy Husband, (*i*) thy Father, and Friend.   (*j*)

Whate'er be thy station the rest of thy days,
Be it thy endeavour to shew forth his praise ;
In pleasure and plenty, or sickness and pain ;
Yea, if death should attend thee, 'twill be for thy gain. (*k*)

And thus, as the stages of life pass away,
If close to thy Jesus, thou livest each day ;
He'll guide thee, (*l*) and guard thee, and bring thee safe through,
And grace make thee more than a conqueror too. (*m*)

And when thou art walking through Jordan's cold streams,
Then Christ will attend thee with his righteous beams ;(*n*)
He'll safely house you on yon happy shore,
Where sickness and sorrow, and death are no more. (*o*)

(*f*) Matthew vi. 26.—"Behold the fowls of the air : for they sow not, neither do they reap, nor gather into barns ; yet our heavenly Father feedeth them. Are ye not much better than they ?"

(*g*) 1 Peter i. 7.—"The trial of your faith is more precious than gold tried in the fire, that it might be found unto praise and honour and glory, at the appearing of Jesus Christ."

(*h*) Lam. iii. 24 ; Psalm xvi. 5 ; Psalm lxxiii. 26 ; Psalm cxlii. 5.—"The Lord is my portion, saith my soul ; therefore will I hope in him. The Lord is the portion of my inheritance, and of my cup : thou maintainest my lot. Thou art my refuge and portion in the land of the living."

(*i*) Isaiah liv. 5.—"Thy Maker is thy Husband."

(*j*) Jeremiah xlix. 11.—"Leave thy fatherless children, I will preserve them alive : and let thy widows trust in me."

(*k*) Read Psalm viii. 5 ; also Psalm cxlvi. 9.—"For me to live is Christ : to die is gain."

(*l*) Psalm lxxiii. 24.—"Thou shalt guide me with thy counsel, and afterward receive me to glory."

(*m*) Romans viii. 31. to the end.—"We are more than conquerors through him that loved us."

[*n*] Psalm xlviii. 14.—"For this God is our God for ever and ever ; and will be our guide, even unto death."

[*o*] Revelations vii. 16, 17.—"They shall hunger no more, neither shall they thirst any more ; neither shall the sun light on them, nor any heat, for the Lamb, which is in the midst of the throne shall feed them, and shall lead them unto living fountains of water ; and God shall wipe away all tears from their eyes."

Then, with holy rapture, thy soul shall partake
Of the glories which Jesus obtained for thy sake; (p)
Then join with thy kindred, who now are above,
And all the redeemed, in singing his love. (q)

'Till that happy moment, be it thy great care,
To be faithful (r) and patient, (s) and watch unto prayer; (t)
That when Jesus cometh thy soul to set free,
With peace and composure, his face thou mayest see. (u)

The following spring, when nature had dressed herself in beautiful green, and the plants and flowers were decorated in azure, scarlet, and gold, I wrote a few verses on Cant. ii. 11, 12, "For lo, the winter is past, the rain is over and gone; the flowers appear on the earth."

How pleasant is the cheerful spring
　To my admiring eyes;
I'll join the winged tribes to sing
　As they approach the skies.

The winter's fled; the rain is gone;
　The stormy winds are past;
All nature puts new beauties on,
　Forgets the nipping blast.

The trees and plants appear'd as dead,
　And 'twas a mournful scene;
But now the death-like sights are fled,
　They're clothed with living green.

The lark mounts up with cheerful voice,
　Salutes the rising morn;
The flocks and herds, and all rejoice,
　To tread the dewy lawn.

The cheerful sun makes haste to rise,
　With his refulgent ray;
And scatters light, which creatures prize,
　And makes a cheering day.

What life and vigour he imparts,
　To every living thing;
Refresh the looks, revives the heart,
　To hail the blooming spring.

The plants and flowers, woods and fields,
　A beauteous prospect shew;
They fruit and food and pleasure yield
　As they spring up and grow.

The face of nature doth rejoice;
　Rocks, hills, and vallies ring;
While every creature joins their voice
　To hail the cheerful spring.

Though nature's spring looks fine and gay,
　And soon fills me with delight;
Yet nature's spring will soon decay,
　And vanish out of sight.
PAUSE.
But thou, my soul, look forward still,
　And wait, and pray, and sing;
'Till thou shalt stand on Zion's hill,
　In everlasting spring.

[p] John xvii. 24.—"Father, I will, that they may behold my glory."

[q] Isaiah li. 11.—"The redeemed shall come with singing unto Zion."

[r] Revelations ii. 10.—"Be thou faithful unto death, and I will give thee a crown of life."

[s] Romans xii. 12.—"Patient in tribulation, instant in prayer, serving the Lord."

[t] 1 Peter iv. 7.—"Be ye therefore sober, and watch unto prayer."

[u] Luke ii. 29, 30.—"Lord! now lettest thou thy servant depart in peace, according to thy Word, for mine eyes have seen thy salvation."

The spring, I trust, is now begun
  In my immortal soul;
For Jesus saith the work is done,
  And he hath done the whole.

I, by my sin, lost all I had,
  My soul, and heaven and all!
But Jesus came, the lost he saved,
  He rais'd me from the fall.

He bore his Father's righteous ire,
  Which was my just desert,
To save my soul from endless fire,
  And endless life impart.

Thou art my glorious Sun, arise!
  Dismiss my winter's gloom;
Let graces spring below the skies,
  In heaven they'll ever bloom.

While in this wilderness below,
  Preserve thy plant from harm;
O make me fruitful, make me grow,
  Beneath thy heavenly warm!

And then, when death shall call me hence,
  My soul shall mount and sing,
Beyond the things of time and sense,
  In heaven's eternal spring.

There fruits and flowers ne'er decay;
  The Sun shall never shade;
New pleasures rising every day,
  No winter e'er invade.

There the bright Sun of righteousness
  Shall shed his beams abroad;
His saints and angels he will bless,
  While they adore their God.

Thus shall the heavenly mansions sound,
  With praises to the King;
And peace and joy run through the round,
  Of heaven's eternal spring.

Penned May 4th, 1812.

Thus have I endeavoured to give some brief account of my life and experience from my earliest remembrance up to the age of twenty-two; and at this time what cause have I to lament over my bad heart, and to acknowledge myself to be a guilty, hell-deserving sinner. Notwithstanding all my profession, how much coldness, indifference, and stupidity have I to mourn over! My backslidings pain me, and my anxieties about this world's baubles are a disgrace to me. My present condition exposes me to many temptations. Satan assaults me—the world allures—the creature entices—the love of money and fine clothes, which may be termed pride and covetousness, sadly molest me—but I feel myself possessed of a greater enemy than these, and that is my desperately wicked heart. Gracious Lord, exert thy power, and subdue my every lust and corruption; extend thy mercy, forgive all my sin, and let thy grace distil upon my heart, that I may adore believingly under felt depravity. O my soul, take courage for yet a little while, and all enemies shall be slain; the messenger death will minister to thy advantage, after his levelling hand has brought thee to the grave. Thou shalt then dwell with Jesus, see his face, and bless his delivering arm who hath redeemed thee from the curse of the law, being made a curse for thee. The resurrection morning will unite body and soul, fashioning me like unto the glorious Lord. Oh! the unknown felicities of that bright morning. Lord increase my faith, quicken my desires, animate my hopes, and meeten me for the heavenly inheritance.

This year my much esteemed pastor Mr. W. Burgess, was called to his promised and expected inheritance. The following letter I wrote on the occasion to a fellow member, named W.

Grey, who was baptised with me, and the others, by our late pastor on the last Sabbath in October, 1809:—

Pinchbeck, December 30, 1813.

MY CHRISTIAN BROTHER:—

I take up my pen to address you on the subject of our bereavement. Our pastor ceased to be a member of the visible church on earth Dec. 11, 1813, aged 59. I love the man, and lament his removal. He was my instructor and comforter; it was under his ministry I was exhorted to flee from the wrath to come, (I was convinced of my sinnership before I sat under him). It was he who pointed me as a lost sinner to Jesus the Lamb of God, who taketh away the sin of the world. To him I listened with attention and diligence. He shewed clearly in his ministry the depravity of man, the enmity of the human heart, the necessity of regeneration, or a new-birth state. He instructed me in the things which accompany salvation; he exhorted me to all that was excellent, and cautioned me against all that is wrong; he aimed at promoting holiness amongst us for present peace and future prosperity. Now, alas! my brother, for us who are left behind, we shall no more hear the gladdening sound of salvation from his joyful lips; his instructive tongue is laid silent in the grave! no more shall we hear his melodious voice in these earthly courts, as heretofore, sounding the high praises of the Lord of our life. No more shall we unite with him in fervent prayer for blessings on the church, the nation, the sick, and the sorrowful; his ardent petitions for the spread of the gospel, the conversion of the heathen, the increase of Zion's progeny, and for more labourers to be sent forth into the harvest. His ardent prayers are now exchanged for delightful praises in the presence of his adored Lord. How oft have we heard him directing poor broken-hearted penitents to the Lamb's redeeming blood; the feeble, the ignorant, the afflicted, and the fearful, what pains he took to advantage them by pouring forth the oil and wine of the consolations of the gospel of Christ into their wounded spirits. With the utmost propriety it may be said of him that "he rejoiced with those who did rejoice, and wept with those who wept."

His eyes are now dried; he is, I doubt not, in the high courts above, where all is bliss and blessedness; while we are here to lament his loss. But let us not mourn as those without hope, for if we believe that Jesus died and rose again, even so them also which sleep in Jesus will God bring with him. May it be our happiness to evince as much humility, patience, and resignation, under trials and losses, as he displayed.

As a preacher, we have lost an able man, and one whose love to the souls of sinners, was ardent: a friend, whose fixedness was admirable, a character, blameless. How few leave such a worthy character behind them; it might be said of him, he lived usefully, and died happy. His usefulness as a preacher, many can bear testimony to. One sermon which he preached from Habakkuk iii. 2, was so blessed to my soul, that while memory lasts, will not be forgotten.—I was labouring under great distress of mind, respecting my eternal state; but while he was elucidating the text, and speaking of God's faithfulness to his promise, my fears subsided, my hope in God through faith in Christ's atoning blood was increased and strengthened; it was a time of love to my soul, and much to be remembered; and I shall always have reason to bless the name of the Lord, who, in his providence, directed me under the sound of his voice. As his labours were useful, so his death was blissful; though oft afflicted, resignation to his righteous Father's will marked him. As he drew near to death, he exclaimed, "What a broad Rock I have got to rest upon." All his hopes were built upon Jesus Christ's atoning blood. O, my friend, may you and I be built upon this Almighty Rock, and all will be well; all other foundations are sand, and will let us sink into hell. At another time he said, "The blood of Jesus Christ cleanseth us from all sins; yes, from all sins." This had been one of his delightful topics; how oft had he announced this glorious truth to the comfort of many poor souls; and now he found it the solace of his own. O, may I experience this joyful truth through all my pilgrimage, and realize it in death, that the blood of Jesus Christ, God's Son, does cleanse from all sin. On his being asked if there was any passage of Scripture he would wish to be spoken from as a funeral text, he said, "Yes: 'My heart and my flesh faileth me, but God is the strength of my heart, and my portion for ever.'" Psalm lxxiii. 26. O, the privilege at such a period, when nature fails, for grace thus to send in her aid; that when the keepers of the house tremble, and the strong men bow themselves, and those that look out at the windows be darkened, and all the daughters of music are brought low, then to enjoy God as my only and satisfying portion, O, how desireable!

"I'm rich to all the intents of bliss,
If thou, O God, art mine."

He exhorted those around him not to weep for him; and presently he exclaimed, being the last word he uttered, "There is therefore now no condemnation to me, which am in Christ Jesus," and calmly breathed his last with such ease, that they who stood by could scarcely tell when he gave up the ghost. Such was the happy end of one of Zion's watchmen.

The loss of him is great, and will be keenly felt by this part of God's Israel. But let us not despair; the Lord is able to send us another tender shepherd who shall feed us with wisdom and understanding; let us be submissive under this stroke, and tremble while we acknowledge that "his way is in the whirlwind, and his paths past finding out;" for the righteous Judge of all the earth will do right. Be it our concern to shun the paths of vice, and to tread in the footsteps of the flock; taking the Scriptures of eternal truth for our guide, both in matters of faith and practice; and however we may be slighted by carnal men, yet we may confidently rely on the divine promise, for he will fulfil all the good pleasure of his will toward us, and the work of faith with power; that he will never forsake us, having said, "I give unto my sheep eternal life, and they shall never perish, neither shall any pluck them out of my hand." Blessed Jesus! help us to love thee for such precious promises to such vile sinners. Help us, O Lord, to adhere to thy truth, to rely on thy faithfulness, and to vindicate the great and glorious doctrines of thy gospel, which are so much despised. Now our pastor is removed, may we be heedful of grieving one another by froward speaking or acting; may we be kept steadfast in the faith, and never be ashamed of Christ and his gospel. And may we strive to comfort and edify each other, in the consideration that we shall soon have to give an account of the deeds done in the body; and then may it be our happiness, when on a dying bed, to repose our heads in Jesu's bosom, saying confidently, "The Lord is my Rock, Fortress, and High Tower;" and then be welcomed into that mansion of rest, prepared for all that love him, when we shall meet our under shepherd and beloved minister, with all the blood-bought family, to celebrate the high praises of the great Three-One for ever, and part no more.

W. BOWCOCK.

The following verses were written on the much lamented death of Mr. Burggs, of Fleet, my late pastor.

Death! 'tis an awful, solemn sound,
  When'er it greets the ear;
The tenderest feelings it will wound,
  And draw the briny tear.

Our nearest friends and kindred dear,
  When we are told they are dead;
With grief and anguish most severe,
  We say our joys are fled.

So when the faithful pastor dies,
  The church's loss is great;
With aching heart, and weeping eyes,
  She mourns her widow'd state.

He was the first that preach'd the word
  With comfort to my heart;
Directed me to seek the Lord,
  And from my sins depart.

He warn'd me of my lost estate;
  Bid me to Jesus fly;
Fly, for thy danger now is great,
  If in that state you die.

"Behold! the Lamb of God," he said,
  "He'll take away thy sin;
Come now, by faith, be not afraid!
  His blood can make thee clean."

Thus was his faithful preaching blest
  To my immortal soul:
But God, the Spirit, gave me rest,
  And Jesus made me whole.

He preached the doctrines of the cross,
  The ruins of the fall;
Repentance, faith, and holiness,
  He testified to all.

His feeling, sympathizing heart,
  Touch'd with such tenderness;
With the afflicted, bore a part,
  And sooth'd their sore distress.

What comfort did his tongue afford;
  What cheering words were given;
Refreshing pilgrims on the road,
  And rais'd their thoughts to heaven.

But now his work is done—he's gone
  To join the saints above,
Adoring stands before the throne,
  And sings redeeming love.

Now he beholds the wondrous plan,
  With pleasure to his eyes,
How Christ redeem'd poor fallen man,
  And raised him to the skies.

Now the deep mysteries of the Word,
  On which men can't agree,
Why some are sav'd and others lost,
  His eyes most clearly see.

With pleasing wonder now he views,
  Jehovah's great decrees,
In choosing some to endless life,
  Or not so, as he please.

There the grand doctrines brightest shine,
  Which some professors hate;
He loves with rapture all divine,
  Now in his happy state.

Jehovah's power, in all his ways,
  His justice, truth and love,
Affords him themes thro' endless days,
  In yon bright world above.

O may I meet the ransom'd throng,
  E'en all the chosen race;
There join with him who now is gone,
  To praise victorious grace.

In copying my productions seventeen years after they were written, I discovered many things that clash with my present views; but when I consider how young in the way I was at the time, there is not any cause for surprise. I thought it most prudent to transcribe them as they were, in my memorandums, that others who may read these pages, may observe with me and advance in scriptural knowledge.

1830.   W. BOWCOCK.

For several years before our pastor's death, there were many additions to the church; but as they were not all Israel who were of Israel, so neither are they all christians who take upon them the profession of christianity; notwithstanding, the church at Fleet enjoyed a large share of prosperity and peace among its members during his ministry amongst them. Having a member, whose profession was great, fallen into disreputable practice, the deacons waited on the person, in the hope of restoring her, but all was in vain. My friend W. Gray, and myself, had much conversation on the subject after I had visited the fallen sister, who was deaf to all expostulation; this led me into a correspondence with W. Gray on christian doctrines. The following are my letters to him.

FIRST LETTER.

Pinchbeck, April 11th, 1813.

CHRISTIAN BROTHER:—

I arose early this morning to write to you, out of esteem as a brother in Christ, seeking your eternal welfare. Let us remember, that whatever we do in the use of means, the power is the Lord's; for who can reclaim the back-slider or convert the sinner but God only? I appeal to your conscience. Do not indulge yourself in vain and foolish language, proclaiming this is Calvinistic, and therefore if we be elected we shall be saved, do what we will, and if not, we shall be condemned, do what we may; such expressions shew that the heart is not right with God. Did you ever know a work to be performed or any end to be accomplished without means? Is it possible for me to come to Fleet without means? Means and ends are connected; how would it sound, if, on my saying "to-morrow I shall be at Fleet," you were to arise and say, " then means to bring you there are excluded; for if you are to go, you will, and if not, what use is trying?" What absurdities some persons run into, through misunderstanding God's Word; for depend on it, if to heaven we are to go, God will set our faces that way, and we shall strive to enter into that straight gate. And where there is no desire, the heart is unrenewed by grace, and consequently, it is under the law, and exposed to the curse. And again, if we think to obtain heaven for our seeking, striving, desiring, or even by our repentance, we shall be equally dissapointed; for it is not to be obtained by merit, but it is the free gift of God; he puts a desire in the heart, having prepared of his goodness, a final home for all the blood-bought, adopted, and regenerate family. To these, he says, "Fear not, little flock, it is your Father's good pleasure to give you the kingdom." Nevertheless, God usually works by means, the Holy Ghost being the efficient cause of conversion, the Word and ordinances the instrumental. When the Spirit, Jehovah, sets in with the Word, then his arrows are sharp in the hearts of the King's enemies, whereby the people fall under him. Psalm xlv. 5. Therefore my brother, be diligent, zealous, and stedfast in the work of the Lord, both by reproof and example, that ye may glorify God in your day and generation. Pray also for me; I am a young man prone to vanity, that you well know. I am in the midst of snares, and carry about with me a deceitful heart. Many lusts that war against my soul, numerous spiritual foes, trials, and difficulties meet me constantly; I have duties to perform, and graces to exercise. O, how shall such a weak, ignorant, trifling sinner as I am, ever be able to encounter all the deadly enemies of my soul? Yea, how shall I stand my ground in times of temptations, unless the Lord uphold me? But though the pathway to heaven is obstructed by many enemies, the grace of God is all-sufficient. O, the grace of God is a delightful theme to a heaven-bound traveller. Grace first contrived the way of saving sinners, grace brings sinners in the way, strengthens them on their journey, and crowns them at last with immortal glory.

> "The grace of God has been my theme,
> And shall be till I die."

I remain yours in the bonds of the gospel,

W. BOWCOCK.

SECOND LETTER TO THE SAME.

Pinchbeck, September, 2nd, 1813.

MY CHRISTIAN BROTHER,

I have been prevented writing so soon as I wished, through my labour. Truly grievous it is to witness poor Lucy's departure from religious things, with all their advantages, to embrace vice, with all its miseries. How awfully is that Scripture fulfilled in her, which saith "The sow that was washed is turned to her wallowing in the mire." 2 Peter ii. 22. And I fear a sow she was, and a sow she remained; washing does not change the nature of an animal; now if the sow then spoken of, was changed into a lamb, I'll venture to say, wallowing in the mire would be impossible. This brings me, my brother, to the Scripture sentiment my soul has embraced the belief of, which truth yields me solid peace, and I live in a cheerful hope towards God through our Lord Jesus Christ. On this point, I am certain that nothing less than a change of heart which is effected only by the gracious operations of the Eternal Spirit can fit a person to serve God acceptably, and meeten a soul for the kingdom of Christ. Yes, there must be a new creation. 2 Cor. v. 17; Eph. ii. 10. For as we by nature since the fall, are born in sin and shapen in iniquity, Psalm li. 5; so to become the subjects of divine grace, we must be created anew in Christ Jesus; we must be born again. John iii. 35. We must be brought out of nature's darkness into God's marvellous light, and from under the power and dominion of sin and satan, and translated into the kingdom of God's dear Son.

Now who can create the heart of a sinner anew but God only. O my brother, let us carefully examine our ownselves, whether we know any thing of the new creature, for if our hearts are not right towards God, externals will avail nothing in the day of trial. Are spiritual things engaging our affections? Is Christ, his person, work and sacrifice dear to us? If not, our profession is vain and delusive. Or if we are seeking acceptance with God by our religious performances, either reading, hearing, praying, repenting, or believing, this is self-righteousness and loathsome in the sight of God. Self-righteous hypocrites are in a worse state before God than the openly profane, because they deceive themselves and others; but let us remember that the heart-searching God is not deceived; such persons also dispose the free grace of God as displayed in election, regeneration, imputation of Christ's righteousness for their justification. Read Romans iv. and v. They think to be accepted and justified before God by their good works, obedience, and observance of religious duties. They say they do what they can, and Christ will make up their deficiencies by his grace; so the dear Jesus is esteemed by them at best only as a partial Saviour. He, say they, hath obtained salvation in part by his sufferings, and they merit it in part by religious duties; they are resolved not to know him as being the author and sole cause of salvation; they cannot brook to the principle that he who hath ordained peace for us, hath wrought all our works in us, and the work of faith with power. No, no, this would be putting too much honor on him, and dishonouring themselves; they contend, that God saves sinners for some good things done by them, thus they are building on a sandy foundation which will assuredly be swept away.

My Christian brother, such characters as this abound in every neighbourhood; our Lord pronounces heavy woes against such in Matt. xxiii; may it be our privilege to trust in, and rely exclusively on, the atoning sacrifice of the Lamb of God, for pardon and endless life.

Your letter surprises me; how unscriptural and opposed to experience is it on your part to think and say that dark, ignorant, rebellious sinners, full of sin and iniquity, haters of God and holiness, that these should do any thing toward turning themselves from the love of sin to love God; my mind is grieved by you, there are so many contradictions to your own statements, when your epistle is compared. A power given to all men, which you affirm God gives, is so at variance with Scripture, where we find it affirmed that God's people shall be made willing in the day of His power. "He giveth power also to the faint, and to them that have no might he increaseth strength;" that is to those who are fainting and panting after the salvation of God; but does the presumptuous sinner, faint and pant after Christ and his great salvation? How is it possible for a carnal man to love spiritual things? For instance, how can you my brother, enjoy the truth as it is in Jesus, find delight in his worship, take delight in the communion of saints, as I trust you do, and after all welcome the company of the wicked, join them in their mockings and blasphemy against God and his Christ? Are not these things revolting to your feelings as a Christian man? but not more so than the things of God are to a natural man. I am certain that it would cause as much pain to an unregenerate man to be in company with the people of God a few hours, provided their conversation was on spiritual subjects, as it would be to a spiritual-minded man to be set down for a few hours where the conversation of the unregenerate ran on the subject of what his depraved nature takes delight in. I pray you, my brother, consider the contrast seriously, and ask yourself this important question, "Who maketh thee to differ?" The Apostle calls up the attention of the believing Corinthians, to the reigning grace that had distinguished them, for saith he, (when speaking of the ungodly,) "And such were some of you, but ye are washed, but ye are sanctified, but ye are justified in the name of the Lord Jesus, and by the Spirit of our God." A new creation is absolutely necessary before a man can act spiritually. "Ye must be born again, and without holiness no man can see the Lord."

And will you continue to affirm that this power, which you say is given to every man, is that by which the soul is regenerated and born of God; for if it be so, then they are heirs of God, and joint heirs with Christ; and in their hearts there is a prevailing desire to partake of his salvation, notwithstanding the workings of inbred corruptions; and the promise is, he will give the desire of their heart. Jesus hath assured us that "they who hunger and thirst after righteousness shall be filled." Let us not forget "God is a Rock, and his work is perfect." Creation and providence declare God's work to be perfect; but in the redemption, justification, new creation, and glorification of a poor, guilty, filthy, helpless, lost sinner—how gloriously doth it appear that Jehovah is a complete deliverer.

Hath our heavenly Father sent his only Son, who is one with him and one with us, into this world of woe, to save sinners? Did Jesus lay aside his glory—empty himself of his riches—become poor—take upon himself the form of a servant, enduring cruel mockings, scourgings, shame and reproach, and at last died a lingering, painful and shameful death on the cross, not for himself, for "he did no sin, neither was guile found in his mouth;" "he died, the just for the unjust, that he might bring us to God?" 1 Peter iii. 18. Bring who to God? The Apostle says us, "even us whom he hath called both Jews and Gentiles." Even all the election of grace. It was for them he shed his precious blood, to atone for their transgressions; and shall the dear Jesus shed his blood for nought? Shall he lay down his life as the price of redemption, and not have the objects of his love and purchase? Will he perform the suffering part, and not go on with the renewing and converting part, for it is equally impossible for man to quicken his own soul, as it is to redeem and justify himself. Christ is a complete Saviour. It is the Lord who begins a good work of grace in the heart; and Paul affirms with holy confidence, the fact that "He which hath begun a good work in you, will perform it until the day of Jesus Christ." Phil. i. 6. No sinner however obstinate, is able to withstand Jehovah's grace. A persecuting soul is constrained to bow at the feet of Jesus and seek mercy of him whom he had persecuted. A Magdalene when touched by divine grace, is found at the feet of Jesus with tears of repentance. So will Jesus ride forth in the gospel chariot by his Spirit, accompanying his truth with power to the hearts of all the adopted, loved, and redeemed people, finally bringing home the top stone to the spiritual temple, crying grace, grace unto it.

You talk about men having power to repent, and again you say, they have not power. Allow me to ask you, my brother, is not the whole bent of the human will, the whole inclinations and desires of the unregenerate heart to conceive and practise iniquity?

And certain it is, God the Holy Ghost can alone rescue the sinner from this awful state, by communicating life to the soul, and light to the understanding, when a sense of pollution, depravity, and carnality causes the man to cry out, "O wretched man that I am, who shall deliver me from this body of sin and death." Mercy is then sought after in good earnest, this fits the poor creature to prize the dear Jesus in all his saving offices, his pardoning mercy, precious blood, and justifying obedience; now he flees to Jesus as his all-sufficient shelter, and cleaves to him as a complete Saviour, saying

> "I trust my whole salvation here,
> Nor shall I suffer shame."

You appear to indulge in hard thoughts against God's eternal purposes in Christ Jesus, in the salvation of his church; should the Lord shed abroad his matchless, measureless and ceaseless love in your heart, it will prove an effectual cure to such daring infidelity. I would never cease loving and praising his dear name for such causeless favour towards my poor soul, entreating him to favour me with further discoveries of that grace by which we are delivered from merited punishment, causing us to make our boast in the Lord, renouncing all confidence in the flesh.

Read this over attentively, and where you see I err, endeavour to correct me by the Word of God, and when you speak or write on these important subjects, do so faithfully, freely, and fearlessly; examine God's book, and may the inspiring Spirit give you and me a spiritual perception of the truth as it is in Jesus.

I remain your affectionate brother in Christ Jesus.

W. B., *Drillman*.

(*Receiving no reply to the foregoing letter our correspondence closed.*)

In the year 1814, I wrote my views of the doctrines of grace; it is sixteen years since I penned, what I called, my articles of belief; and at this time, while I am transcribing them, I see no reason to expunge or renounce any part thereof; but I have made some additions thereto, having been led into fellowship with truths which, at that time, I was ignorant of; especially the antiquity and glory of the Lord Jesus Christ as the complex person, by whom the purposes of the Eternal were to be carried out to their glorious accomplishment. This is that mysterious Him, God and man in one Christ, who has effected our complete salvation, according to the stipulations of that covenant into which he entered with the Father, on the behalf of God's chosen before this world was made by him. It was his divine nature which gave worth to the sacrifice which he offered when he gave himself a sacrifice for sin. The covenant of redemption rendered it necessary that the Agent, on whom the conditions rested to be accomplished, should be a complex individual. The Lord Jesus stood forth as Zion's representative in covenant relationship; but abstract Deity could never represent creatures: our Lord Jesus, the anointed Christ, represented his church in a sameness of nature from the beginning. The apostle affirms him to be Jesus Christ, the same yesterday and for ever; the same in the beginning as in the days of his incarnation; (his body excepted, which is not essential to his complex personality,) and he will ever remain the same glorious Emanuel, the all-competent, anointed, and appointed Saviour, the one glorious High Priest, Prophet, and Prince of his people. My views of truth have exposed me to reproach, many epithets have been applied to me; they have left me as they found me, a lover of free grace, an adorer at Jesu's footstool, and a confider in his perfect work; and my prayer is, that I may walk in the light of his countenance, enjoying a sense of his love; under the sacred guidance of the infallible spirit I am hoping to be led, strengthened and cheered on my homeward course to my heavenly Father's house above; I know whom I have believed and in whom I confide, and the Lord hath assured me, by his word, "That blessed are all they that trust in him." Psalm ii. 12.

I. I believe in the doctrine of the Trinity of Persons subsisting in the one glorious Jehovah, the Father, the Son, and the Holy Ghost. These divine Persons comprehend the One indivisible Godhead; each glorious Person possessing every essential attribute peculiar to God. This great God is an uncreated, self-existent being, "From everlasting to everlasting thou art God." Psalm xc. 2.

II. I believe in the perfect unity of the adorable Trinity, that there is no inferiority or subordination in the divine Persons; that the divine nature of Christ is no more begotten of the Father than that of the Father's was the product of the Son. Neither is the Deity of Christ founded upon such God dishonouring ideas; for that which is produced, brought forth or begotten, cannot be eternal and self-existent; but each of the glorious Persons in the one self existent God, are eternal, immutable, and incomprehensible. Hence, I conclude, that Sonship always involves our Lord's creature nature: he was, and is, the Son of God, in a much higher sense than angels or man, in his innocent state, or than saints ever will be in their glorified state; for he was brought forth in union with the Divine nature. He is said to be the beginning of the creation of God, the first-born of every creature; but, that which is self-existent and eternal can never be begotten, or brought forth and formed by another. Being, therefore, brought to adore the Lord Christ as God over all, blessed for ever. I find all these phrases, *begotten*, *possessed first brrn* and *image*, most expressive as referring to him as a complex agent. It was as God-man that he covenanted with the Father on behalf of his Zion; he stepped forth as the Man of God's right hand as a representative and surety for the many sons and daughters love adopted; engaging to meet the law's requirements; delivering his Hepzibah from merited wrath, and investing her with a right and title to live everlastingly. Accordingly, we find him, in the fulness of time, dressed in flesh: this Word, which was the beginning with God, becomes the incarnate Word, fulfilling the law, ending the curse by enduring the judicial sentence passed upon the election of grace for faults committed; and before he yields up his life a sacrifice, exclaims, " Now, O Father, glorify thou me with thine own self, with the glory I had with thee before the world was !" John xvii. 4. What language could be used more appropriate to set forth his primeval glories as our ancient Interposer, as the God-man, I am at a loss to conceive of. This is the doctrine the Holy Ghost teaches in testifying of Christ in the Word. Read John i. 1, 2, 3; Col. i. 15, and following verses; Heb. i.; Rev. iii. 14; 2 Cant. viii. 9: together with the 6th chapter of John.

III. I believe that God, in his Trinity of Persons, created the world and all that is therein, out of nothing, by the Word of his power; he spoke, and it was. Gen. i. 1, 2; Acts xvii. 26.

IV. I believe that the covenant of redemption and salvation was entered into by the sacred Three in God on the behalf of elect sinners, on whom grace and glory was settled for ever in Christ their covenant Head before the world began. Psalm lxxxix. 3, 28; Eph. i. 3, 4; 2 Tim. i. 9; Titus i. 2; 1 Cor. ii. 7. The Father chose them in Christ, gave them to Christ, and stored all blessings in Christ for them to be bestowed in grace through his meriting life and death to the glorification of Christ, and to the honour of his eternal Majesty.

V. I believe, that according to the stipulations of that well ordered covenant, Jesus Christ did appear at the pre-ordained time, to save sinners, even the vilest, so that none need despair: "For whosoever believeth on the name of the Lord shall be saved:" not for believing, for faith is not a condition of salvation, but a new covenant blessing, by which he enjoys the deliverance Christ hath effected for him: Jesu's errand here, was to purchase his church with his own blood, to justify her by his own acts, to save her from the tyranny of the devil, the dominion of sin, the claims of the law, terror of death, and the victory of the grave. Let me examine myself here. Have I an evidence in my soul that Jesus is mine and I am his? Truly, my soul believes in the finished work of my adorable Lord Jesus Christ, and to him I have committed my soul with all its momentous concerns.

VI. I believe that justification is God's gracious act, whereby he reputes a lost, guilty, criminal, just for the alone sake of what Christ has done and suffered for him; his deeds being computed to him for righteousness. These gracious acts of a covenant

God are made known to the sinner by the Holy Ghost through the; Word the soul taking fast hold of the righteousness revealed as its justifying and adoring robe, pleading before God this law-honouring work of Jesus as its only ground of acceptance in his sight. The glorious gospel of our God is an exhibition of Christ in his love, blood, and obedience; faith becomes conversant with the theme, love takes delight in it, sweet peace of mind ensues, the fear of God pervades the bosom, and subjection to the gracious rule of Emanuel is the issue. Our honourable justification is by grace, through the redemption that is in Christ Jesus. Rom. iii. 24. Hence, are we said to be justified by Christ, (Galatians ii. 16, 17,) by his blood, (Rom. v. 9,) by his knowledge, (Isaiah liii. 11;) may we be favoured to enjoy the soul-satisfying benefit of justification through faith in the glorious justifying obedience of the Lamb, who was stripped and striped, that we might be clad and fed.

VII. I believe that God created man holy; but by disobedience he fell and lost his original righteousness and purity, and that the whole human family fell in him as in their common parent: and that since the fall, every son and daughter of our apostate parents are born into this world shapen in iniquity and equitably condemned by God's righteous law, so that infants are not saved because of their innocency: but they, together with all adults who are saved, escape merited punishment by an act of sovereign grace, reigning through the finished work of the God-man Mediator.

VIII. I believe, that Regeneration is a change and renovation of the soul by the Spirit of God. John i. 13; and iii. 5, 6. It is denominated a new birth, and consists in the impartation of spiritual life, whereby the soul becomes capable of performing spiritual acts, and living to the praise and glory of God. Prior to which change I believe no man can act spiritually; "The natural man discerneth not the things of the Spirit, neither can he know them, for they are spiritually discerned." Peter saith to the scattered saints, "Being born again, not of corruptible seed, but of incorruptible; by the Word of God, which liveth and abideth for ever." Our God is the living God, and all his family are made really alive. He has no dead children, or lifeless subjects in his spiritual kingdom, but they are born of God, love God, subjecting themselves to his righteous rule. Therefore, a mere profession of christianity, without vital union to, and communion with Christ, will end in confusion and ceaseless misery.

IX. I believe, in the final perseverence of every believer, which doctrine is clearly revealed in the word of God. John x. 28; 2 Tim. ii. 19; 1 John ii. 19. Which truth affords the greatest consolation to a tried and tempted christian. "Being confident," saith Paul, "of this very thing that he, which hath begun a good work in you, will perform it until the day of Christ. Phil. i. 6. The immutable love of God, the redeeming death of Christ, and the inhabitation of the Spirit, all attest the absolute certainty of the endless bliss of a chosen people, which people are visibly set apart for God in the day of these heavenly, holy, and effectual callings. My soul can sing with solemn satisfaction and unwavering confidence,

> "Grace will complete what grace begins,
> To save from sorrows and from sins;
> The work that wisdom undertakes
> Eternal mercy ne'er forsakes."

X. I believe, in the resurrection of the whole human family at the last day, and this will be effected by that Almighty Him, who entered the territories of the dead, and who is the resurrection and the life, and who now possesses the keys of death and hell, having conquered death and him that had the power of death; and that this gracious Life-bringer will watch the dust of his saints, bringing them up from the sleeping chamber of the grave, under the covert of his cross, summoning his enemies to appear at his equitable tribunal. The doctrine is at large declared by Paul. 1 Cor. xv.; Rev. xx.

XI. I also believe, that then will be the period of God's righteous judgment, when he will openly appear before an assembled world to avenge the wrongs of his afflicted Zion, and manifestively display his power and glory in her complete deliverance from all her enemies; so that satan, sin, death, and the grave shall be entirely vanquished; not one member of Christ's body being left under the curse of God's law; but every individual for whom Jesus shed his precious blood shall then be advanced to his right hand, and possess the mansion love ordained. Then will be the great day of separating the sheep from the goats —never again to be blended. The tares will be gathered from the wheat—the righteous from the wicked—the sheep on his right hand—the goats on the left. Then will the gracious award be made to the poor, humble despised, followers of the Lamb—"Come, ye blessed of my Father, inherit the kingdom prepared for you;" while the doleful proclamation will be made, which will kindle a fire of never abating despair—"Depart from me, ye cursed, into everlasting fire, prepared for the devil and his angels." Infidels, unblushing sensualists, and hypocritital professors may sport with the solemnities of the day now, but the day is approaching when they will be clothed with confusion. O, the momentous affairs of that all-important period! My soul, how art thou expecting to appear before a sin-avenging God without confusion? Surely it is by being found in his righteousness, which makes a sinner just, and through which God appears just in thy justification, being found in Him, not having on my own righteousness, which is of the law, but that which is through the faith of Christ. The righteousness which is of God by faith is my soul's only hope of exemption from endless dismay.

XII. I also firmly believe, (and pray that I may be assisted to practice my principles,) the ordinances which Zion's King ordained in his church when he tabernacled among men; such as assembling together with saints, publicly to worship the Lord our God in preaching and hearing his holy word, singing his praises, and calling on his great name; attending to christian baptism, and communing together at his table in the use of the symbols his wisdom appointed. These are institutions appointed in great mercy, and in attendance to them rich blessings are poured out upon the faithful followers of the Lamb slain, so that in waiting upon the Lord spiritual strength is renewed. On the ordinance of baptism some things I have said on pp. 13, 14, and something more will be found in the prosecution of my memoir, I therefore leave it for the present.

XIII. As to the ordinance of the Lord's Supper I believe that there is no authority from the word of God for any person to appear there unless he has confessed the Lord in the ordinance of baptism. The ignorance pleaded of not seeing the necessity is of no avail; the commands of Zion's Deliverer are the rules for our direction. "Teach them to observe all things" is an injunction not to be trifled with. A person who lives, therefore, in the neglect of attending to baptism is not justified in approaching the table of communion. Baptism does not remove my guilt, but in attendance to it my Guilt-Bearer is honoured. Our acceptance arises from the obedience and blood of the Lamb; but to disobey Jesu's command is a crime of no small magnitude, for "his yoke is easy and his burden is light." The wilful ignorance that marks the professing church of Christ is painful to witness; what else can account for the attestation of many that they were scripturally baptised in their infancy, while there is not a sentence in the volume of inspiration that can fairly be construed to have the least reference to such a practice ever being commanded or attended to. Every person, therefore, that has not been baptised after our Lord's example, and, according to his command, is as yet unbaptised, and can have not the least warrant to communicate at the Lord's table.

Thus have I eadeavoured as a humble drillman to state in a few words my belief of the fundamental doctrines of the gospel of our Lord and Saviour Jesus Christ, as they are plainly revealed in the written word; and we know that "All scripture is given by the inspiration of God, and is profitable for doctrine, for reproof, for correction, for instruction in righteousness, that the man of God may be perfect, thoroughly furnished unto all good works." 2 Tim. iii. 16, 17. The Lord grant that these truths may have their due influence on my heart, and copied out in my walk and conversation. And while my ears are saluted, and my eyes perceive arminianism spreading, the truth of God being derided and condemned, may the everlasting gospel be more highly prized, its Author adored, proclaimers of it increased, and its defamers silenced. Through the grace given unto me I am hoping to live in the love of the truth, and to die in the embraces of Him who is " the truth." Certain I am that the doctrines of rich, free, and distinguishing grace, accompanied with power to the heart, will stimulate the soul to diligence and activity in divine things. As the main-spring in a watch keeps the wheels in motion, so God's immutable, immense, and inseparable love shed abroad in the heart by the power of the Holy Ghost will produce righteousness of life, humility of heart, and tranquility of mind.

Suppose a nobleman had settled upon me a large estate before I was born, it might be thought nothing of by me in the days of my childhood, but as I advanced in knowledge, its value became obvious to me, and my future prospects dilated me; farther discoveries are made to me respecting my patrimony; it is disclosed to me that my inheritance is so settled that it cannot be sold, stole, lost, or forfeited by any means, would the possession on such a permanent basis, lead me to admire or contemn the donor? The answer is easy—

> " 'Tis love that makes our willing feet
> In swift obedience move."

But slavish servitude God abhors; hypocritical worship is a stench in God's nostrils.

> " Their lifted eyes salute the skies,
> Their bended knees the ground,
> But God abhors the sacrifice
> Where not the heart is found."

The Lord secures the heart and best affections of his family by shedding abroad his love in their hearts by the Holy Ghost, which is given unto them. It acts like leaven on all the powers of the man, producing love to God, obedience to his commands, sets in active employment all the graces of the Holy Spirit, and there is a running the christian race with patience, alacrity, and delight.

It is plain from God's word that sinners are brought out of a state of darkness, rebellion, and unbelief into a state of grace and salvation by a revelation of Jesus Christ to the soul; and this is the gracious work of the Holy Ghost, according to our Lord's own declaration, John xvi. 13, 14; for he reveals Christ to the elect in the glories of his person, the riches of his grace, and the aboundings of his mercy and goodness in pardoning sinners, sanctifying the unclean, and saving the lost. A Saul of Tarsus is a witness to the fact.

I fear this is a day in which thousands are contenting themselves with a form of godliness, denying the power of it, from which source arises the abhorrence to the pure doctrines of distinguishing grace, and a denial of man's apostacy, depravity, and imbecility. The necessity of a new creation is rejected; the representation of a sinner being drowsy and not dead is pleasing; the testimony of a man being in a salvable condition, instead of being saved by Christ, meets with a greedy reception. Eternal thanks to Him who hath taught us better. Proud nature cannot brook to the humbling truths of the gospel, and it is not to be doubted but what some of our most blazing professors would, if it was in their power, persecute the lovers of the truth as it is in Jesus with as much cruelty as Saul of Tarsus did. Such is the enmity of the human heart against the soul-animating truths of the everlasting gospel. But when the Holy Ghost takes of the things of Christ and reveals them to the soul, then these heretofore enemies become the real friends to Christ and his interest. See in Paul's case. What a mighty change! This bloodhound became a patron, a nurse, and a caterer to the flock he unsparingly persecuted. Oh blessed change! happy is the soul who experiences it—out of nature into grace, but not *vice versa*, out of grace into nature. Nothing but a transition from death to life can fit a soul for communion with God here, and fellowship with him in the world to come. May the infinite love of the sacred Three who bear record in heaven be more and more revealed to my soul as the undecaying pledge of my interest in Christ's sacrifice, righteousness, and ever prevalent intercession. May I be preserved from every false doctrine and froward conduct, that I may neither turn to the right hand or the left, but be kept on in the good old way—the way of holiness, which is the way of peace, safety, and prosperity, and made truly thankful and joyful in what he hath done for my soul.

From the year 1807 to 1812 I lived at Fleet and Gedney in farmer's service, during which time I began to write the former part of this narrative, regularly attending the ministry of my much esteemed, pastor Mr. Burgess. Having saved a little money, and being desirous of leaving servitude, by the providence of God my mind was directed to make a purchase of a corn drill, intending to commence the occupation of a drillman in Holland Fen. Providence directed my course to Pinchbeck Fen, where the Lord blessed my efforts to obtain a living exceedingly, so that the next spring my means warranted me to give orders for a new thrashing machine, and there is abundant cause for me to bless the Lord for his kindness in crowning me with abundant success. His providence smiled on me in all I put my hands to. The Lord also smiled on me in spiritual matters, for I became a boarder in the house of my uncle Shepperson. I had heretofore met with opposition from him on account of my conduct in pleading for, and attending unto, the ordinance of believers' baptism, as I have related before on p. 13. My uncle was a God-fearing man, and a deacon of an independent church, with him I have enjoyed sweet communion on divine subjects; much pleasure have we had in conversing on the glorious truths revealed in the Scriptures, the amazing love of God to his chosen people, its sovereignty, immensity, and inseparability, shining forth to our view in the person, headship, and mediatorial work of Christ. It pleased the Lord to love, to bless, and to save is the only cause we shall ever arrive at. He hath done whatsoever it hath pleased him. What wisdom, majesty, and grace breaks forth to view in the adoption, redemption, and salvation of sinners in, by, and through Christ Jesus! He would suffer his people to deserve hell, but would not suffer one to go there. Justice shall be glorified, the law magnified, and richest grace exemplified in their complete deliverance by Christ; for it is redemption through his blood, the forgiveness of all sin, according to the riches of grace. Divine faithfulness, love, and power are all displayed in our emancipation by our exalted Lord Jesus Christ. O how great was that love and condescension of Jesus in becoming poor that we should be enriched—in humbling himself that we should be elevated—in being stripped and striped that we should be clothed and caressed, so that he might ultimately present the church to himself "A glorious church, not having spot, wrinkle, or any such thing, but that it should be holy and without blame before him in love." His resurrection and ascension into heaven proves that his work of mediation is complete; for when he had by himself purged our sins, he sat down at the right hand of God, and this is the immoveable basis of a sinner's hope, the death, resurrection, intercession, and dominion of the Lord Christ, who is the Head, Representative, and Saviour of his body the church.

What a miracle of grace is the church collectively and distributively! Concerning each one and the whole it may be catechetically put "Is not this a brand plucked out of the fire?" What a description of our apostacy and impotency we have in Ephes. ii. 1—3; and what a tide of mercy is opened up to us in the following verses, in our deliverance by grace, the spring of our deliverance—the matchless love of God, and all to issue in the praise of his glorious grace.

Oft hath my soul been refreshed in communing with my uncle; and for three years I attended with my uncle and aunt the ministry of that good and venerable servant of the Lord, Isaac Woodward, pastor of the Independent Congregation at Pinchbeck, whose ministry was congenial with my views of the doctrines of grace, and was oft very refreshing to my soul; but the sprinkling system annoyed me, and I often entered into controversy with many of my friends on the subject. But, in the absence of Scripture command or precedent, my mind remained unmoved, affirming it was safe and honourable to follow in the footsteps of the flock, and simply to obey the mandates of Jesus, who commissioned his apostles to go and teach all nations, baptizing them in the name of the Father, Son, and Holy Ghost, Matt. xxviii. 19, 20. Observe, first teach, then baptise them which believe; teach them to observe all things whatsoever I have commanded you; and how evident it is that baptism was one among the all; connected therewith is his promised presence and blessing. Although the apostles lived many years to testify of the truth and correct the abuses, negligence, and errors that arose, setting also in order the things that were wanting, yet not a word of reproof for neglecting to sprinkle their babes, nor a word of commendation because they had practised such a thing; evident it is that such a practice crept into the church in modern times. We read "there is one Lord, one faith, one baptism;" and it is affirmed that "believing men and women were baptized," Acts viii. 12. Verse 38th assures us that "they both went down into the water, Philip and the eunuch, and he (Philip) baptized the eunuch." And "Jesus, when he was baptised of John, came up straightway out of the water." We also read of "rivers" and "places of much water," in which believers were baptised; but our friends are content with a little water in a basin, into which they immerse their fingers, sprinkling a few drops upon the face of an infant. What a departure from the command of Christ is such a practice!

Through gracious instruction, I am aware that little, much, or no water, used on a person, can make any real change of the state of the individual; but is it not sinful to alter the mode and manner of attending to a positive command, issuing from the lips of Zion's deliverer? Let us be careful how we countenance a worldly maxim in the place of a gospel ordinance, which preaches some of the most important truths to us. It is painful to behold men who profess to revere God's Word, following the maxim of the wealthy and worldly-wise in their political establishments and state policy, introducing their offspring into a mere profession of religious conformity, after the commandments of men; so crowding the streets of Zion with mere formalists and hypocrites; who, while professing themselves to be wise, they become fools. Surely such practice is provoking to the eye of our Lord. May we not look for God's anger to be displayed, as against his professing Israel of old? for though he was a God that forgave them, yet he took vengance of their inventions, and certainly a future posterity will be raised up, to say concerning the practice of the greater part of our professing Israel, "Surely our ancestors inherited lies, vanities, and things wherein there is no profit." Jeremiah xvi. 19.

There are some who affirm, if we are born again, and baptized with the Spirit, water baptism is needless. Certainly this evinces a wrong temper, and an erroneous judgment; let such a person ask himself seriously, as in the presence of God, whether the baptism of the Holy Ghost be an ordinance—and who was, or is, to be the administrator—when, where, and under what circumstances people are to attend to it, and in what manner it is to be performed. Surely such serious queries would cause a conscientious man to be silent! As well might we ask whether regeneration be not an ordinance—who the administrator—who the person—what their character, and where the place it is to be attended to. How painful to see persons fleeing from an ordinance which Christ commanded, his apostles practised, and the primitive church attended to reverently; and which will be regarded by some to the end of the world. To be born of God, and to be a partaker of the Spirit Jehovah, are no more ordinances for us to attend to, than our election and adoption into the family of God, or our justification in the righteousness of our great Surety. All are equally acts of grace towards us, made known to his people in effectual calling, they being entirely passive in the affair.

How often are we hearing it said, it matters not whether we are baptised by sprinkling, pouring, or dipping—whether in infancy, or in adult years—we are at liberty to act as conscience dictates, or the custom of the people amongst whom we dwell. Such reasoning is a proof that the heart is not right with God. Alas! alas! for poor erring sinners to imagine that they are at liberty to alter or change the standing ordinances of Jehovah's worship, attending to it just as suits their own convenience and inclinations. Oh that the Lord Jesus himself may preserve his saints from all the superstitious and foolish reasonings and inventions of men, delivering us from all the errors of Popery, which are infesting the minds of men. Open thou our eyes to see, and our hearts to receive all the doctrines, promises, and precepts of thy word; and help Zion to adhere to, and love the means of grace, and to walk in the ordinances of thy house blameless. I beg of God to preserve me from slighting any of his institutions, notwithstanding the opposition of friends and foes.

I continued with my relatives, and followed my employment, as drill-man, and machine-man, the Lord prospering me, so that I cleared annually more than £100. Here I was surrounded with mercies in great abundance—upper and nether spring blessings abounded. But how uncertain are all earthly enjoyments! A relation envied me my success; refused to pay me for labour done; used abusive language; grieved me exceedingly; and became the cause of my removal from my esteemed relatives.

I now removed to Gosburton, and took up my abode with my mother; and although this removal was inconvenient for my work, yet I was led to see the hand of the Lord in it, as it led to a connection and train of circumstances which I shall, through the Lord's goodness, attempt to detail.

On coming to reside at Gosbuton I was invited to assist as a teacher in the Sunday-school. This is an excellent and praiseworthy act, and I rejoice to hear of the good effect arising from such institutions, yet I must confess that I am not possessed of that meekness, patience, and forbearance which is so necessary for the discharge of such an office. So when I came to reside at Boston I was solicited to become a teacher, to which I consented, expecting to find the children under better management than at Gosbuton. But in this I was doomed to disappointment; and as I found the duties of a school on a Sabbath day interrupted me in acts of spiritual worship, I conscientiously, after much prayer to God for direction, resigned my office, intreating him to bless the efforts of others who could, without interfering with spiritual devotion, continue to instruct the rising generation, wishing that God would impart his Holy Spirit, and make many wise unto salvation. But to return.

When at Gosbuton I became acquainted with Mr. Joseph Anderson, a respectable farmer, and deacon of the general baptist church in that place. We often conversed freely on religious subjects. His views were Calvinistic. I used to express my surprise at his continuing among the general baptists, but he had his reasons, which he thought sufficient for his abidance. I often went to the meetings, and assisted in teaching the scholars. A Mr. Bampton was the preacher, who left and went to India as a Missionary. With this person I frequently talked over the leading subjects of his ministry. After preaching one Sabbath evening he invited me to his house on purpose to discuss the points of doctrine relative to faith and repentance. We continued our debate until morning; our views were diametrically opposite, and so they continued. In a few days I addressed the following letter, dated—

March 12th, 1816.

SIR:—

I have reflected seriously on the charges made by me against your ministry when I was with you on Sabbath last, and I do believe the charging you with preaching error to the subverting of the truth is substantially true. Your testimony is calculated to teach sinners that their salvation depends much more on their own performances than upon the vicarious sufferings of God's dear Son. This is the tendency of your ministry, and it is building poor sinners up in self-righteousness. You are always putting the sinner and his doings first, as though repenting and believing were the causes of salvation; and lest this mode of preaching should appear too barefaced for some of your hearers, you introduce the name of Christ, and his obedience and sufferings, as a helper, to make up their deficiency. It is a well-known fact, and you know that it is a principle you espouse, that there is more dependence to be placed on a sinner doing his duty as well as he is able, than upon the life, sufferings, and death of the Lamb of God. The procuring cause of salvation by Christ you despise, and Jehovah's infinite and eternal love to the sinner you deny. You affirm that you will by no means believe that the death of Christ was intended absolutely to accomplish the salvation of any body; he died provisionally for all, but intentionally for none. It puts sinners in a salvable state, is your note. They now all have an opportunity you aver; secure none are, but all may be saved if they like.

How at war are such statements with the purposes of God, the purchase of Emanuel, and the official work of the Holy Ghost. What a denial of the mission of Jesus, who came into this world to lay down his life for his sheep, who gave his life a sacrifice for sin, and has, by his one offering, perfected his church for ever.

I am grieved that you should exhibit Jesus the Saviour of sinners in such a despicable light—as having only made a provision if they will accept. Your words from the pulpit are, "It will avail nothing that Christ hath suffered for you—it will be of no use to you that Christ hath atoned for your sins, except you repent, believe, and obey. So you make the acts of a creature the cause of his salvation instead of the incarnate Jesus serving and suffering in his stead. It is because he died for me that I am brought to believe, repent, and act spiritually. How horrifying to hear you proclaim Christ suffered equally for those who are lost as for those who are saved; how at variance with Paul's testimony, "He loved me and gave himself for me."

You ask the question, Can a sinner be saved without repentance and faith? These are blessings of the New Covenant, and a part of that salvation which God bestows in grace. These are not conditions of salvation, but blessings Christ is exalted to bestow on all the redeemed. Repentance is an effect arising from God's favour. You are constantly placing the effect for the cause. It has been from such misrepresentations made by you that has caused me to tell you your testimony is contradictory; how repeatedly are you calling unregenerate men to perform spiritual acts, and then declare that the natural man discerneth not, neither can he understand the things that are spiritual. What a contradictory tale your's is, when you again affirm every man that comes under the sound of the gospel hath power to repent and believe to the saving of his soul. What saith the lip of truth, "The carnal mind is enmity against God, it is not subject to the law of God, neither indeed can be." The Scripture saith, "We are created in Christ Jesus unto good works, which God before ordained that we should walk in them."

Ephes. ii. 10. Now, sir, you insist upon good works being brought forth by the sinner before he is created anew in Christ Jesus.

> "We cannot act before we live,
> And life proceeds from grace."

Sir, you are awfully mistaken about the eternal truths of the gospel. Were you tasting the measureless love of God, displaying itself in storing up all spiritual blessings in Christ for all his seed, and living by faith on the atoning death of Jesus, your language would be different; you would not be sending poor sinners to feed on the husks of their creature performances, but you would exhibit a salvation complete in Christ, by Christ, and with Christ. If you are really made acquainted with your own condemned state and entire helplessness, compare your statements with your sensibilities, and see if such principles as you publish are true. What must be the final issue? even ruin—ruin endless.

While you are labouring to propagate such soul-distressing and God-dishonouring principles, how grateful ought I to be that I (an untutored man as it respects natural learning,) am preserved from falling into those errors which you are labouring with all your might to disseminate. May the Holy Spirit lead me in the paths of truth, and preserve me from all these refuges of lies, and help me to trust alone in the finished work of Him who exclaimed with his latest breath, "It is finished."

It is an unspeakable mercy that we have a faithful High Priest over the house of God, one that hath compassion on the ignorant and such as are out of the way. He came to seek his poor, lost, wandering sheep, to bring them to himself, to feed upon his all-sufficient fulness, receiving from him grace and strength, enabling them to bring forth the fruits of righteousness to the praise of his grace.

Mr. Bampton, your proclamation grates on my ears, "Christ's atoning blood is no security unless we repent." Again you say, "Christ atoned as much for those who are now lifting up their eyes in hell, being in torments, as for those who are gone to glory." Then sir, Christ's death secures none from perdition, and his sacrificial death is no foundation for a sinner's hopes to rest on. This is worse than mangling the gospel; this is an annihilation of everything that is gladdening to a sensible sinner. How can a poor, distressed, tempest-tossed, and law-condemned soul, that is labouring under an apprehension of God's just indignation being poured out upon him,—one who knows the plague of his own heart, and is mourning under a sense of the same, and longs for deliverance from his awful state, meet with any relief under a testimony like your's? So far are you from directing such an one to the fulness of Christ, his grace, merit, and mercy, that you banish the poor soul hence, and direct him to his own acts; you conceal the fountain, and drive him to a cistern that is broken, and can hold no water: "you must repent and believe." And if it was asked you what he is to believe, your answer would be as vague as your views of repentance are. It is such preaching as your's which makes sorry those whom the Lord would have made glad, feeding hypocrites, and starving the hungry souls of the Lord's poor saints. Alas, sir, where is the Holy Spirit all this while? He is not only kept out of sight, but he is insulted and denied. When I asked you if repentance did not flow from conviction of sin on the conscience, and whether this was not the product of the Spirit of God; you said you did not know whether you were justified in telling sinners that such was the case, for they got such notions as those into their heads soon enough of themselves.

I ask, is not this doing despite to the Spirit of Grace? Our redeeming Jesus told his disciples he would send forth his Holy Spirit. Do you think he will not fulfil his promise? He also told them what would be his work—First, convince of sin, of righteousness, and of judgment to come. Secondly, to receive of the things of Christ, and reveal them to the soul. Thirdly, to teach them all things, and lead them into all truth, and comfort them in the way to heaven.

The Eternal Spirit, as one of the Sacred Three in our glorious Jehovah, delighteth in testifying to the love, blood, and merit of Christ. The Father loves whom he will; Jesus redeemed whom he would; and the Spirit quickens whom he will. We are, by generation, born into this world in a state of depravity and condemnation through the rebellion of our great ancestor; so in the day of God's power we are brought into spiritual life by the regenerating grace of the Life-giver; and as certain as Jesus hath redeemed his people, so certain it is that the Holy Ghost will, in due time, make known the adopting love of the Father, and the complete redemption of Jesus to the delight of the sin-distracted soul.

You, sir, do not believe that Jesus by his blood-shedding, actually ransomed any one of Adams' sons and daughters; the all he effected, was, he placed them in a salvable condition; so that the helpless, hopeless, and forlorn sinner, might, by his work of repentance, faith, and good works, be saved. Your cuckoo note is, Christ's obedience and blood avails nothing of itself. If such were the case, satan would triumph, justice would inflict condign punishment on all mankind, and heaven would possess no inhabitant from this land of trespassers. But I have not so learned Christ. He hath made the atonement, many receive it, (while you deny it,) and joy in God through our Lord Jesus Christ; his righteousness alone is their boast, and his Word their delight. You, sir, are leading them from Christ, to take comfort in their own acts; building them up in self-righteousness, endeavouring by all means in your power, to instil into the minds of your hearers, an awful apprehension of those very truths by which a poor sinner can be saved to the honour of law, the rights of justice, and the glory of the God of immaculate purity.

Now, sir, you are either resting your soul's salvation on Jesus Christ's atoning blood and righteousness, or upon your repentance, faith, and obedience; and as your faith, such will be your testimony. By what drops from your lips, it is evident the latter is what your hopes *are* founded on; that it is a sandbank and not a rock, the lip of inspiration clearly determines. As a teacher of such unsound doctrines you are in a perilous position, deceiving both yourself and your hearers.

I would bless and praise Him whose I am, and whom I serve with my spirit, that he hath delivered me from those errors you are propagating, and given me to know and love his truth. His sovereign grace alone accounts for his love to me, redemption of me, and instruction imparted to me. The Eternal Trinity of Persons in the all-glorious God, break forth to view in salvation's mystery, by Christ Jesus our Lord. "It is by the grace of God I am what I am."

A lover of the truth,

W. BOWCOCK, *Drillman.*

SECOND LETTER TO THE SAME,

July 21*st*, 1816.

Not long since, your testimony from the pulpit was little better than the performance of a mountebank. Your affirmation was— "If persons say we cannot repent, they tell lies; they will not repent; that is the reason why they do not." I ask you, is this preaching the gospel? Suppose a poor sinner was distressed in his mind, and longed to know more about the way of salvation, and was complaining like the apostle, " the good that I would I do not," so far are you from leading such a soul to Jesus and his fulness, and to encourage him by the Word to look for pardon and complete salvation by Christ, that the tendency of your testimony is to drive a poor sensible sinner to the borders of despair. He must, he ought, he can, and if he does not repent, to hell you must go; so says Mr. Bampton. He groans, being burdened with sin, a hard heart, a depraved nature, and a tempting devil. Poor soul, thus mourning and complaining, he hears the orator prolaim, " You can melt your own frozen bosom, repent at your pleasure." Should he in answer say, "no, it is not so," he is accosted with the sound, " You tell lies; woe, woe, woe, to him that tells lies in God's name." I read repentance and remission are both blessings, which the Lord Jesus Christ is exalted to give. It appears to me, sir, that you never knew what it was to groan under a spirit of bondage; and, consequently, are a stranger to that liberty wherewith Christ makes his people free; and those whom he makes free, they are free indeed. It is by his Spirit that he blesses them with a sense of pardoning mercy, justifying righteousness, and adopting favour; thus sealing them as joint heirs with Christ to the heavenly inheritance. But your proclamation is, "Free yourselves you must, by repentance and a new obedience." Can any thing be more at war with God's truth? It is the work of that foe of Christ, that serpent who bruised Christ's heel, and whose head Christ bruised, to instil into their minds erroneous views of the Word of God, the person, offices, character, love, and grace of Christ.

Oh, how absolutely necessary is it that a person who stands up to teach poor sinners God's method of saving sinners, should be spiritually enlightened, and be alert to see that the doctrines he declares, should be according to the written Word. If thou hast any concern for truth, and hast any sensibilities of your state as a sinner, examine whether your own experience harmonizes with that of the saints in all ages, and also reflect on the doctrines you declare, and see if the condition you are in, does not require a salvation far more gracious and glorious than what you have been wont to speak. Your ministration distresses those whom God will have comforted; they are safe in his hands, and if you are lead by God's Spirit, you have some painful and profitable lessons to learn, that will be seen and known by that people, who discern all things, yet they are judged by no man. This, I expect is a riddle to you at present.

However much you may treat this subject with derision, and go on teaching the people that salvation is very precarious and uncertain, it will be found to the confusion of the abettors of such principles, that God's salvation is both sure and certain to all the seed of Christ. You are called a servant of the Lord; (I fear it is a libel,) would the servant rebel against his Lord's sovereignty? If the Lord God Most High, sees fit to save his people by an act of free, unmerited grace; and declares he loves them, notwithstanding their guilt and vileness; for be it remembered that his choice of them does not go upon the ground of worthiness; would a servant of the Lord's rebel against these gracious acts? Suppose the Righteous Judge of all had left all mankind to perish in their sins, would he not have been the just Jehovah?

But we read that he hath chosen a people for himself in Christ, before the foundation of the world. To write down the Scriptures which affirm it, and confirm the sentiment, would be to transcribe the greater part of the Testament. The Father hath made Christ to be the Head over all things to his body, the church; he hath blessed us with all spiritual blessings in him, and in the fulness of time, Christ, according to covenant arrangement, laid aside his glory, took upon him a body of flesh, stood in their law place, obeyed all its righteous precepts, suffering all its penalties, and so, by his obedience and blood, delivered them from the curse of the law. In the virtue of whose blood, the Spirit descends, opening the eyes of the blind to see, and the ears to hear, the good news of salvation; leading the ransomed to rejoice in their Liberator, and causing them to walk in his ways by choice, and teaching them to honour him as their all-competent Saviour. To misrepresent Scripture truths, is equally hateful in God's sight, as to deny them; you are frequently employing your moments in ridiculing the truths of God's Word; and villifying the characters of those whom God in mercy hath called to acknowledge his truth; receiving the forgiveness of all their sins through faith in the atoning blood of the Lamb. There were some in the apostles' days did as you do now, and the apostle rebuked them, with a holy abhorrence of their conduct—"Nay, but O man, who art thou that repliest against God?" This faithful, affectionate, and God-honouring servant of the Lord, was not like those who are now styled ministers of Christ, who teach men that salvation is designed for all men, and that it is to be obtained or not, according to their resolves, but as a wise master builder, who needed not to be ashamed, declares that salvation is founded in God's everlasting love, and is made known to the sinner in a way that opens up God's councils and decrees. Paul delighted to dwell on those heavenly mysteries of distinguishing grace, which you, with thousands more in this land of Bibles, despise, condemn, and deride, but which will be found, are truths influential on the hearts of God's saints, productive of fruits of righteousness to his eternal praise.

It is to be feared that most of you crouch to your employment for a morsel of bread, and your pulpits are the rostrums where you can, with an appearance of sanctity, pour forth your venom against the distinguishing truths of the gospel.

The apostles and subsequent ministers of the gospel were not time-servers, flesh-pleasers, self-seekers, nor merit-mongers. Hear Paul's acclamation, "Who hath saved us and called us with an holy calling, not according to our works, (as Mr. B. teaches,) but according to his own purposes and grace, which was given us in Christ Jesus before the world began." Again, he says, "Having predestinated us unto the adoption of children by Christ Jesus to himself, according to the good pleasure of his will, that we should be holy and without blame before him in love; for whom he did foreknow, he also did predesinate to be conformed to the image of his Son; that he might be the first-born among many brethren; moveover, whom he did predestinate, them he also called; and whom he called, them he also justified; and whom he justified, them he also glorified." Here is the golden chain which secures the heirs of heaven as permanently as the throne of the eternal.

God permits rebellious worms to lift up their puny arms against his truth, and while they try to extirpate, God overrules their malice, and causes his word to run and be glorified: enemies always mean destruction. The Lord purposes propagation; his councils stand—he is doing all his pleasure in the salvation of the vessels of mercy, whom he afore prepared unto glory. Who shall lay anything to the charge of God's elect? You may affirm there is no elect. You rise and say God justifies none; man is his own justifier. Your contention is with God, Christ, and the justifying Spirit: may the Lord cause you to cease from your unholy contest, and lead you into the grace of the apostle's doctrine: "Who is he that condemneth? it is Christ that died; yea, rather, that is risen again; who also even liveth to make intercession for us." In the eighth of Romans, he commences with, "There is no condemnation to them who are in Christ." He closeth the same chapter with, "There is no separation from the love of God in Christ Jesus."

Is it not a proof of great blindness having happened to our professed teachers of the gospel, when you hear apostolic doctrine defamed by them; justification a free act of favour; perfected redemption by the work of Jesus, are denounced as erroneous principles, leading to consequences tremendous? Hence, to mention election by grace, predestination to life, renewing, quickening, sanctifying, and leading God's family home to glory, by the Spirit's energy, is ridiculed by you and your associates; and with daring effrontery you affirm that wheresoever these doctrines are taught and imbibed, there licentiousness and profligacy is the result! What a matter of lamentation that such discerning men as you were not present, to have checked the apostles in their unsparing use of language which conveys such contrary principles to what you approve? They unhesitatingly declared to the followers of the Lamb, "That they were chosen to eternal life in Christ, before the world began, and that pardon of sin, and a title to endless bliss, was secured to them through the righteousness and blood of Jesus, their divine Surety and Redeemer, without any regard to their works or worthiness." You have never believed these doctrines, therefore you are as unable to speak of the effects they produce on the mind, as a blind man is unable to speak of colours; but there is an old adage "Fools will be meddling." There was such characters in the apostle's days, who affirmed that what they said amounted to the fatal issue of doing evil that good may come: of such defamers, he said, "Their damnation is just." Rom. iii. 8. But modern preachers can boldly stand up and say, that they do not preach anything that wicked men could construe to such a bad use, for we derive all those sentiments that teach the sinner to look for his perfection in Christ.

Sir, you know how ready you, with your fraternity are, to say that the calvinists believe they shall be saved, do what they will, if they do but believe they are the elect. Beware, sir, how you charge men with crimes of which they are innocent. It is the principles which you hate, that induces you to lodge such charges at the door of the man who receives the truths of the gospel. Remember the apostle's denouncement, because they wilfully belied the saints as saying, "Let us do evil that good may come." You know, or might know sir, that the real election of grace give proof of their character by their being called into fellowship with Christ, walking apart from the despisers of his gospel, and walking in communion with his people, word, and ordinances. God's everlasting love, upon which election is founded, is the source from whence all holy principles proceed, and all righteous practice is secured. It is from this source that the Holy Ghost descends and takes up his abode in a poor sinner's heart, adorning their souls with all his heavenly graces, such as faith, hope, love, joy, peace, and patience, leading them to see more and more of their internal depravity, external deformity, and entire imbecility, in connection therewith; giving to see the freeness of God's grace, the fulness of Christ's redemption, and perfection of his salvation. His teaching I pray to be under—his influence I pray to feel, that I may follow on in the footsteps of the flock, and never be allowed for a moment, apparently, to join with the enemies of his truth, who reject those soul-elevating truths which secures man's salvation and the Saviour's glory.

Your affirmation of my opposing myself should be reversed, for you are always opposing the fundamental parts of the gospel: you are so partial of having a hand in procuring your own salvation, and you are of a piece with yourself in this matter in your ministry, zealously teaching others to do the same, by telling them that their salvation depends on their doing their duty. On one occasion you proclaimed from the pulpit, that those who did not believe that Christ had made an atonement for every human being where unbelievers. Now, I hesitate not in saying, that had you been a partaker of the faith of God's elect you would not have uttered such a falsehood; for saving faith is a living principle, wrought in the soul by the Holy Ghost, and is an evidence of that indissoluble union which subsists between Christ and his church. If those very persons, whom you contemn as high Calvinists and presumptuous creatures, were to say for themselves absolutely what you say of yourself, it would be considered by you as savouring of presumptuous boldness. You say, I know, from God's word, that Jesus Christ has made a complete atonement for my sin. There are but few of those, whom you brand with arrogance, who can unhesitatingly say, "He loved me, and gave himself for me:" think of these things.

Again, you scarcely ever finish a sermon without exhorting your hearers to give all diligence to make their calling and election sure, and at the same time, you deny the doctrine of election. Alas! what inconsistency is here? This proves you to be a contradictory testfier, and shews your ignorance of some of the fundamental truths of the gospel. Remember, there is a day coming, it is that day when the Lord Jesus shall be revealed from heaven with his mighty angels, in flaming fire; he shall send his angels with a great sound of a trumpet, and they shall gather together his elect from the four winds of heaven. They will be known and acknowledged by the Son of God as his elect in the last day, to the astonishment and confusion of thousands. May you reflect, sir, on your principles, and resign those sentiments which will be falsified, in that day, when Christ gathers his ransomed and gives up the kingdom to his Father, with a "Here am I, and those whom thou hast given me—not a hoof is left behind." Nay, he who opened the eyes of Elijah's servants to see those fiery chariots and horses round about them for their protection, open your eyes that you may see and duly estimate those glorious truths, which at present you despise; and then you will acknowledge to the praise of sovereign grace, that those who are with the Lamb are called, chosen, and faithful: called because they were chosen, that they should be faithful.

W. B., *Drillman.*

To these letters I received no answer; but he censured me to others, affirming that I was warm, and that it became him, as the servant of the Lord, to be patient and gentle; but he ever after looked very shy at me. However, I thanked the Lord, who enabled me thus far to act faithful to my own conscience, in reproving this man. But I soon found I had made myself more work from others of the same stamp, who attacked me with their Arminian tenets, as the subsequent pages will explain.

When at Gosbuton, the Lord answered my prayers and supplications in the matter of directing me, in his providence, to a female, with whom I might be united, who is a Christian indeed. My esteemed friend, Mr. Anderson's daughter Ann, appeared that character; possessing much meekness and patience. I oft conversed with her about spiritual subjects, and found her views more congenial with my own than could have been expected, considering she was brought up among the Arminians: believing she was one that was united to Christ, and a living member of him, the true vine; and knowing that such an one was the true character, with which we could expect to walk through the wilderness comfortably together, I made suit to her, and then followed several letters to and from each other; some of which, I have looked over with pleasure since we have been united.

It would be well for young people, and especially for Christians, when writing what is termed love letters, if they would avoid all immoderate expressions which is calculated to enkindle unhallowed fire, and state more freely their views and experience of gospel truths, and their thoughts and intentions respecting practical godliness; this might be of advantage to each other in future life, as well as afford satisfaction to them when they reflected on the steps taken in early life.

I will here transcribe an extract from one of my letters which I wrote to my, then intended, future companion; because I find the truths therein contained, to be according to the doctrines of the gospel, and advantageous to the practiser of those things enforced; and I do wish my life and conduct was more of a practical exemplification of what I then said: it is as follows:—

My Esteemed Christian Sister,

Family worship is the subject I intended to write a letter on: may the glorious Lord assist me, a poor worm, in my meditations, while I endeavour to pen a few thoughts on, first, the object of divine worship; secondly, the nature of worship; thirdly, the manner in which it is to be performed; and, lastly, the holy tendency.

First, the object of all worship is God; even the poor heathens who knew not the living God, formed to themselves gods, the works of their own hands: and hence, we read of some who made gods or rather idols of gold, others of silver, others of brass, stone, wood, clay, in order that they might have an object of worship. Oh! what deplorable ignorance to bow down and pray unto senseless idols! Let us praise the name of Jehovah, our adorable Creator, who hath revealed himself in his glorious Trinity of Personalities in the everlasting gospel, as the object of our supreme adoration, hope, expectation, and delight. But, alas! how little is he prized as the God of salvation by deluded mortals, whose delight is in riches, honours, or pleasures, arising from carnal gratifications; how many are adoring the creature more than the Creator, Ransomer, and Sanctifier; may the Lord preserve us from every species of idolatry; the Lord Jehovah, Son, and Spirit, is the only object of supreme adoration. May we be led to contemplate his covenant character as the Triune God of Israel's hope and security, he having chosen us in Christ, his first-born and heir of all things; who, in the fulness of time, according to covenant arrangements, became incarnate, and ransomed our souls from hell by his own most precious blood; and now, as our Advocate with the Father, ever liveth to intercede for all his people. Yes, blessed Jesus! thou art the helpless sinner's almighty Friend. The Holy Spirit may we ever adore as our teacher and sanctifier, who takes of the things of Christ and reveals them to our souls; thus may we always be able to set the Triune Jehovah before us as the object of our adoration, thanksgiving, and praise; methinks you will add to it your hearty Amen.

Secondly, the nature of Christian worship is spiritual. Those that worship him, must worship him in spirit and in truth. It is not outward forms and ceremonies that constitute man a worshipper. A man may be a constant attendant on all outward forms of worship, both public and private, and yet his heart not right in the sight of God, a mere formalist, and his hopes built on his performances: he worships the means, dishonouring the God of them. It is to be feared that many in this, our day, content themselves with the form of godliness, denying the power; live strangers to prayer and supplication, which arises from a felt sense of want, weakness, sin, guilt, temptation, and depravity; they attend preaching, and make a saviour of their devotions, which is a stench in God's nostrils. Oh, that it may be our privilege to enjoy the worship of God in our domestic walk, and his public ordinances, sweetly living in a diligent use of the means, and mercifully preserved from living on the means! I wish to enjoy much of God's grace in my own soul, hoping to promote spirituality of mind in all about me, who know and fear God. [Alas! alas! what convictions of my faultiness break in on my mind now I am transcribing my letter into this manuscript.]

Thirdly, the manner of performing worship. Our God dwelleth in the heavens and filleth immensity with his presence: blessed be his name, he is not confined to time, place, or attitude; but in every place at any time, and in any posture, we have the priviledge to draw near to his throne of grace in, by, and through the blood of the covenant.

As it respects family worship, if practicable, the household should be assembled morning and evening, to reverence and adore Him who hath preserved them safe through the hours of day or night, and to implore his blessing and protection through the dangers of night or the toils and exposures of the day: in some situations this is impossible. Should such be our case, let us remember for our comfort that there is no employment in which we may be occupied that can possibly prevent us from mentally offering up our morning sacrifice to the Father of all our mercies: he reads the heart, and when the heart is right with God, his worship will be regarded. And, methinks, all men who are at the head of a domestic establishment and fear God, might attend to family worship by a little judicious arrangement. Surely, a Christian man, having been preserved and helped through the toils and snares of a day, could not be better employed than in acknowledgement of the goodness of God, and a prayerfully seeking the Lord's blessing to rest on them through the silent hours of rest and retirement. Weariness of body may oft be pleaded, this is a temptation from the enemy; unfitness in the temper of mind will oft be felt. A ground of argument may be fetched therefrom; that the greater need there is for my begging the blessing of a righteous spirit at his hand, who alone can renew the face of my soul. If the man be spiritually minded he will wish to honour Christ in his family. Nor will the Christian woman be less alive in uniting with the partner of her bosom in such heavenly and profitable exercise.

My thoughts of conducting family worship is somewhat as follows:—Whatever valuable books may be read in the course of a long evening or at other times, let all be laid aside except the Bible and hymn book; if practicable, let an appropriate hymn be sung, then a portion of God's Word be read, and as the Lord may afford help, drop a few thoughts as we read, to promote each other's edification, afterwards make an effort to approach the Father of mercies and God of all grace, in the dear Redeemer's name, making confession with supplications and thanksgiving, pleading the virtue of Jesus' blood and righteousness, to cleanse and justify our filthy and guilty souls before God, even the Father, through the application of the eternal Comforter, that we may rest in peace.

I by no means wish to lay this down as a rule to go through, in order to satisfy conscience, by performing a duty, as the formalist, who is as barren as was the fig-tree Christ cursed; but this, so far as our covenant God shall enable us, is the path I wish we may be helped to pursue. Let us aim at drawing near to the throne of grace; let us earnestly beseech the Lord to preserve us from all hypocrisy, intreating him to make us spiritual worshippers, that we may enjoy his presence, and that the Holy Spirit may evidence to our spirits that we are his adopted children. If we are thus alive to God and our best interests, we shall not be prevented by trifles from enjoying our privileges. I do not say but that there may be circumstances occurring in the Lord's providence, which may alter the case; but let us watch against wilful negligence. Sickness may prevent singing, but the book of God should be read, for he can bless a word, and make our hearts glad; it is his blessiug "maketh rich, and addeth no sorrow." Thus may we live, pleading his promises, seeking his direction, and imploring his aid, trusting alone in his great name. Should we be called to sustain losses, or carry weighty crosses in our family or our circumstances, our harps will then probably be hung on the willows, and we more ready to weep than sing. Yet then the Bible will be our best resource to fly to; there we shall be apprised that nothing has happened to us but what is common to man, and God is faithful, who also will make a way to escape, that we may be able to bear it. The richest, wisest, greatest, holiest, and faithful among the Lord's saints, have had their trials, afflictions, and bereavements—but in all their afflictions he was afflicted, and the angel of his presence saved them; yea, he bare and carried them all the days of old, saying "Fear not, thou worm Jacob, I am with thee, yea, I will strengthen thee, yea, I will uphold thee with the right hand of my righteousness." Isa. xli. 10—14. Yes, thou ever-blessed Jesus, thy saints have found indeed, that the consolations of thy gospel are neither few nor small.

> "The Volume of my Father's grace
> Doth all my griefs assuage;
> Here I behold my Saviour's face,
> Almost in every page.
>
> "O, may those heavenly pages be
> My ever dear delight;
> And still new beauties may I see,
> And still increase in light.

Fourthly, Family worship hath a holy tendency; it tends to solemnize the mind, and advance a spiritual temper. By daily intercourse with heavenly subjects, we shall find our best interests maintained, the Lord will animate our spirits, renew the face of our souls, and invigorate our powers to run the race set before us. But if we neglect his worship, public or private, we shall insensibly grow cold and indifferent, and become unfruitful. The kind Lord help us to muse on the Person, love, grace, and work of Jesus, our anointed Saviour, when our hands are employed in the necessary business of the day.

Again, family worship and secret prayer, will tend to preserve us from rage and violence. The God-fearing man who maintains and enjoys daily intercourse with heaven, will feel a concern that his practice may not be impeded, and his character disgraced, by bursts of passion, and conduct disreputable to the profession made. His desire will be maintained in the employment he is daily in the exercise of, that the Lord would fortify his mind against temptation, and endow him with patience under all his trials, losses, and crosses.

Again, it hath a tendency to preserve us from spending many an hour in vain and idle communications by the fire-side. I have often been pained to witness this practice among those of whom better things had been looked for. To spend hour after hour of a winter's evening in foolish jesting, and that too, among christian friends, is shameful, wasteful, and painful; how dishonourable to the Lord, and deadening to the soul. If conversation on better things cannot be maintained, why not have recourse to reading? There are many valuable works well worthy of perusing attentively, and would afford much instruction to the mind. And then there is that Book of books, the blessed Bible, which is on our perusing that, going to the fountain head. Oh, that the Word of God may be our daily companion and guide; may we love it more and more.

Miss Anderson and myself kept up correspondence by letter and conversation for about thirteen months; I then hired a house and garden at Pinchbeck, and we were married on the 19th of June, 1817. I continued to work my drill and machine, the Lord prospering me exceedingly.

The following year, I purchased eighteen acres of land in the Fen, with the crops growing thereon. After thrashing my corn and disposing of it, I took a grocer's and draper's shop at Pinchbeck, and entered into that business on the 16th of October, 1818. I then sold my land, putting the money into my trade; shortly after, I sold my drill and thrashing machine, thinking to become a tradesman; but in my new occupation I was introduced into trials that I had been altogether ignorant of. In this occupation we remained two years, but many customers got so much in my debt, without any prospect of my ever having it paid; this, together with my not liking the confinement of the shop, it being so contrary to my former manner of life, brought me to the determination to part with my shop as soon as the Lord opened a door for my exit.

Knowing a young tradesman, (with whose father I once lived as a servant,) who was anxious to take my shop, we arranged for his taking my stock at cost price, and enter immediately; which he did on the first day of June, 1821. We then had apartments at a neighbouring house, until a situation presented itself for our departure. Here I must leave the historical part of my narrative for the present, and refer to that which immediately concerns my soul, and the religion of Jesus.

After the decease of Mr. Burgess, the pastor of the church at Fleet, a Mr. Rogers became the pastor. Standing at this time a member, living at the distance of sixteen miles, I could attend only on the day of our table communion; on the other Sabbaths, my attendance was on the ministry of good old Mr. Woodward, at Pinchbeck. On one occasion, when at Fleet, Mr. Rogers said to me, "I shall pass through Pinchbeck on my way to Bourn, do you think Mr. Woodward will let me preach in his pulpit on the Monday evening?" On my return I asked Mr. Woodward, who consented; and notice was given of it on the preceding Sabbath. Mr. Rogers preached from Eph. ii. 18. At another time, Mr. Rogers and Mr. Everard, of Spalding, with another general baptist minister, came to see us; my wife was absent. Mr. Rogers, the pastor of the church of which I was a member, soon commenced his defaming tongue against the Calvinistic sentiments which he knew I had greedily embraced; and among other things he said, he believed that poor sinners were brought to the knowledge of the truth much sooner under Arminian preachers, than they were under Calvinistic, and that Calvinistic doctrines always had a tendency to keep poor souls in a state of darkness, doubt, and uncertainty; and that it is Arminian ministrations that are blessed in the conversion of souls, far more than Calvinistic. At the time, my health was impaired, and I was unable to say much; my feelings were alive, and my mind was grieved to hear a professed minister of Jesus Christ ridicule and libellously declare things against the gracious truths of the gospel. After their departure, I had resource to the throne of grace, lifting up my heart to the God of my salvation for light and direction in the matter. My thoughts were much employed on what had passed : I was induced to take my pen in hand, and addressed him as follows.

Pinchbeck, May, 1819.

To Mr. Rogers:—

It surprises me, that you, as a minister, should have no more reverence for the name and work of Jehovah, than to attribute the new creation or new birth of an immortal soul, to the system and creeds of sinful worms. When speaking of Calvinists, their preaching kept back sinners in nature's darkness, you said, while arminianism brings them out of that state. If sinners, say you, would but attend arminian preachers instead of Calvinists, their conversion would be effected much sooner. What reflections are these on that Being who can both kill and make alive, and who alone can impart life to the dead, and give to the living a sense of pardon and justification through the obedience and blood of the Lamb. You laugh and make sport of God's Almighty arm being stretched out to save a sinner sovereignly, graciously, and energetically; saying as you did, and do, that if a king exercised his supremacy in such a way, that such a monarch would deserve to be dethroned; such a temper is as much at variance with christianity as Judas's.

It is impossible for a man to read the book of his maker, without meeting with constant declarations of his peerless sovereignty, and rich distinguishing grace; but your eyes perceive it not. He passed by sinning angels, he has resolved on saving sinners of the human family. He passed by the old world, and left them to perish in the flood, choosing to save Noah and his family alone; and why was Noah and his family saved? because of their worthiness? dare you say it was their worth? I dare say, that it was his sovereign favour towards them, and the exhibition of his justice in drowning the rest. See in the choice of Abraham, the promises he gave him, and the care God took of him; and then say if God saves supremely, he is unworthy of holding the reins of government.

God called Abraham alone, and blessed him, saying, that in his seed should all the families of the earth be blessed; and in order to cut off all carnal notions about family descent, or family holiness, in this day of fleshly profession, the apostle tells us that this seed is Christ, and none but those who are chosen in Christ, and regenerated by the Holy Ghost, are blessed with faithful Abraham. Here we see sovereign grace and freest favour towards the lost, helpless, and forlorn.

The Lord elected prophets of old to be his messengers; and he sovereignly employed them, and not others. Christ chose his agents; he did not go to colleges, but he poured contempt on the self-important, and instead of taking rabbis, he elected fishermen, a custom-house officer, and a bloody persecutor. You may quarrel with his Majesty, but you will be laughed at; he will hold you in derision; if you are a minister of his—which many doubt of—but supposing you are, or ever will be, it will arise from him having made choice of you, and qualified you for his service; in which occupation you would exult in that grace which is given you, to preach among Gentile sinners the unsearchable riches of Christ. Truly, when I look around, I have ample testimony of God's sovereignty, in the calling of first one and then another, from nature to grace. Yea, I am a miracle of mercy, a living testimony of the Lord's grace, being free; and daily I can sing—

> "Why was I made to hear his voice,
> And enter while there's room,
> While thousands make a wretched choice,
> And rather starve than come?"

My reply is not—I was more tractable than others—more worthy than others; it was not by human might or power, but by the Lord the Spirit. There is the same sinful propensities in my heart—the same vile affections—much darkness, wickedness, and wantonness, as in others—much work for lamentation do I find; and if grace was not as free and sovereign in all her bestowments to me now as it was in my arrest, all hope must cease from this moment; but grace reigns, and I am brought to love and serve my covenant God in the person and bloodshedding of Emanuel. It is not for any work or worthiness in me that the Lord changed my heart and altered my ways, hopes, and desires; but it springs from his sovereign goodness to poor sinful me; and he has been pleased to reveal these things to my soul, through the life-giving operation of the Spirit of grace.

These things I acknowledge with thankfulness to the God of all my mercies, but you ascribe the conversion of poor sinners to something else, and not to the sovereign grace of God; yea, Arminianism must have all the glory; certainly you are in a great error.

You said, I never come nigh you. Can you be surprised at that, sir? It is not altogether the distance, (sixteen miles,) but the wide distance of our views. How can I unite with a man who professes to be a minister of the New Testament, who treats a change of state with such a decided opposition to what the Scriptures exhibit it and experience confirms; to talk about all men may have a new heart and a right spirit if they will, and all men may become saints if they like; this is not speaking half in the language of Ashdod and half in the Jew, but this is wholly Ashdod. I wonder how you dare, with a New Testament in your hand, assert such things, ascribing that to the creature which is the prerogative of God the Holy Ghost to effect; your testimony denies that regeneration is the work of the Lord the Spirit.

Sir, were you acquainted with the honour of God, the rectitude of his government, and man's condition, you would not preach, talk, and act as you do. Remember that it is the glorious Jehovah, Israel's covenant God, that quickens sinners who were dead in trespasses and sins, bringing them out of darkness into his marvellous light, blessing them with all spiritual blessings, according as he hath chosen them in Christ Jesus, before the foundation of the world; Eph. i. 4; and he hath promised to do them good and help them forward amidst all their tribulations, and finally to bring them home. "Where I am," saith Jesus, "there shall ye be also." John xiv. 3. Then let the ransomed shout, "Not unto us, not unto us—not our diligence, goodness, humility, penitence, or patience; for these are the fruits of his favour, and not the causes. I conclude with David's words, and, I trust, in David's spirit—"The Lord liveth, and blessed be my Rock, and let the God of my salvation be magnified." Psalm xviii. 46.

W. B., *Drillman*.

I received a reply to this, so full of bitterness and derision, that grieved me. To transcribe it would be worse than useless. However, I sat down, and attempted to answer it.

Pinchbeck, September 30, 1819.

DEAR SIR:—

Your's, dated July 26th, reached me the 23rd of September; and pained I was to find such unjust accusations lodged against me as to call me a persecutor, and under a delusion. Certainly, if such be the case, censure for the first of these charges is my desert, your commiseration and energies to deliver me from the latter, as my pastor, is your duty, pointing out to me scripturally where I err. You affirm that I cherish an unchristian temper and an hypocritical spirit. Would it not be well had you taken Paul's advice, "Brethren, if a man be overtaken in a fault, ye which are spiritual, restore such an one in a spirit of meekness." Really, sir, I am at a loss to imagine your motive in loading me with the following opprobrious names—"insolent," "self-deluding," "unchristian," "impudent," "hypocritical," "ungracious," "blind zeal," "an inquisitionist;" and then you return thanks to God "that such a fiery bigot as the Drillman has no power to imprison and burn you." Surely, my good sir, you do not mean what you say; or, as you said to me, what is most probable, "you don't know what you mean."

You know, my conversation with you at the time you allude to, was confined to no particular doctrine; and but little dropped from my lips to talk of me, and then of my principles, dressing up their idols in a fool's coat. When we affirm that the justification, and new creation of a sinner, arises from the immutable love of God, the deeds and death of Christ, and the sovereign energy of the Holy Ghost, without any regard to the sinner's worth or desires, in such assertions of yours, sir, the heart is exhibited through the lips, as not being right with God. You ask me why I did not oppose you at the time you was at my house. Bodily infirmity was one cause; and distress of mind, arising from such God-dishonouring assertions made by you and one of your associates, the other. Sinner's hearts would be sooner changed under arminian preachers, than under Calvinistic ones, was your note. Alas! thought I, where is the Holy Ghost? in what does his work consist? Surely life from the dead is God's work, independent of the parson or the laity. Means are useful to the living, but to translate from death to life is his prerogative alone, who said to Tabitha, "arise;" to Lazarus, "come forth." "You hath God himself quickened, who was dead in trespasses and in sin."

I perceive you want to shift the question about salvation being of God's rich, reigning grace; and you point me to Mr. Andrew Fuller's testimony, (recorded in his diary, you affirm,) where he asserts it as a matter of his belief, that he should have found soul rest much sooner, had he have sat under different doctrines to those he did. You infer, of course, that he refers to bondage, by hearing Calvinistic sentiments; and that his liberty came in by his views of the sufficiency of the atonement of Christ for all the world. A query arises here. Did Mr. Fuller himself ever find rest for his soul, on the notion of universal sufficiency, or the personal efficiency of the atonement, by which justice became satisfied, and the sinner personally saved? Hear what this champion says, who used his pen artfully, and his lips constantly, in proclaiming against those truths which are the basis of a sinner's salvation, and God's endless honours as the gracious deliverer. Mr. Fuller's biographer asserts, that when drawing near to his dissolution, he, as many of the Lord's saints are, was labouring under much bodily pain, darkness of mind, and depression of spirit. One of his attendants, possessing a temper natural to every man, addressed him thus—"I know of no person, sir, who is in a more happy condition than yourself: a good man, on the verge of a blessed immortality;" in which it is said he humbly acquiesced, and hoped it was so. But we are told that he afterwards lifted up his hands, and exclaimed, "I am a great sinner, and if I am saved, it must be by great and sovereign grace—by great and sovereign grace."

Mr. Fuller, we are told from another quarter, expressed himself thus—"I am a poor guilty sinner, but Jesus is an Almighty Saviour; I have no other hope of salvation, than what arises from mere sovereign grace, through the atonement of my Lord and Saviour. With this hope I can go into eternity with composure." A few days before he died, he thus expressed himself, —"I have preached and written much against the abuse of the doctrines of grace, but that doctrine is all my salvation, and all my desire." How much better had Mr. Fuller's time been spent, had he written and spake more of that grace, which now he found to be the only subject that could cheer his mind in the dark valley of the shadow of death. Before you come to the swellings of Jordan, I pray God that your lips may be employed under a feeling sense of the worth of the things to commend that grace which now you ridicule.

A child of God may be labouring for a time under great darkness, guilt, and misery, from a sense of his sinnership, helplessness, and depravity. He may cry out as one of old, "Oh that I knew where I might find him." God may meet with such a soul by the ministration of his truth through the agent of his electing, and cause him to enjoy rest and peace by believing. But our conversation was not about the sorrows and joys of saints, but about a change of heart—a translating a man from satan's kingdom into the kingdom of God's dear Son. That a man is more blessed under one ministration than another, I am a living witness. Your testimony has neither instructed, consoled, or satiated me; others I have heard who have ministerially clothed, cleansed, instructed, cheered, reproved, edified, and satiated my poor soul, so that had your conversation been on one ministration being blessed more than another to the living family of God we had agreed at once; but no: Arminianism it is which new creates the soul—our preaching it is, you affirm, by which sinners are converted or regenerated.

It appears strange, sir, to me, that you should enter into my house with two others, enemies to the doctrine of distinguishing grace, which you know were themes in which I delight, and commence with a volley of abuse against the Calvinists, representing them as cruel, ignorant, vile, &c., as though they were destitute of common sense, affirming that, with those whom you were acquainted, it was evident that it was the arminian part of their creed which converted sinners, which is evident to me that the popular system of what is called moderate Calvinism, and which obtains so much applause in this day of great profession, is strongly tinctured with arminianism; and while you were inveighing against the truths of the gospel, your sarcastic looks and laughter evinced so much enmity that my soul was grieved.

You, I suppose, intended to grieve me; hereby you accomplished your desire. Also you hoped to laugh me out of the truths of God's word; here you failed: and you make me out as an enemy to you, and that had I it in my power, fines, imprisonment, and death would be inflicted on you. As a man I wish you well, and would not oppress any for his views in religious matters, but your sentiments I unhesitatingly declare that I have an implacable enmity to.

Although I have endeavoured to state my views as clearly as I can upon Jehovah's sovereign, rich, and distinguishing grace, yet you wilfully pervert my writings, and let out your enmity against

God's manner of saving sinners, which precludes a poor saved sinner from having any communion with you.

You charge me with indulging in my heart, hatred and strife at the time you called. Such as I had you were made welcome to, and no such thought could you indulge in from my conduct, but because I have made an effort to convince you that salvation is of God and not man, therefore some false charges you must lodge at my door. Let me counsel you in future when you assert any thing let it be according to truth.

Your manner of treating with scurility the subjects of justification by the imputed, imperishable obedience of the Son of God, full, free, and endless remission by the blood of Christ, and personal, effectual calling by the Holy Ghost, made me ashamed of you, instead of making me to loathe or leave those eternal verities, wherein are contained all my salvation and all my desire. You charge me with setting aside means. When have I been found practising anything that would warrant your aspersion? Sentimentily I am as far from it as the east is from the west, believing Jehovah has ordained means adapted to the ends designed, and that they always have, and will effect the design of their Author.

Your constant asseveration is, that we Hyper-Calvinists make the Divine Being a sovereign tyrant—an Egyptian tyrant, and that these blasphemous and wicked views are identically my own. Really, sir, such awful things you may find pleasure in asserting; to live in a practical and sentimental denial of them is my privilege, and to him I appeal before whom the secrets of all hearts are manifest. It is with elevated hopes and heart-felt gratitude I ascribe the whole of my looked-for salvation to unmerited mercy and rich grace, and not to faith, repentance, or reformation. On Christ's atoning blood I rest.

If this is the picture of the *hyper* you abhor, God keep me the subject of your abhorrence until he give you a new heart and new eyes.

Now let me ask you this simple and serious question,—Is repentance, faith, obedience, patience, and perseverance causes or consequences of God's love to sinners. I think the answer is plain; but you will probably strive to muddle it. As the following is so to the point, expressive of my own sentiments, and truly scriptural, I shall transcribe it.

> "How helpless guilty nature lies,
>   Unconscious of the load:
> The heart unchanged can never rise
>   To happiness and God.
>
> "Can aught beneath a power divine
>   The stubborn will subdue?
> 'Tis thine Eternal Spirit, thine,
>   To form the heart anew.

> " 'Tis thine the passions to recall,
>   And upward bid them rise;
> And make the scales of error fall
>   From reason's darken'd eyes.
>
> " To chase the shades of death away,
>   And bid the sinner live;
> A beam of heaven—a vital ray—
>   'Tis thine alone to give.
>
> " O change these wretched hearts of ours,
>   And give them life divine;
> Then shall our passions and our powers
>   Almighty Lord be thine."

With such acknowledgements of the poet I must conclude, fully convinced that the sinner is altogether passive in the work of regeneration; that Jehovah herein displays his sovereignty and grace, bestowing life to the dead; then he that was dead is fitted for spiritual activity; and conversion to God, is an effect of life imparted.

When I look over what has passed between us, I feel certain that your conduct is highly reprehensible in treating divine subjects as you have, and charging me with entertaining blasphemous views of the divine being.

I confess, in looking over my epistle, that I have not expressed my thoughts in a style that is polished and gentle; but a plain man may find a shelter here; truth has been my object, and education I have never had to fit me for the polite. Plain dealing is best, in my judgment, on subjects so important: but to inveigh against a man in satirical language, and heap falsehoods on his head as you have done is not plain dealing, but wicked devices.

You affirm it as your belief, that I wish to withdraw from the church, and have therefore sought a pretext, by quarrelling with the ministry—here you greatly err. My intention was to seek a home among friends with whom I could heartily unite in principle, then to have sought an honourable dismissal, which is the plan I shall yet pursue, unless you, as a minister, thrust me out as an implacable enemy. But I request you to act otherwise, and part with me as unblemished in conduct; but of a different opinion respecting the glorious method of God's salvation. For I again declare it as my belief, that such is the depravity of human nature, and so averse is the carnal heart to everything that is holy, that we all to a man should be content to live in ignorance, unbelief, and rebellion against God and his Word; and so perish eternally, were it not for that rich and unsought grace of our sovereign Lord Jesus Christ, who calls poor sinners from darkness to light, according to covenant settlement with the Father before the world was. To the Three One, Jehovah, Father, Son, and Holy Ghost, be ceaseless praises. I remain, &c.,

W. B., *Drillman.*

After waiting nearly six months, and receiving no reply, I wrote nearly as follows:—

Pinchbeck, March 6th, 1820.

Sir,

I have been waiting, with much solicitude, for something from you of a conciliatory nature; but as you have remained so long silent you will allow me, for the last time, to state my views to you as concise as possible on the new creation of an immortal soul. You profess to take God's Word as the only rule of direction; now, here we are informed, that man is born in sin, and that he is shapen in iniquity; that we go astray from the womb, speaking lies; that the mind is enmity against God, not subject to his law nor can be; and in this state we live and die if grace prevent not: and then, as enemies to God, we must be cast into outer darkness, where there is " weeping and wailing and knashing of teeth." Now, as it is generally allowed among you Arminians, that the soul must be born again, or it cannot enter the kingdom of God, the question is, who is the Author of regeneration? I answer, God; and that this work is perfect at once as the creation was. Quickening into life is instantaneous; independent of all means. "You hath he quickened who were dead in trespasses and sins." Enlightening the quickened soul, feeding the new created, and clothing the sensibly naked transgressor are acts performed by the Life-giver in the use of means heaven has elected, appointed and honours. The Holy Ghost's continual working on the mind in convincing the sinner of his depravity, ruin and helplessness are gradual; and in the use of means his Almighty work on the already regenerated is progressive; enlightening the soul by the Word, the ministry, the ordinances, and Christian communion, to see more of Christ's personal glories, his redeeming wonders, and justifying deeds. Our gracious Emanuel declared to his living family, it is needful for you that I go away, and if I go away I will send you another Comforter, who shall abide with you for ever; and this shall he do, he shall guide you into all truth—he shall take of mine and shall shew it unto you, and he will shew you things to come. The Lord Jehovah the Holy Ghost, in covenant with the Father and the Son, is the efficient cause of our new creation, and all spiritual acts spring therefrom, under the Spirit's enlightening, teaching and sanctifying operations. He setting apart visibly a people to the Lord Jehovah's endless praise, guiding and preparing them for ultimate glory.

Now, sir, let me ask you seriously whether you do upon mature deliberation, think it a dishonour to Jesus Christ and his great work, when we attribute the whole of salvation to him as the meriting cause, and to the Holy Ghost as the efficient cause in the heart of a sinner? Or, do you think it is more to his honour and glory to say, that, although he hath made an atonement for all the sins of all men; yet the salvation of those who are saved cannot be attributed to the atoning death of Jesus, or to the unpreventable energies of the Holy Ghost: but that their diligence, goodness, attention, and compliance with his proffers, gives efficacy to his death, and makes their salvation certain? Surely, if you have any reverence for God's Word, and any experience of truth in your own bosom, the conclusion will be what I am pleading for—salvation is by grace.

Rather than debate further on such downright absurdities and self-evident contradictions as you plead for, I desist, and sing with the poet:—

> "Not all the outward forms on earth,
>   Nor rites that God has given;
> Nor will of man, nor blood nor birth,
>   Can raise a soul to heaven.
>
> "The sovereign will of God alone,
>   Creates us heirs of grace;
> Born in the image of his Son,
>   A new, peculiar race.
>
> "The Spirit, like some heavenly wind,
>   Blows on the sons of flesh;
> New models all the carnal mind,
>   And forms the man afresh.
>
> "Our quickened souls awake and rise,
>   From the long sleep of death;
> On heavenly things we fix our eyes,
>   And praise employs our breath."

The Scripture asks, "How two can walk together unless they be agreed?" The difference between us is here; we cannot agree respecting the glorious Author and causes of our salvation; so that in my ascribing the honour and praise of the sinner's deliverance, to matchless, ceaseless, and unpreventable mercy, reigning through the Mediator, is at war with your acclamations; which ascribes the praise to the pliable and docile creature man, who has rendered effectual the work of Christ by his acts of faith, repentance, and affection. I have reflected much on what you, with others of a kindred spirit have experienced; also, on the principles I have embraced; and the more I think upon them, the more I feel satisfied, that it is not by works of righteousness which we have done, but of his own mercy he saveth us by the washing of regeneration, and renewing of the Holy Ghost, which he shed on us abundantly through Jesus Christ our Saviour; that being satisfied by his grace, we should be made heirs according to the hope of eternal life.

Your views being so very different to this, and other parts of Holy Writ, together with my locality, sixteen miles distant, I think it will be much better both for the church and myself to withdraw from her community, for I cannot any longer unite with that minister and people who ascribe the work of a soul's new creation to the creature.

My supplication is, that the God of all grace will pardon our sins, and wash our souls from all defilement in the blood of the Lamb, whose precious blood was shed for the remission of sins that he might obtain eternal redemption; nor will it appear to all eternity that his blood was shed in vain. To his dear name, with the Father of mercies, and the Inspiring Spirit, be endless hallelujahs given. Amen.

W. B., *Drillman*.

P. S. Pray, sir, with what face will you meet the apostle Paul in the day of judgment, for such a scurilous reflection and palpable contradiction which you have cast on his word by a note inserted by you in the margin of Mr. Booth's book, which I lent you for perusal, entitled "Divine justice essential to the divine character?" Your note runs thus, "Reconciled to God when we were enemies! strange kind of logic this, and as false as it is strange!" Verily, sir, I should not wish to be found in your temper and in your position.

To this last letter Mr. Rogers wrote, saying he very cheerfully accepted my resignation, being confident that with my litigious spirit, there would be neither peace or quietness. What ridiculous conclusions some men can arrive at in wrapping up a bad argument. When a man pleads for the sovereignty and freeness of divine grace in the bestowment of spiritual blessings, according to covenant engagements and covenant love, he must be set down as a bad tempered, litigious person, and a disturber of the peace of the society. This is one way of getting rid of a bad argument —giving a man a bad name, and send him adrift as a dangerous fellow. So much for this arminian prelate.

About this time (1821), a Mr. J. Yeates, successor to Mr. Bampton, of Gosbuton, preached three sermons, in which he laboured to prove that faith is not the gift of God. The text he chose as a foundation for his sermons was "Ephes. ii. 8, 9, "For by grace ye are saved, through faith, and that not of yourselves, it is the gift of God, not of works, lest any man should boast." These sermons excited the people's attention, and although some were disgusted with his dogmatical arguments and levity, yet he made some vaunting remarks over his performances and the effects produced. In telling his tale to another of the like fraternity with whom I was acquainted, he exultingly exclaims, "I have silenced two or three of my Calvinistic hearers, and now I will have a turn with Bowcock." Not long after, he made his appearance at my house, with as much self-sufficiency and enmity against the truth of God as the devil could well fill a man with.

D

Faith not being the gift of God was his text. My text was, "This is the work of God, that ye believe on Jesus Christ whom he hath sent." We talked the subject over for more than three hours, and left off as we begun.

The next morning he wrote me six propositions, promising me if I would give my sentiments in writing he would answer me in the same way. The following are his propositions verbally, and my answers follow in substance.

What is believing? An act of the mind by which we assent to a thing proposed according to the evidence deducible in support of such proposition, therefore not the gift of God, but the act of man. Faith is the name of the above act—I think so.

First. Because it is said nowhere in Scripture that it is the gift of God.

Second. Faith is no where promised.

Third. Faith is not included in New Covenant blessings.

Fourth. Every figure made use of in the Scriptures conveys the idea of personal action, such as laying hold, putting on, running unto, &c.

Fifthly. Because unbelief is always represented as the condemning sin.

Observe, I do not deny, 1st., that the moving cause of believing is the Spirit of God, nor that Jesus is the Author and finisher of my faith.

2nd. I admit that God gives the power, but leaves man to exercise it.

3rd. This is in harmony with scripture and reason.

To the above propositions I wrote as follows:—

Pinchbeck, March 17, 1821.

DEAR SIR:—

I have been thinking and re-thinking over the subject of our late conversation, together with the propositions given. I have prayerfully sought the Lord's assistance. On the aid of the Holy Ghost I rely to preserve me from error and falsehood, and I would counsel you to do the same, that all our investigations of divine truth may be attended with his blessing to our edification.

In the first place, I agree with your first proposition, that believing is an act of the mind, and when it is exercised upon our Lord Jesus Christ it is called faith. And before we proceed any further, let us not forget that saving faith flows from a living principle in the soul, and is an evidence of that soul being born of God; yet you, sir, say this faith is not the gift of God! This assertion I consider derogatory to the honour of that Jesus who is the Author and Finisher of faith; therefore we must turn to his own word, and listen to what he there attests. Now for the text. "For by grace ye are saved, through faith, and that not of yourselves." Observe, and that faith, "Not of yourselves, it is the gift of God; not of works, lest any man should boast." Then let us notice the next verse—the reason why faith is said not to be of ourselves. Now note particular the Author and the work. "For we are his workmanship, created in Christ Jesus unto good works, which God before ordained that we should walk in them." "Without faith it is impossible to please God." Faith is is an inwrought principle of spiritual life implanted in the soul in the day of God's power. "Whom," saith Jesus to Peter, "say ye that I am. Simon Peter answered and said, Thou art the Christ, the Son of the living God. And Jesus answered, Blessed art thou, Simon Barjona, for flesh and blood hath not revealed it unto you, but my Father which is in heaven."

When the apostle speaking of God having made choice of him, that by his mouth the Gentiles should hear the gospel and believe, he says, "And God which knoweth the heart, bare them witness, giving them the Holy Ghost even as he did unto us, and put no difference between us, purifying their hearts by faith. What a precious act of Jehovah, Israel's covenant God, to give his Holy Spirit unto these poor idolatrous Gentiles, quickening them into life, and purifying their hearts by the faith of his own operation.

The apostles prayed also unto the Lord for an increase of faith. How could he increase that which he had not given; and which is not his to bestow according to your hypothesis? As faith is a living principle implanted by the Holy Ghost in the new-created, so it is called the faith of God's elect, they alone are in the faith. This accords with James i. 18, "Of his own will begat he us with the word of truth." Mark, his own will is the efficient cause of the new birth, and the implantation of those abiding principles which appear in the saints, such as faith, hope, joy, peace, patience, and all other graces are the products of Him who is styled the God of hope and the God of patience, so that if we trace the little that is found in us that can be called good to its Author, we shall soon discover that every good and perfect gift cometh down from the Father of lights, with whom there is no variableness nor shadow of turning. Now, sir, do not exclude faith from these good and perfect gifts; because if you do, they must be of nature's production; but surely you are better taught than to put natural acts in competition with the gracious workings of God's Spirit. "Being" says Peter to his scattered and persecuted brethren in the faith, "born again, not of corruptible seed, but of incorruptible, by the Word of God, which liveth and abideth for ever."

You see, it is not by reading or hearing the written Word men are born again, but by the living Word, who is God over all, and blessed for ever, that men are born again to a lively hope through faith, which is wrought in them by the mighty power of God.

All spiritual acts, you must allow, flow from a spiritual nature—the product of God. It would be absurd to expect the child to act and speak before its birth; but not more so is it to suppose that faith and repentance is produced by depraved nature. If we take a view of the scriptural account of man by nature, we shall find that he is unclean; his heart is deceitful above all things, and desperately wicked. The carnal man is enmity against God, and that he understands not the things of God, neither can he know them. Why not? Because they are spiritually discerned. See what a picture of human nature the Holy Ghost has drawn in 1 Cor. vi. 9. 10. He also tells us who effected the great change passed upon them—"But ye are washed, but ye are sanctified, but ye are justified, in the name of the Lord Jesus, and by the Spirit of our God." Hence it is plain by the above scriptures, with many others that might be quoted, that the Holy Ghost is the Author and Giver of spiritual life, and is the efficient cause of that holy abiding principle within, from whence flows our faith in, and affiance on the crucified Lord of glory; and this is according to the purpose of Him who worketh all things after the council of his own will, having predestinated us unto the adoption of children by Jesus Christ, to himself, according to the good pleasure of his will. Here we come to the Fountain Head, from whence our salvation flows, with every covenant blessing; such as regeneration, pardon of sin, adoption into the family of God, sanctification and ultimate glory. These are blessings freely given to us of God, according to the good pleasure of His will, who hath made us accepted in the beloved, to the praise of the glory of his grace, and every fruit of the Spirit that in us appear, such as love, joy, peace, longsuffering, meekness, temperance; and let not your reverence exclude faith from among the number, as being the product of the Spirit Jehovah. Consider 1 Peter i. 1., "To them that have obtained like precious faith with us." Now how did they obtain it? did they purchase it, merit it, steal it, or produce it? or rather, did not they receive it as the free gift of God—as a living principle within, from whence their act oozes, as a pure stream from a pure fountain?

However you may feel disposed to tell the Most High that faith is not his gift to poor, fallen sinners, be it my constant practice to exclaim with the apostle, "I am nothing, and have nothing that is worth calling good, but that I have received freely of my God," in answer to that simple, but all-important interrogation, "what hast thou that thou hast not received?"

Now, sir, if you would establish your first and second propositions, you must have recourse to logic, and not revelation, for I am thoroughly convinced that there is nothing in God's Word to prove your hypothesis, nor any thing from which you can draw the slightest inference that faith is not the free gift of God,

Further, you say that faith is not promised, nor yet included, in the blessings of the new covenant. To the law and testimony my soul, and not to bold assertions of presuming men. Is faith a spiritual blessing? I ask, if not, what is it? A natural good treasured up in nature's barren soil? This conclusion I dare not arrive at; but consider faith a cardinal blessing settled upon the church unforfeitably, in Christ their Covenant Head, Representative, and Saviour. Read that unearthly proclamation from him whose education qualified him to write facts not to be questioned, but to be received as infallible truths; Eph. i. 3., "Blessed be the God and Father of our Lord Jesus Christ, who hath blessed us with all spiritual blessings in heavenly places in Christ." Again and again the Lord hath promised what he will do for his people; and God's redeemed and quickened family find their joys come in by contemplating on what he hath done, is doing, and hath promised what he will do. Hear his proclamation still further, and then say, if you can, that in all he has promised, a believing heart is not among the many things he will bless his people with —" Behold the days come, saith the Lord, that I will make a new covenant with the house of Israel. After those days, saith the Lord, I will put my law in their hearts, and in their minds will I write them; and I will put my fear in their heart, and I will give them a heart to know me; and I will be their God, and they shall be my people; for I will be merciful to their unrighteousness, and their sins and iniquities will I remember no more."

I recommend to your serious perusal the above cited Scriptures; you will find them recorded in Jeremiah xxiv. 7; xxxi. 31, and three following verses; Heb. viii. 8—14; and x. 16, 17; and then see if new covenant blessings do not include that faith which is denominated the faith of God's elect. Allow me to say, that if your faith and mine, as our acts, do not proceed from the principle of faith implanted in the soul, without our deserts or desire, it is a dead faith, a false faith, and not that faith by which the soul enters into rest, by the reception of the truth as it is in Jesus. From the Scriptures, it appears plain that both your second and third propositions are unfounded, and that saving faith is the gift of God, and included in the blessings of the new covenant.

You say, every figure in Scripture denotes personal action. This is cheerfully allowed and experimentally practiced, by all the heaven-taught travellers; but our limbs and life, by which we act, are God's gift. The gracious Lord does not intend to conceal his grace by our acts, but manifest it. In my looking into Jesus by the eye of faith, in my fleeing to Jesus, taking hold of Jesus, trusting in Jesus, walking after Jesus, and taking delight in Jesus, the faith by which I perform these acts, the God of my salvation supplies me with. These are not acts of mere reason, as your ideas insinuate, but effects arising from an inward fitness, to welcome to the truth of Christ being a Rock, a Fortress, a High Tower, a Hiding Place. The power by which my soul flees unto Jesus, hopes in Jesus, and feelingly exclaims,

> "Other refuge I have none,
> Hangs my helpless soul on thee."

The power by which my soul performs such mighty spiritual feats as these, is God's gift of grace. The faith which makes Christ precious, springs from the same grace which gave Christ to us, and us to Christ. It is

> "His Spirit moves our heavenly lungs,
> Or they would breathe no more."

May the same Almighty Spirit who first enlightened my understanding, still continue in rich abundance his life-giving influence, that my acts may be more under his guidance; it will then be my continual effort to live and acknowledge that all spiritual deeds are the effects of his special favour towards me.

Your next proposition is, unbelief is the condemning sin. Upon this point, there is no disposition on my part to controvert; for the Scripture saith, "They could not enter in because of unbelief." Heb. iii. 9. Here, however, I would just ask you, whether you do not believe that this would have been the case with us all to a man, were it not for the sovereign distinguishing grace of God. Yes, sir, I firmly believe but for the immutable, immense, and inseparable love of Jehovah to poor sinners in the person of Immanuel; yes, sir, but for the voluntary and vicarious sacrifice of Christ, by which his people's sins were atoned for; yes, sir, but for the unpreventable grace and energetic influences of God the Holy Ghost, in changing the sinner's heart—there would not be one of Adam's guilty posterity that would escape the wrath to come; but since this is the case, there will not be a loved child, a redeemed sinner, a quickened soul, but what will taste everlastingly the Father's love, admire perpetually the Saviour's meritorious death, and praise eternally the Holy Ghost for his life-giving and life-perpetuating influence. Here the song of the ransomed commences; and oh, the grace that softened my hard heart, cleansed my guilty conscience, and taught my lips to pray by faith in a Mediator, and tuned my heart to sing the note, "Not unto me, not unto me, but unto thy name be all the praise, for present comforts and future prospects, in an ultimate arrival at that kingdom where my character will be perfected, and my bliss consummated."

You yet say, I do not deny that the moving cause is the Spirit of God, and that Jesus is the Author and Finisher of faith. This, sir, is all I have contended for in your presence and by my pen. But really what a paradox; to deny faith to be God's gift, and to say the Spirit is the first moving cause, and Jesus the Author and Finisher. Will you inform me by writing, how the Spirit is the efficient cause, and Christ the Author and Finisher of his people's faith, and yet faith is not his gift.

Again, you say, God gives the power, but leaves it to them to exercise that power, according to the inclination of the poor, depraved creature. How does this tally with that heavenly proclamation, "Thy people shall be willing in the day of my power!" Do you mean that faculty of the mind, reason, whereby we are distinguished from brutes, and by which we determine on any given proposition, and nothing further? Sir, you will find an insurmountable difficulty to prove, by Scripture, that faith of affiance and attachment to Christ, consists in the mere exercise of this faculty—"It is not by might nor by power, but by my Spirit, saith the Lord of hosts." Zech. iv. 6. The apostle affirmeth that he giveth to the saints the Spirit of power; not power as you nakedly affirm, but the Spirit of power; not that only, but the Spirit of love, and of a sound mind; intimating that while in a state of nature, we are beside ourselves as to spiritual objects and subjects; but in regeneration, the Spirit of a sound mind is imparted; then it is we think on spiritual truths interestedly, anxiously, and savingly.

The Scriptures speak of some being rooted and built up in him, and established in the faith. This establishment is the fruit of favour and the product of God the Holy Ghost. Col. ii. 7. 12, 13, "Buried with him in baptism, wherein also ye are risen with him through the faith of the operation of God, who hath raised him from the dead." Again, hear what Paul saith of the faith the Ephesians displayed, i. 19. 20., "That ye may know what is the exceeding greatness of his power to usward, who believe according to the working of his mighty power, which he wrought in Christ when he raised him from the dead, and set him at his own right hand in the heavens."

It appears evident from the Word of God, and the experiences of God's family will confirm it, that faith, as exercised on the Redeemer's person, love, blood, and grace, is the gift of God planted in the heart in the day of God's power, and drawn forth in continued acts, on the truth of God, and will issue in the ultimate vision of God in the person of the Redeemer, without a vail to intercept. The opposite you labour to establish now. If you fulfil your promise by writing, I entreat you to abide by the Scriptures, and give me the meaning of those quoted; don't run into philosophical reasoning, grammatical distinctions, and other translations of the Word of God. May the Spirit Jehovah chase away the mist of error from our minds, and reveal unto us the truth as it is in Jesus. I remain, &c.,
W. B., *Drillman*.

Although Mr. Yeates set this subject on foot himself, commencing an attack upon me, wrote the foregoing propositions, requesting me to write, and promised to answer me, saying he would set the subject in a clear light, "for" said he, "it is of great importance;" yet after these declarations, his word is forfeited; he proving himself unfaithful. It is now eleven years since he made his proposal and promises; the last time I asked him why he neglected to fulfil his promise; he said "The older I grow, the wiser I shall become;" and there he left it. This sort of conduct I consider very unbecoming any one, but in a professed minister of the gospel, it is truly disreputable; it is a breach of promise, and begets a suspicion of a man's christianity. About three or four years after this, Mr. Yeates became a professed deist.

Alas! what worms we are—how vain and sinful! we embrace this and the other doctrine, then fancy ourselves immoveable; self-conceit springs up, we become vain in our imaginations, and our foolish heart deceiveth us. We profess this, and avouch that, confidently, until our doctrines are brought to the standard of God's Holy Word, and cut up by the root; then finding that we have not a "Thus saith the Lord" for what we have said or written, pride is mortified, we start aside like a broken bow, shrink back, break our promises, and become unfaithful and sinful.

What an unutterable favour for we, poor guilty helpless sinners that our great High Priest did not shrink back from his engagements. Blessed be his dear name, he well knew the nature of his undertaking with the Father; he knew how his church would disgrace herself, and become abominable, filthy, and vile in her conduct. He knew what law and justice would require at his hands as her Surety, Husband, and Redeemer; nothing but his life poured out at the altar of burnt offerings could meet the claims of indignant justice. Jesus well knew the potent enemies he had to contend with, in bringing many sons and daughters to glory; but nothing could frustrate him in his love, or turn him from his purpose. In the fulness of time he appeared here in a state of humiliation and suffering, with his heart full of love and grace, and he voluntarily endured all the malice, rage, ignominy, reproach, and contempt his enemies heaped upon him, with all the afflictions, pain, and shame incidental to his abasement; and last of all, and the greatest of all, he endured the hiding of his Father's face, the frowns of his brow, which kindles a hell of never-abating despair, when it falls on any, except this Almighty HIM whom the Father spared not—but inflicted that curse on Him, his beloved one, that the many loved ones should escape to the glory of Divine Justice, and the honour of the Divine Ransomer, he having redeemed them from the curse of the law, by being made a curse for them. Was ever love like this?

Here faithfulness and truth appear cheering and lovely. Say

ye, will he not be faithful to his promises? Yes; blessed be his holy name, he will. What hath he promised? Why he hath promised that all the Father hath given to him shall come unto him, and that whosoever cometh, he will in no wise cast out. He hath graciously promised to send the Holy Spirit, even the Spirit of truth, whom the world cannot receive, and assures us that he will guide us into all truth, and shew you things to come —"He shall glorify me; for he shall receive of mine, and shall shew it unto you." Now I would ask—since Jesus has poured out his soul unto death, to redeem his people from deserved wrath, and just condemnation, will he leave them in nature's darkness, to perish in a state of enmity and unbelief! No, no; he will not; he will seek out his own, and bring them to seek forgiveness in his name, and possess them with those blessings he has acquired for them. Yes; blessed be his name, he will gather his people one by one; he will take away the heart of stone, and give them a heart of flesh, and cause his people to walk in his ways; "they shall look upon him whom they have pierced, and mourn;" and "I will pour out my Spirit upon you, and my blessing upon your seed; I will rejoice over them to do them good." I would have my brethren look over the sixteenth chapter of Ezekiel, and after considering carefully the Lord's love, as the cause of salvation, behold the covenant into which he enters with his church, threatening to punish her for her criminality and idolatry, yet, notwithstanding her baseness, he affirms he will not cast her off, but establishes his covenant with her for an everlasting covenant, and brings her down to his footstool, with shame and confusion of face, for all her abominations. This is how the Lord deals with all his children, whom he hath begotten with the Word of truth. He gives them eyes to see, and hearts to feel both their own pollution and the exceeding riches of his pardoning grace, through the blood of atonement. Christ will not leave the purchase of his blood unconquered by the Spirit. Regeneration, like redemption, is altogether the work of Israel's triune God in covenant. There is a sacred connection between purchase by price and conquest by power. One runs parallel with the other. All the bought will be possessed, and the regenerated will be known by repentance, faith, hope, love and delight in the good news of salvation, which all evince God's everlasting love to such souls. Strangely mistaken are my opponents, who are endeavouring to persuade men that repentance, faith, and obedience are, some way or other, the conditions of salvation under the gospel dispensation. Now these are blessings of salvation—the fruits of divine favour; Christ is exalted to give repentance and remission; faith receives remission, not procures it. The Comforter leads to Christ, where the soul finds all it needs—perfect righteousness, complete atonement, honourable redemption, and unforfeitable sanctity.

Salvation originates in the Father's will; is acquired for sinners by the work of Christ, and made known by the inspiring Spirit; all declaring the immense, immutable and unceasing love of the Three-One Jehovah. The soul's new birth is not by blood, nor by the will of the flesh, nor of the will of man, but of God—"Of his own will begat he us with the Word of truth, that we should be a kind of first-fruits of his creatures." See how the Spirit wrought on Philip, and on the heart of the eunuch, bringing him to receive the truth through the lip of Philip; and on his being baptised by Philip, he went on his way rejoicing, having communion with the mystery of the Lamb of God being slain to put away sin. It was the same Spirit that led Philip, which opened this Ethiopian's heart, and that opened a Lydia's heart, and so he does every heart that receives the truth in the love of it. I love the mission of the Holy Ghost; on him would I depend for instruction and guidance. O that he would lead my soul into clear discoveries of the glorious doctrines which exhibit my Lord in his eternity and antiquity, his Omnipotency and weakness, his self-existence and derived existence, that I may adore at his footstool, while I possess a holy familiarity with him, as my Brother who was born for adversity. May the Lord the Comforter, lead me into such a useful discovery of the gracious mysteries of salvation, that I may exultingly triumph in redeeming grace, dying love, and justifying righteousness; with a heart of gratitude, I pray to be kept giving my gracious God thanks for faith and repentance, as well as for every other new covenant blessing; so that while one is denying faith to be the gift of God, and another is affirming that repentance is the creature's product and a condition of salvation, be it mine to remember the words of my Redeemer, that "grapes cannot grow on thorns, nor figs on thistles; but that the tree must be made good, and then the fruit will be good also. These graces, or heavenly fruits, such as faith, repentance, meekness, love, humility, peace, and patience cannot grow in nature's garden, but are the products of the Spirit, fruits of favour, and inseparably connected with endless felicity.

I hesitate not to say, that it is in virtue of the Saviour's blood, according to covenant arrangements between the eternal Three, that the Holy Ghost quickens the sinner who was dead in sin, brings him to discover his real state and condition, as a transgressor against God, brings him to feel that he is justly exposed to God's curse, and leads him to cry, "What must I do to be saved?" And with eyes, hands, and heart lifted up to heaven, he cries, "God be merciful!" "Save, or I perish!" These are the cries of a living soul; and this fits the sinner to welcome the good news of salvation by Christ, and which subject the sacred Spirit opens up to the soul gradually, as he pleases and begets hope, peace, and joy, as faith is increased.

The natural man may be alarmed—unregenerate men have their fears, but they are strangers to the nature of that sentence of condemnation which the holy law awards to transgressors, and which the Holy Ghost makes known to the quickened soul, from which springs repentance, godly sorrow, and an hatred to evil. Onward the soul is led, by the same Spirit, to the blood of atonement, the sacrificial death of the Lord Jesus, which alone taketh away all sin; he is mercifully helped to look to him, and commit his soul into his hands by humble prayer and faith, knowing, as taught by the Spirit, that there is no salvation in any other. Thus Christ, the exalted Prince and Saviour of his people, through the ministry of the Spirit, by the word and ordinances, works faith, repentance, and love in them; and then follows peace from him which the world can neither give, nor take away.

Blessed Jesus! it was in this way thy good Spirit wrought upon my mind; and when a farmer's lad in the field, and pondering over the Word, and musing over the Lord's providence which had attended me from one servitude to another; and how I was at length favoured to attend regularly the Word preached, with a fear that I remained unprofitted by it, and that I knew nothing of the gospel—I hear of salvation, that the blood of Jesus Christ cleanseth from all sin. "Do I not need cleansing?" arose in my mind; "my heart is certainly very hard and very base; my thoughts very filthy and abominable; what will become of me?" Condemned I felt, and almost overpowered with a sense of guilt, and under the fear of Divine vengeance; being employed in the field alone, the Lord the Spirit led me to seek mercy under a feeling sense of my miserable estate. This was that never-to-be-forgotten day by me, recorded at the early part of my history, when I stopped the mare I was driving, crept behind the roller, and under a sense of my just deserts, lifted up my soul to God in prayer, with "Lord! save, or I perish!" "God be merciful to me a sinner!" whose ear was open, and whose mercy I found to the joy and rejoicing of my heart.

Great and many have been the changes, convulsions, and revolutions of my mind since that period! Many a time have I had to lament over my fickleness, folly, levity, and carnality. But thanks be unto the Lord for his sovereign unchangeable love and unutterable grace, he dealeth not with his children as their conduct deserves; but "as a Father pitieth his children, so the Lord pitieth them that fear him;" for notwithstanding all my ups and downs, I have enjoyed many precious seasons at the throne of grace, and have had a sweet sense of pardon sealed home on my soul; and down to this moment he indulges me with a sweet sense of his pardoning mercy, and preserves me in a cheerful hope of acceptance through the precious blood and righteousness of the Lamb that was slain.

May I live in a continual sense of the cleansing efficacy of that blood which purifies from all defilements, and that righteousness which justifies from all sin; in this robe I am hoping to appear at the wedding feast with all the redeemed for ever.

Having stated a few particulars respecting the Lord's dealings with me in a way of providence and grace, down to the year 1821, I shall proceed to state a few more of those changes which the Lord called me to pass through.

Being now quite out of business, and having some property, one of my near relatives consulted me about embarking with him and his brother in business. Being desirous of employment, and also of an enterprising turn of mind, I consented. The plan proposed was, to open a concern in the drapery business, on a large and respectable plan, in a large market town. Here, perhaps, I erred; being brought up at the plough, and used only to farmer's service most of my days. However Boston was spoken of; thither we went, seeking about the market place, being resolved to have an eligible place for business, wherever, or whenever we commenced. At last we arrived at the Bridgeport, where we found a shop to be sold: this we purchased for the sum of £1400. We entered into articles of partnership, removed to our new habitation on Tuesday, the 5th day of February, 1822, and fitted up our premises in a manner adapted to carry out a respectable trade.

On Monday, March the 13th, we commenced business; the the Lord prospered us exceedingly from the commencement until I withdrew; every thing went on smoothly for a season. But— ah, this *but*! I often think of what our pastor reminded us of the other day, that in all our prosperity and enjoyments in this life, there is sure to be a *but!* but *this!* but *that!* There is always something to interrupt our joy and disturb our tranquility. Certainly it is right it should be so; for if we had everything that heart could wish, we should be for making this our home, forget our dependence on the Lord, and rob him of his rights. Therefore, let us not only observe, but admire the Lord's ways who overturns and overturns man's projects, in the accomplishing of his own gracious purposes concerning his family. Let us remember, also, that our sorrows and afflictions are frequently brought upon ourselves, by our follies, pride, and evil tempers. Blessed be the name of our covenant God and Father, who dealeth not with us after our deserts, or we should soon perish from the way; but according to his mercy and faithfulness, he guides and preserves his stumbling babes.

Things arose which occasioned me to expostulate with one of my partners; his unrelenting spirit and unkind replies grieved me much; his practices I would not keep silent about; and his resolvedness to pursue his own will in the matter, led me to seek as speedy a retirement from the concern as possible. This I made known to my partners, and much unpleasantness arose. I however, proposed to buy my partners' shares in the premises, and then let it to them on a lease for fourteen years. This was amicably arranged; and on the 10th day of April, 1823, we closed our partnership, and I, with my wife, went to live in Norfolk Place, near the Grand Sluice, living on our interests.

When we first came to Boston, we assembled with the people commonly called, Particular Baptists, meeting for worship at Salem Chapel, Liquorpond Street, under the ministry of Mr. John Hinmers. We derived some benefit to our souls; and wishing to unite with them, we requested our dismission from the church at Pinchbeck, which was granted in a very affectionate letter to the church in Liquorpond Street, recommending us to the grace of God, and to their care. Mr. Hinmers was a man possessed of a kind and friendly disposition towards all his people, often calling upon us for a few minutes' christian converse, which we found pleasant and profitable.

What cause for thankfulness! Bless the Lord, O my soul! for his goodness towards such poor sinful creatures, in permitting us to assemble with his saints, in all places whither his providence has conducted us, and for having given us a name and a place in the church militant. This is a prelude I hope of having a place in the glorious kingdom of our God above.

Mr. Hinmers was very affectionate and laborious in preaching, expounding, exhorting, and instructing poor sinners in the things that accompany salvation. By his exertions, union prayer meetings were established, and held alternately every month, at the different dissenting places of worship, in Boston; and Bethel prayer meetings every Sunday morning, at seven o'clock, on board some ship in the haven. These things appeared kind and charitable towards all. But, ah! that but, alas! for me, I soon began to feel a want: the great and distinguishing doctrines of rich, free, and sovereign grace were kept back, as is always the case where there is an attempt to amalgamate with all; salvation is sure to be a mingle-mangle affair where there is an effort to unite with all: God's family become pained and grieved, where salvation is misrepresented to be sometimes of grace, and sometimes of works, sometimes election, and anon free-will takes the lead in the harangue. My soul was dissatisfied, and I cried, "my leanness, my leanness!" for, notwithstanding these frequent meetings and means of grace, so called, in uniting with the Methodists, Independents, General Baptists, &c., how dull, stupid, and barren, my soul felt. And why? because the grace of the gospel was concealed by them who should have published it, denied by others, and ridiculed occasionally by some. The love of God to his people, chosen in Christ Jesus, the life-giving influences and power of the Holy Ghost in regeneration, and the substitutionary work of Christ was never heard of. Such things as a soul's translation out of darkness into God's marvellous light, their unalienable and unforfeitable right and title to all spiritual blessings here, and to the heavenly inheritance above, on the foundation of being redeemed from the curse of the law, and out of the hands of primitive justice by the precious blood of Christ, the royal robe of Christ's righteousness, which is to all and upon all that believe, in which they shall be justified and shine gloriously into all eternity, in the kingdom of their Father — these, with other sacred truths, which are the food of my immortal mind in this land of drought, this state of sin and transgression—to keep back these eternal verities is the case now most woefully; until little more is preached than moral virtues, human ability, and creature-performances: and sinners are being taught what they should do, instead of being directed to what Christ did when he made an end of sin, and brought in an everlasting righteousness. Examine, O my soul! how matters stand betwixt God and thee: hast thou an interest in the finished work of Emanuel? Truly, last Monday night, I felt some sweet out-goings of soul in prayer, some sacred longings of soul that the Lord Jesus would come down, by his Spirit, and visit this plantation of his grace; quicken our souls, increase our faith, cause our love to abound, and glow with holy ardour! "Awake! O north wind! and come thou south, blow upon this garden, that the spices thereof may flow out. Let my beloved come into this garden and eat his pleasant fruits." Cant. iv. 16.

February 24, 1824.

Having but little employment of late, I have had Neal's History of the Puritans put into my hands. It contains much useful information respecting religion; giving an awful account of the instability and enmity of the human heart against Christ and his family, while it presents to us the favour of heaven in supporting his servants and maintaining his cause in the teeth of his foes. Who, that has read the account with a love to God and his cause, but is led to admire the rich grace and sovereign mercy of our covenant God to his poor afflicted children, in enabling them to confess his dear name before merciless tyrants and fawning hypocrites. There were hundreds, if not thousands, of the Lord's faithful ministers ejected, silenced, put down, and many of them banished from their native country, others imprisoned and perished in noisome dungeons, treatment the most cruel, which makes human nature to shudder and recoil! their only crime was worshipping God, rejoicing in Christ Jesus, and renouncing all confidence in the flesh, their unoffending wives and families were ruined, houses plundered, property confiscated, with every insult that mortals could devise to render life miserable; and these afflictions were inflicted by men, who even professed the gospel of peace, but in fact, were traitors to the blessed Jesus, and the bitterest foes to his saints. Mark the conduct of that archbishop Laud, who under a pretence of defending the cause of Christ, inforced with rigour and cruelty, almost all the mummery and superstitious ceremonies of that man of sin, the Pope. What could appear more superstitious than Laud's conduct at the consecration of Creed Church, London, on Sunday, January 16th, 1603? On his approach, persons appointed, exclaimed, "Open, open, ye everlasting doors, that the King of glory may come in!" Immediately this sinful Protestant bishop entered, he fell on his knees, and with eyes upwards directed, and hands spread abroad, presumptuously proclaimed with his unholy lips, "This place is holy, the ground is holy: in the name of Father, Son, and Holy Ghost, I pronounce it holy." At the same time, he was most bitterly persecuting those characters, of whom it is said, "The Lord hath set apart, him that is godly for himself." And even King Charles 1st, who had taken an oath to defend the Protestant religion, and protect his subjects from the cruel paw of the bloodhounds of Satan, perjured himself; being a Papist at heart, as appears by their idolatrous worship in the chapel royal, conducted by Popish recusants. Witness the cruel and terrible massacre in Ireland, wherein more than one hundred thousand Protestants were slain in one night! and upwards of two hundred thousand in a few days, not supposing anything of the kind was meditated against them! The infuriated Papists, like so many monsters let loose from the infernal regions, entered the houses of the Protestants at midnight, when the poor unoffending people were in a defenceless state, and cut them to pieces with the edge of the sword, old and young, without distinction. Abusing many young women, using them barbarously, even cutting off their breasts, ripping open their bodies, pricking others of them in various parts of their body, with their swords; driving them out of towns, villages, and cities, naked; and as cattle, drove to the slaughterhouse, so hundreds were driven naked at the point of the sword, into rivers and there drowned. Some fled into woods and to mountains, and there perished.

Now, all this cruelty and bloodshed was instigated by the king and queen together, with the archfiend Laud and emissaries, inflicting greatest calamities on innocent persons, infringing upon the rights of the subjects, and betraying the liberties of the people.

How can I help exclaiming against such kings and bishops, who take upon themselves the christian name, only as a cloak to hide their wickedness? And, instead of being helps and guides to the church, they set themselves up, the one as head over the church, the others as something more than human; even arrogating to themselves such dignities and titles as, the Lord Bishop, Archbishop, Right Reverend Father in God, &c. Under these specious titles, assumed by themselves, or derived by tradition, from their forefathers in wickedness, they wish to appear outwardly religious; and to be thought so by men. But, verily, there is but little doubt that the generality of bishops, even down to this, our day, are enemies to the cross of Christ, and bitter enemies to those who love Christ, walk in his ordinances, departing from the pomps and vanities of this wicked world.

It appears evident to me, by their principles and practices in church and state affairs, that was the Lord, in his providence to give us, his poor followers up into the hands of our English bishops and the bigotted clergy, that we should have no more mercy shewn us from them, than Job had from his arch-enemy. Yea, except Jehovah Jesus laid the same restraint upon the bishops and clergy as he did upon satan, saying, "Only spare their life, they would not hesitate to take that also."

But why harbour such thoughts against men who are the rulers of the church? They are no rulers of Christ's church; but they are Antichrists in spirit and tendency; they are the descendants from that mother of abominations, the mother of harlots, the scarlet whore. Our established religion, its character, conduct, aim, end, and design is worldly, fleshly, sensual, and devilish. As an illustration of it, mark the conduct of those at the head of this ecclesiastical estabishment in the senate house; see their political movements in oppressing rather than relieving a burdened people; seeking by every means to increase their revenues, and exalt themselves in worldly greatness, levying tythes, dues, and imposts; extracting, even from the poorest people, money for burying their dead; and extra money for breaking up the ground, as they denominate it, when, shame on them, the ground has been publicly set apart for ages past for the very purpose of depositing the dead. And then, in many parishes where the parson's living is, from the great tythe alone, from £600 to £700 per annum, and then exacts so much money per head for fire hearth, Easter offering, &c. The wonder is to me, how an enlightened people should so greatly submit to these things? If Dissenters were to unite their moral force, such things could not continue seven years. Proud prelates must soon seek to obtain a living in an honourable way; the nation would rise in a scale of greater importance; Christianity would appear in her native simplicity; and men's consciences freed from those manacles in which they are often fettered. The Lord reigns! and thanks, eternal thanks, to his name, whose watchful eyes are over his own people for their good. We have unspeakable privileges in the land of our nativity, we are setting under our own vine and fig tree, worshipping the Lord our God, according to the dictates of our own consciences, as directed by God's Word, and aided by the Holy Spirit; none, not even priests or prelates, daring to make us afraid. These privileges we should soon be deprived of, had the dominant Hierarchy its full sway, which I pray God to prevent.

April, 1824.

I have been perusing a book written some time back by Edward Fisher, with copious notes. It is called, "The marrow of modern Divinity." It is the best work I have yet met with on the subject, distinguishing between the law of works and the law of Christ, shewing how all mankind are under the law as a covenant of works, and are, by transgression, justly exposed to its awful curses, and how believers are delivered from it as a covenant of works, so that they have nothing to fear from it, or to hope for from it. Their keeping its righteous precepts cannot save them, and their breaking it cannot condemn them; and for this plain reason they are not under it as a covenant, and "Christ is the end of the law for righteousness to every one that believeth;" he having honoured its commands for them in obeying its dictates; and he having glorified that law for them as a broken covenant with a curse incurred, which he has endured to his endless praise, and to his people's gracious and honourable emancipation. The salvation, therefore, of all the redeemed is secured to them by the covenant of grace, without the deeds of the law, and yet the righteousness of the law is fulfilled in them "Who walk not after the flesh but after the spirit."

Christ appeared here to magnify the law, and all Christ's disciples delight in that law as it is in the hands of their redeeming Lord, living not without law to God; but this arises from a work of grace on the heart. Their obedience to him is voluntary, springing from a view of Christ their Law-fulfiller. He having redeemed them from the curse, and secured to them an inalienable right to eternal life by his perfect work, accomplished meritoriously when he gave up the ghost; so that justice is glorified and mercy is manifested by the cross, to the joy of the contrite, the confusion of enemies, and glorification of God's character as Lawgiver, Judge, and Deliverer.

How very wrong in their statements are all those who affirm that man must first turn to God and seek him dillgently, then God will turn to him and have mercy on him; while the fact is, God acts mercifully towards the sinners in Christ, then acts mercifully on the sinner's heart by his Spirit, then the soul acts graciously under feelings which declare that the man's stony heart is removed, and a heart of flesh is imparted. Repentance, then, arises from the love of God as the moving cause, from redemption as the meriting cause, and from the Spirit Jehovah as the efficient cause.

"Repentance," saith Calvin, "doth not only follow faith, but is a fruit arising from it." "There is," saith Poole in his Annotations, "a repentance that goeth before faith; that is, (saith he) before a believing apprehension of pardoning mercy through the blood of the cross; though true evangelical repentance and godly sorrow on account of sin, is promoted by faith's apprehension of the love of God in Christ Jesus, and pardon enjoyed through the atoning sacrifice of the Lamb."

Lightfoot says, "Faith or believing, in the order of grace, is before repentance, faith being the parent grace of all others. Yet her children are first seen and heard, and we know the mother is keeping house by the family walking into publicity."

The difference of the law of works and the law of Christ is material. The covenant of works saith, "Do this and live; and if thou do it not thou shalt die the death." The law of Christ speaketh on this wise, (Ezek. xvi. 6.) "And when I passed by thee, and saw thee polluted in thine own blood, I said unto thee, Live." "And whosoever liveth and believeth in me shall never die." "If ye love me, keep my commandments, &c." "If they break my statutes, and keep not my commandments, I will visit their transgressions with a rod, and their iniquities with stripes. Nevertheless my lovingkindness will I not utterly take from them, nor suffer my faithfulness to fail." Thus you see both these laws say "Do this;" but here is the difference, one saith, "Do this and live;" the other saith, "Live and do this." The one saith, "Do this for life;" the other saith, "Do this from life." The one saith, "If thou do it not thou shalt die;" the other saith, "If thou do it not I will chastise thee with a rod." The one is delivered by God, as he is Creator and Judge of all, the other is delivered by Jehovah, as he is a Redeemer in Christ, and Saviour of all who are in Christ. In answer to the querist, whether the ten commandments may be called the law of Christ, Mr. Fisher's reply is, "So long as we find that Christ and his apostles did require and command the things that are therein commanded, reproving and condemning those things that are therein forbidden, it is quite sufficient to prove it to be the law of Christ."

A christian man is not at liberty to do those things that are ungodly; and if the doing those things the law forbids does not displease Christ—if they be not repugnant to the righteousness received of him—then let a man do them, and guilt can never be contracted.

The same author says, when speaking of marks and signs of grace, "Indeed I must confess that in these days of professed christianity that many reprobates appear, making a shining profession, performing all duties with a great shew of zeal, partaking also of a measure of inward illumination, and have a shadow of true faith, repentance, and attachment to Christ, his truth, ordinances and people; there being no grace effectually wrought in the faithful, a resemblance whereof may not be found in the unregenerate. A true christian's acts flow from the inward emotions of his soul and his inward sensibilities as arising from an internal work of grace began without his desires, and carried on without his deserts. The work on his heart is to be accounted for by electing favour, justifying righteousness, and ransoming merit. The eternal Comforter is the Author of that life of faith —he now lives on the Son of God, Christ Jesus the Lord of Zion. Thus the man of God's sure mark of safety is, he has fled for refuge and taken hold of the hope set before him in the gospel. In faithful dealing we say that every one who hath the form of godliness hath not the power, yet every one who hath the power venerates the form. It is an old adage that "It is not all gold that glisteneth;" yet all gold doth glisten; and therefore I tell you truly, if you have no regard to make the law of Christ your rule, by endeavouring to do what he requires and to avoid what he forbids, it is a very evil sign. In this the children of God are manifested, and also the children of the devil. Whosoever doeth not righteousness is not of God."

In perusing over this book respecting faith, repentance, and regeneration it caused me to review what I had written on the subject in my letters to Messrs. Bampton, Yeates, and others; it afforded me some satisfaction to see how the Lord had graciously led me in the footsteps of the flock, and given me to embrace those God-honouring and soul-elevating doctrines which others had written in defence of; and that my experience tallied with those saints who are now in glory, and though dead yet speak to us instructively by their words written. All conspire to tell the church there is one faith, one Lord, and one baptism; that it is the same spirit of truth who teaches the same things to the saints in all ages and in all places; indeed the church of Christ is but one and the same family; she has but one Spirit— the infallible Guide into all truth, and that eventually the church will be presented by Christ perfect in her number, completed in her character, and consummated in bliss.

> "Thanks to thy name, thou sovereign Lord most high,
> For all thy favours thus bestowed on me;
> I still would praise thee, Saviour, till I die,
> And after death may I ascend to thee:
> There to unite with all thy saints above,
> And aid the angelic powers to chaunt thy praise;
> There rapturously adore thy wondrous love,
> And prostrate mingle in harmonious lays."

"Behold the Lamb of God which taketh away the sin of the world." John i. 29.

What grace is here exemplified! The mysterious subject is ushered in with a Behold—a note of wonder, surprise, admiration, and attention. Take notice, this is God's precious Lamb. This name is significant; it denotes his innocency, and spotless purity of his nature. Lambs were offered under the law to take away sin typically, pointing immediately to this one great sacrificial Lamb, who, by his one offering, hath put away sin, which offering was a sweet smelling sacrifice to our offended Lawgiver.

The apostle Peter reminds his brethren that they were not redeemed "With corruptible things, such as silver and gold, but with the precious blood of Christ, as of a Lamb without blemish and without spot." Sin is so offensive to infinite majesty, that his infinite holiness will not allow it to go unpunished; hence the early appointment of sacrifices to remove it typically manifested his abhorrence of evil, and his determination to pardon by satisfaction being given by an unoffending victim. Thus to our first parents, immediately after their revolt, was made known the Lord's gracious will to accept an atonement through the blood of an innocent victim, and which victim was to spring from the seed of the woman, and by whom the serpent's head should be bruised. But further disclosures of the all-important mystery was revealed to Abraham and his posterity, for in him and his seed God promised all the nations of the earth should be blessed. This seed is Christ.

The Lord sovereignly chose this people for himself, setting them apart from the rest of the nations; he increased them like a flock, and led them by the hand of Moses and Aaron; with them he established the priesthood, gave them his laws and ordinances to observe and do, appointing all those offerings and sacrifices for sin which we read of in the Levitical dispensation, and was ordained to preach Christ as the great and precious Priest and Sacrifice who alone could take away sin.

The people of Israel being thus favoured of the Lord above all others, made them very tenacious of their laws and religion. To this the apostle bears them witness, "For," says he, "they have a zeal for God, but not according to knowledge."

Now it appears evident, through the writings of the Evangelists and Apostles, that the Jews had entertained erroneous views of the promised Messiah, both as to his Person and offices. They even look at the time of Christ's appearance for the fulfilment of the predictions respecting his appearance as their Deliverer; and although they were at the time of Christ's incarnation ready for the reception of their Messiah on his appearance, they rejected him with disdain, and the cause was, their expectations were that he whom they looked for would appear in great worldly splendour, and that he would establish an earthly kingdom in great glory, delivering them as a nation from the Roman yoke, and exalt them to national distinctions and carnal greatness; so that when John the Baptist pointed them to the meek and lowly Jesus as the Messiah, the holy and only Lamb of God, he does it with a *take notice*; be assured this, this is he.

But, notwithstanding John's testimony of Christ, and Christ's own testimony of himself, together with the works and miracles he performed before them, they would not receive him; but treated him who was truth itself, as an impostor—conspired against him, and put him to death. Here we have a clear proof of the enmity of the human heart, the deceitfulness of sin; this is the awful state we are all in, by nature, being led captive by the devil at his will. We must be born again to enter into Christ's kingdom, until our eyes are anointed with eye-salve, we can see no beauties in King Jesus to admire; but when our eyes are opened by grace divine, we see a beauty in this Lamb, and derive comfort while gazing on this sacrificial Lamb.

He taketh away sin. This is expressive of the continual efficacy of his one offering, and that we need a sacrifice which takes in a removal of our every day's transgressions, and that our High Priest ever lives, presenting the memorials of his death, making intercession for all who come to God by him, which truth a sweet poet expresses in a forcible manner by the lines below:

> "Father! he cries, forgive their sins!
> For I myself have died;
> And then he shews his open veins,
> And pleads his wounded side."

With such a faithful, compassionate, and merciful High Priest and Intercessor before the throne of God, surely, my brethren, we have abundant reason to take encouragement to approach in his name. Let us commit the cause of our souls into his dear hands, since

> "Jesus pleads and must prevail,
> While Justice keeps the throne."

The sin of the world, saith John. What a world of iniquity we have in ourselves! But, blessed be Jesus, the precious Lamb of God, his blood cleanseth from all sin, and all that believe are justified from all things. Jehovah hath laid on this sacrificial Lamb, the iniquities of us all, and by his stripes we are healed: the healing extends to "*the all*" whose iniquites he bore. I have known many apply this passage, universally; affirming that Christ endured and ended the punishment due to every individual in the world: but so it will not appear at the end of the world, Jesus never put that away which is to be brought forward at the last day; Christ never ended that punishment which is to be inflicted another day. Sin is a transgression of the law; punishment is the just demerit of sin; it must be inflicted on the criminal or a substitute: if on the former, his case is hopeless and easeless; but if on the latter, atonement is the object reached at by the inflicter and by the afflicted, punished substitute. "Awake! O sword, against the man that is my fellow! smite the shepherd, and the sheep shall be scattered; but I will turn my hand upon the little ones." "If (says Jesus) ye take me, let these go their way." "There is, therefore, now no condemnation to them that are in Christ Jesus." If Christ has ended the punishment due to all men, there will be found none at the left hand of the Judge, and there is no hell to be endured: it will be found at last, that the sins that Christ atoned for are concealed, never to be revealed to the confusion of the ransomed. Jesus, in that memorable prayer which the Arminian feels little interest in, has more of the gospel in it than any chapter in the four gospels, (John xvii.) "I pray not for the world, but for those whom thou hast given me, thine they were, and thou hast given them unto me; and I give unto them eternal life, and they shall never perish." It was for these the Son of God took flesh. Hear him again; "I lay down my life for my sheep, none shall pluck them out of my hand:" and he will seek out his own in the dark and cloudy day, he will gather them one by one and bring them to Mount Zion above; here he will fit them for the mansion ordained. In this world his people are distinguished from the rest by their dependence on him, cleaving to him, and delighting in what he has done, and in what the scriptures say about him, at his footstool, they adore, and of his fame they speak. The word *world* here, as in many other places, is to be taken in a limited sense; the reason why the Holy Ghost directed men to use it, doubtless, was this— the Jews being the only people chosen of God, and blessed with a revelation from heaven, their carnal hearts were lifted up with pride; they despised all other people, and boasted of their parentage and privileges, as the descendants of Abraham. Hence, they thought every thing of a religious kind would always belong to them, to the exclusion of all other nations under the sun. They rejected, and still do, that any of the blessings promised under the Messiah's reign belong to the Gentiles; not crediting that the nations of the earth were to be made partakers of the blessings of salvation. When Paul declared his conversion and call to the apostleship, they gave him audience until he spake of being sent unto the Gentiles, and they lifted up their voices and threw dust into the air, and exclaimed, "Away with such a fellow from the earth, for it is not fit that he should live."

In order, therefore, to meet the prejudices of these Jews, the sacred writers made use of terms the strongest, such as the world, the whole world, all men, every man, &c., and thereby gave them to understand that idolatrous Gentiles are interested in this precious Messiah, the Lamb of God; and that they shall be saved through faith in his blood, as well as the Jews.

So again, (1 John ii. 2.) "And he is the propitiation for our sins, and not for ours only, but also for the sins of the whole world;" that is, for Gentiles, for heathens, for men of all classes, and of all climes. Now, this is a fact. But it is not a fact that all men of all climates and grades, are redeemed from the curse of the law, by the precious blood of Christ. John, in his vision, saw a number that no man could number, out of every nation, kindred, and people, standing clad in white robes, having palms in their hand; and they overcame satan, sin, death, and hell, through the blood of the Lamb.

Neither are we to think that original sin merely is meant here;

for, if the Lamb of God only removed original sin, then we should all sink under the vast load of actual transgression: but such views are erroneous, and tend to subvert the mystery of the real vicarious work of Christ. Every exercised Christian knows that pardon of sin is a free bestowment to the sinner, through the expiatory death of Christ, and that unless Christ served and suffered for him, he must be equitably punished; but, that as Jesus died to put sin away, that if he suffered for him, he shall as certainly escape as it is certain Christ was punished; and through faith, in Jesu's atoning death, he has joys which a stranger intermeddleth not with.

Blessed be the name of the Lord, who taketh away the power of sin by his Spirit, as it is written, "Sin shall not have dominion over you, for you are not under the law, but under grace." The blood of Jesus Christ cleanseth from all sin! An application thereof, by the Holy Ghost, to the conscience of a poor burdened soul, purgeth from the defilement and pollution of sin, and gives an evidence and satisfaction to the man that his sins are forgiven, that he is accepted, justified, and in due time will be glorified. He is associated with the family, and he is on his journey to the family mansion, and shall soon arrive there though death and hell obstruct his way; for he is under the convoy of grace, and shall be welcomed at the family home with shouts of joy.

It is evident that the Lord's people are not travelling in multitudes. A remnant shall be saved; narrow is the way to heaven; few there are who find that way. It is a truth, and can never be falsified, that the Lamb of God put away all the sins of all the elect world, and if this offend general professors, they stumble at God's word, and blame will never be lodged at the door of any man who adheres to the truths of God's book. A fact! It will be eternally evident that all the Father gave to Jesus, for them Jesus died to ransom; and all those whom he ransomed, he will possess by his Spirit; to them righteousness is imputed without works, and heaven will be possessed by them without a spark of merit on their part.

It may well be called a world, for their number will be more than any man can number, who are redeemed from among men and redeemed to God. O may I stand among them at the right hand of God, singing for ever unto Him that "Loved us, and washed us from our sins in his own blood."

The use I would make of the subject are these:—

1st. I would pray to be indulged with a believing apprehension of this Paschal Lamb as our all-sufficient Sacrifice to take away our sins, and as our Advocate with the Father, ever living to plead our cause, and ever prevalent through the merit of his offering.

2nd. To yield myself up unto him as a devoted follower, walking in his ordinances, meditating upon him as God-Man

Mediator, and upon his finished work as the Procurer of perfect salvation.

3rd. So to walk that my light may so shine before men, that my Father which is in heaven may be glorified thereby, and Christ be honoured as King and Law-giver in Zion.

4th. Live depending on the Holy Ghost daily to be led into all truth, and mercifully preserved from all errors and false doctrines which the professing church is deluged with, and that we may be lead on in the way in which we should go, and that we may be found of him in peace.

W. B.

Written for the Sabbath-evening Conference, Oct. 27, 1821.

"I love the Lord." Psalm cxvi. 1.

"Blessed be the Lord God of Israel who remembered me in my low estate, for his mercy endureth for ever."

I love the Lord—I love his Word—I love his worship—I love his people—I love his ordinances.

1. I love the Lord as my Creator, because he hath made me a rational being, capable of knowing, loving, and enjoying him. My body is a display of his skilfulness; rightly framed, and put together curiously. I praise his holy name for right shape and make, while many are decrepit around me; he hath given me an immortal soul, and endowed me with faculties and powers, by which I think, observe, and admire. Sometimes I contemplate Jehovah in his works of creation; ranging through fields, I observe endless varieties in the vegetable kingdom. What a gradation from the smallest spire of grass, to the fragrant rose, whose lovely blush and sweet perfume, cheers and delights the senses; and from the meanest shrub to the wide-spreading oak, whose stately trunk defies the storms of winter's blast, and endures for ages, when other trees and plants have crumbled to dust, and fallen into decay. It is by the use of my reasoning faculties, that I observe and admire the wisdom of God in the production of such multitudes of living creatures of various forms and size; endowing them with animation and instinct. Their natures and movements are various; some grovelling in the earth, others crawling on its surface, others flying in the open expanse of the heavens, and building their houses on the rocking boughs, while others can only exist in the liquid elements.

And here again what matchless wonders appear from the shrimp to the monster of the deep—the whale. Again my eyes are directed upwards, and here what ceaseless wonders appear; those mighty orbs that fly swiftly round in their endless circles, and shine to their Maker's praise, who first formed them and continues them by his power, and directs them by his wisdom. How vast their number! how stupendous their size! with what velocity they perform their revolutions! When my thoughts are drawn forth in meditation upon the works of Jehovah, as Sovereign Creator, I admire and adore him, thanking his Eternal Majesty for endowing me with rational faculties; but more especially when I obtain a believing view of the Lord as my Redeemer and Saviour; I then can say, "I love the Lord."

I was not only born in sin and shapen in iniquity, but even the noblest powers of my mind, by which Jehovah designed I should know and serve him, were devoted to sinful pursuits. Yea, I have revolted from God, and am justly exposed to his righteous curse; I was going post-haste with the unthinking multitude, in the broad road that leadeth to destruction. There is not a doubt in my mind, but what that course would have been pursued by me and all men until we dropped into hell, had not the Lord stretched forth his hand, and plucked me, with many others, from the wrath to come. Thanks to the Lord, he hath done great things for me, whereof I am glad. He convinced me by his Spirit through his word, that I was in the way to endless ruin; he enlightened my eyes to see my ruined condition as a condemned sinner. I trembled under the discovery made to me; I cried for mercy, and he heard my cry, and delivered me from going down to hell, for his dear name's sake; for I was not only guilty, but I found myself as helpless as I was vile; to help myself was impossible, therefore help and salvation was what my soul coveted, and the Lord has proved himself to be the helper of the helpless, and the Saviour of the lost. He has brought me up out of an horrible pit, and out of the miry clay, and set my feet upon a Rock, even the Rock of ages, which is Christ Jesus; having enabled me to cast myself as a lost, helpless, guilty, yea, and as a filthy creature, upon the rich mercy and boundless love of God in Christ Jesus; believing, that if ever I am saved, it is entirely by virtue of the atoning blood of the Lamb of God.

His blood to cleanse my leprous soul, and his righteousness to justify my person in the sight of God, is my only hope. Thus hath the Lord brought me from the brink of despair, and raised me to a cheerful hope in his mercy, through the redemption of Christ; he hath put a new song into my mouth, even praise to his holy name. Salvation through electing love, redeeming blood, and sovereign grace, are delightful themes in my ear. O, I say, love the Lord because he hath heard the voice of my supplications; he hath from of old blessed me, with all his people, with all spiritual blessings in heavenly places in Christ Jesus, according as he hath chosen us in him before the foundation of the world, and hath made me acquainted with it, and satiated my soul by it; he hath brought me by his grace into the highway of holiness; promised me strength to pursue my course, saying, "Fear not, for I am with thee;" he will give peace in the midst of trouble, and he will subdue our enemies before us; the God of peace shall bruise satan under your feet shortly; he hath established my goings, and is leading me on graciously, and will bring me off more than conqueror, at last, over death and the grave.

Behold what manner of love the Father hath bestowed on a rebel—one that deserved the hottest place in hell!! How can I sufficiently praise and adore my covenant God. O that I could but love the Lord with an ardent, abiding, and undivided love, all the moments of my existence! Lord Jesus, I beseech thee, shed abroad thy matchless love in my poor heart, by the Holy Ghost, that it may purge my conscience, mortify my pride, subdue my corruptions, and produce supreme love to thyself, until thou shalt bring me into those pure regions, where the love of God shall be the atmosphere in which I shall breathe, and be the bliss of my soul eternally.

II. I love God's Word. The Bible is the Lord's Book, and a revelation of his mind and will towards offending men; it is here I learn what a transgressor against God guilty man is; it lays open man's pollution, deceitfulness, wretchedness, and entire ruin. Here is disclosed to us the origin of our misery—"By one man sin entered, and death passed upon all, for all have sinned in him." This Book of books makes known how it is that men sleep at ease, with such a gulph before them—"The god of this world hath blinded our eyes, and we love darkness, because our deeds are evil."

Bless the Lord, O my soul, for that Word which not only makes known our ruined estate, but discloses to us the way of salvation—"Herein is life and immortality brought to light." It is by the Scriptures we are informed, for our profit, of God's Omniscience and Omnipresence—"Known unto God are all his works." Jehovah hath gone forth in acts of covenant favour, with his bosom Son, for the salvation of the people whom he hath loved eternally;—but permitted them to sin foully, taking occasion from their baseness, to illustrate his rich grace gloriously, by their deliverance from their thraldom, by Jesus Christ, their Elder Brother, serving for them—dying in their stead, and raising them to a more glorious standing than what they had by creation interest; for the Adam interest was an earthly paradise, and a forfeitable one, but interest in Christ places us in a heavenly paradise that is unloseable.

Now, it is by that Book, which is the Volume to correct all other testimonies, that we know these gracious mysteries. Take away God's Book, and what darkness we are plunged into! In this Vocabulary we are taught that "The Lord Jehovah is one Lord," and that there are Three distinct Persons in the Divine Essence, and that these Three are One; that Jesus, the adorable Emanuel, is a complex Person, verily God, and verily man; not two Persons, but One glorious Person, God-Man, one with the Father and Spirit, and one with the family, loved, adopted, and saved. He, their chosen Head and Representative, before his brethren were brought into being. Hence he is denominated, "The Son of God," "The first begotten of the Father," "The beginning of the creation of God," "In the beginning was the word, and the word was with God," "The first-born of every creature." The above expressions have to do with Christ, as a complex Person, as a divine Person, begotten, produced, or proceeded from none; but as a complex one, we see him the product of infinite wisdom, grace, and power; and thus was he brought forth as a fit agent for all the after acts of his glorious Majesty, which he, in love to his brethren, undertook to accomplish, and "in the fulness of time" accomplished; manifesting himself to be the Son of God, in truth and love. He was set up as the elect Head and Representative of his (to be brought forth) brethren, he undertaking to accomplish his Father's will in the salvation of his brethren, by his vicarious obedience and death. In heaven he was capacitated to undertake the work—on earth he must appear to accomplish it; and "in the fulness of time" he appeared to do the work which his Father gave him to do, and which he had voluntarily undertaken to do.

I cannot envy those men their feelings, or sentiments, who obstinately deny that the Lord Jesus Christ was a complex Person, before he was an incarnate one! Indeed, their own experience and expressions cotradict, very often, such an idea. How the divine Being, the Lord of all, could represent his fallen polluted creatures is a matter the Scriptures never aver, and to me the idea is monstrous! He who stood forth as the Bondsman was the Man, the Lord from heaven, our Kinsman, God, and brother, in whom the right of redemption rested; right stands in his relation to the church—might to redeem, in his relationship to the Father, as one in the essence of God.

In this glorious Christ we have a complex agent entering into a covenant of life and peace, restoring what he took not away, honouring law, establishing the rights of justice, in the remission of sin, by his own personal acts, according to his own personal undertaking. It was the same glorious Person who appeared at the brazen altar to put away sin—that had antecedently appeared around the council table in heaven, and undertaken so to appear. Men may say these are bold assertions and prove nothing; but I still appeal to God's Word; and let us take the obvious meaning of the passages above quoted, as well as those which follow, without wilful twists to evade the true import of the words, and it will appear that bold as my affirmations may appear, they are most certainly correct. Hear the language of the Son of God himself—"Jehovah possessed me in the beginning of his way; before his works of old, I was set up from everlasting, from the beginning, or ever the earth was; before the mountains were settled; before the hills were brought forth; before the creation of the heavens and the earth I was by him, as one brought up with him; and I was daily his delight, rejoicing always before him." Prov. viii. 22—30. The above language cannot apply to the wisdom of God as an attribute, any more than it can to any other essential perfection; neither can it be applied to the Divine nature of the Son of God in an abstract sense, any more than to the Divine nature of the Father, or the Holy Ghost. Hence it is evident these things are spoken of him as a complex Person, in whom all divine perfections essentially exist, and in whom subsists man's nature, as "the first-born of every creature," and who is the glorious God-Man, the Head of the church, and the Saviour of his body; and by his church he will be approached, as her "Brother born for adversity," and adored as her God, all-sufficient, all-glorious, and perfect Deliverer; being delighted with their Father's contrivance to bring rebels to his footstool, hopefully; "For it hath pleased the Father that in him should all fulness dwell."

The blessed book it is that tells us that Jesus Christ, who was rich, "became poor, that we through his poverty might be made rich;" "Father, glorify me with the glory I had with thee;" my plea is founded on the perfection of the work done. Evident it is that Christ alludes to his glorified state, as the God-Man and Head of his church, before he descended to that work which would have annihilated all creatures, had they attempted to perform it. Let us adore our covenant God, who hath favoured us with his Scriptures, which make known the antiquity of the Lord Jesus Christ, as the "Man of God's right hand," whom "he made strong for himself;" this Jesus being the God-Man, Mediator, Redeemer, Saviour, for it is written— "The Redeemer shall come and turn away ungodliness from Jacob." Blessed be his dear name for ever and ever, he has come and manifested himself strong enough to save and weak enough to suffer; Omnipotence and weakness; Infinite knowledge, and limited understanding; real ubiquity, and yet limitation; self-existence, and derived existence; independence, and dependence; all these appear in the Person of our Lord! His incarnation, sorrows, death, resurrection, and ascension, manifest him to be the Son of God and Saviour of his people.

What know we about the true God, sin, holiness, heaven, or hell, except by the Word of God. Here we discover "God is just, and yet the justifier of the man who believeth in Jesus; herein we discover God's love to guilty sinners; his grace, wisdom, mercy, and goodness, in pardoning the criminal and yet punishing for the crime, in the Person of Jesus, the criminal Substitute, Surety, and Ransomer; here we discover the law honoured, justice glorified, the sinner escapes, but his delinquencies marked with abhorrence; here Jehovah makes himself known as the friend of the vicious and the foe of his vice; the embracer of the defiled, but the remover of his defilement. To the cross of Christ the Word directs us, and the Spirit leads us to behold all this. The Son of God, this strong Lord, cheerfully undertook the cause of his sinful brethren, and he exclaims, " Lo, I come to do thy will, O God, thy law is within my heart;" the covenant, or counsel of peace was between them both; and the Spirit beareth witness, because the Spirit is truth; for the Spirit searcheth all things, even the deep things of God—" Now we have received not the spirit of the world, but the Spirit which is of God; that we may know the things that are freely given to us of God."

Under the Old Testament dispensation, the saints of God were directed to the promised Saviour, and the law sacrifices assisted their faith in him, as the glorious object of hope. The priest, the altar, the sacrifices, the sprinkling of the blood, the temple, the, ark, the mercy-seat, the golden censor, and the incense, were all shadows and types of the Lord Jesus and his great work, which he, "in the fulness of time," achieved at Jerusalem, when he offered himself up as an atoning sacrifice, which heaven accepted; at which time the middle wall of partition between Jews and Gentiles was removed, and a way into the holiest of all was made for Jews and Gentiles, by the rending of Emanuel's flesh. So that now, by faith in his sacerdotal office, we poor outcasts, are brought experimentally to enjoy privileges which the Hebrew house never enjoyed by their priests, sacrifices, and altar. And after Christ's advancement, as our Atoning Victim, he sent forth his servants to proclaim the good news of sins forgiven, peace established, and righteousness brought in for the guilty, helpless sons of men; and that all who come to the Father, by him, he lives in the heavens to intercede for. The efficacy of Christ's intercession is demonstrated by the descent of the Holy Spirit, who beareth witness to, and maketh application of the blood of Jesus to the souls of the redeemed, working faith in the hearts of all God's people, leading them to Jesus, for pardon, purity, righteousness, and endless life; disposing their hearts to love him, and inclining them to walk in the paths of righteousness. The Bible is endeared and highly prized; precious Scriptures! What a treasure! O how I love thy law!

Here I discover precepts and admonitions suited to every state, relationship, and circumstance. As disciples of the Lamb, what counsels, cautions, and promises are afforded us! How to walk as those who have obtained mercy. It is a written rule, promulgated by Zion's Legislator, Saviour, and Head, instructing ordinances. Here we see encouraging promises and soul-animating doctrines. To live under the influences of those gracious doctrines is the privilege of none but Zion's progeny; to feel the sweets of encouraging promises is happy sensibility; and to walk in the ordinances of the Lord's house cheeerfully is a temper becoming the child of his care. If persons can treat the Lord's precepts with negligence, and omit to attend to his positive institutions, it is a fearful sign that they are deceived. How necessary it is that the Christian man should think for himself, and act as in the fear of God; not swim on with the tide of customary professors, who are substituting human inventions in the place of God's institutions, altering that mode of worship his wisdom has commanded. Let it be remembered that Jehovah is a jealous God, and he will visit for these things. Let all our acts of worship be as his gracious Majesty directs, and never let us who are of the family of God, be drawn aside from the simplicity of truth, by the custom of professors, or by the sophistical argument of academical parsons, with which our dissenting interest is infested; nor by ancient fathers, doctors, or councils. May we avoid all innovations, evasions, and substitutions, keeping close to God's revealed will, the only test which will abide, when all flesh-pleasing and soul-entangling schemes will be swept hence. When we look around at the inventions of men, and behold the forms introduced in God's worship to please and attract the carnal heart, what a favour to have God's sure Word to guide us amidst the "lo here, and lo there." The Lord says, "All thy children shall be taught of God;" the Holy Ghost is still in office, and ever will attend to the trust reposed in him—to teach all the redeemed, taking of the things of Christ and revealing them unto them.

III. I love his worship. Yes, I can testify to the honour of my God, that he hath fulfilled his gracious promises repeatedly in my experience—"They that wait upon the Lord shall renew their strength." How oft have I found the means of grace to be gracious meal times; sanctuary services have been sacred opportunities, wherein the Lord has broke in upon my mind, and dilated my bosom; dullness, deadness, and carnality of heart has been counteracted, giving birth to thoughts that have been pleasant and profitable; God's praises have been sung with vigour, and his name adored with reverence; the plan of mercy has been shewn me again with joy-creating effects; Jesus has been again seen; his person loved; and his saving acts delighted in. What pleasure have I had, when the Lord the Spirit has called up my thoughts on the great things of God; his purposes of grace, in the salvation of his people, by Christ, the first begotten, set up as the head of the family, he covenanting to save all the election of grace, musing on all the wonderful transactions and great work which Jesus undertook, and in part has accomplished, is sacred and salutary employment; and it affords me unutterable delight at seasons when I am led to believe that I shall ere long see him, be with him, and be like him. Then shall those transforming visions of the mysteries be had, and the endless praises of my Redeemer be sung by me without weariness or imperfection.

Many moments have I spent in private musings on the adorable Lord Jehovah; yet it has been in the house of God, in the public worship, where my soul has been oft blessed and banquetted with those rich provisions of his goodness, spoken of by Isaiah, (25th chapter 6th verse,) "And in this mountain shall the Lord of hosts make unto all people a feast of fat things, a feast of wines on the lees, of fat things full of marrow, and of wines on the lees well refined." In his house the Lord hath oft revealed himself by his Spirit to my soul; 'tis in his temple by a preached gospel, that the faith of his people is increased and established; their hope oft abounds, while the love of God is shed abroad in their hearts by the power of the Holy Ghost, and the soul is constrained to say, "I love the Lord."

What a privation to a man of God, whose soul is alive to the honour of God and the welfare of Zion, to be shut out from the public worship. He, wearied with the toils of the week, vexed with the temptations and snares waylaying him, the Sabbath returning, but he at a distance from the means of mercy, and away from those whom his soul is united to—he keenly feels the loss, and rejoices in the fact that God is not confined. On his name he calls, and in his truth he exults, and begs God's blessing on the tents of Jacob, while he implores the Lord Christ to meet his saints where they are assembled to call upon his name, seeking forgiveness, acceptance, and assistance. How often have the Lord's people found the truth of God's Word demonstrated in their experience, "Where two or three are met together in my name, there am I, and that to bless; before they call I will answer, and while they are yet speaking, I will hear." Many a time have I assembled with his dear children in this profitable part of divine worship, when the sweet savour of Jesus' name, his person, love, and sacrificial death has refreshed my soul; God's servants have been helped to preach Christ crucified for the salvation of poor, sinful, wretched, guilty, helpless worms—open up and explain the precious truths of the gospel—making known ministerially the love of the Father, absolute redemption by the blood of the Son, testifying of the person and ministry of the Holy Ghost, whose sacred work is to subdue the disobedient will, give life to sinners who were dead, and lead them with weeping and supplication to the cross of Christ, for pardon, peace, and acceptance; by the truth, God's elect are spiritually sanctified to the service of God; "for as many as are led by the Spirit of God, they are the sons of God;" he leads them on in the christian warfare, and oft comforts their heavy hearts on their journey to the heavenly Canaan; hence he is called the Comforter, who comforts with the cordials Christ has prepared meritoriously. O, how delightful to the new-born soul to sit in the assemblies of saints, in the gates of Zion, when the sent servant of God is directing the thoughts to the triune Jehovah, as the alone object of worship, and expatiating upon the richness, freeness, fulness, and suitability of God's salvation to our case; how the Eternal Three covenanted, and are equally interested in the salvation of a beloved people. The Father chose them in Christ, before the foundation of the world; the Son, in the fulness of time, took flesh, and offered himself a sacrifice, without spot, to put away sin and make the atonement, hence we have redemption through his blood, the forgiveness of sins, according to the riches of his grace." The Holy Ghost imparts life; and by the preaching of the Word begets hope in Jesus, attachment to him, and a reverence to his sacred name; the Spirit abides in and with his church, as in a temple, succouring and assisting them under all trials, temptations, and afflictions, and will

"Cheer the humble soul, when nature melts away."

Ye ministers of Jesus Christ! never be afraid to publish all the great things of your divine Master, for fear of offending the sinful creature, man. Human nature in its unregenerate state, never can bear the doctrines of sovereign grace, because it cuts at the root of all human merit. I greatly fear that all this noise about duty and obedience, in the present day, is not genuine, but springs from a self-justifying spirit, and from an ignorance of Jehovah's sovereign system of salvation. The motives are base in many of those task-masters, for they say, and do not; and it is to be feared that many are so deluded, that they think they are doing God service, and bring him in their debtor; but alas! it will be followed by a rebut, "I never knew you; depart from me ye workers of iniquity." There can be no works acceptable to God, but what flows from the love of God shed abroad in the heart, by the Holy Ghost given unto us; this blessed love of God makes the soul alive and fruitful to every good word and work, directing to a right end—the glory of the adorable Three One Jehovah, Israel's glorious Deliverer.

I felt the force of our minister's remarks yesterday, while speaking from those words, "Having a form of godliness, but denying the power thereof." 2 Tim. iii. 5. And I lamented that multitudes of such are round about us, who are lulled to sleep in a regular round of duties; to church or chapel they go, the Bible they read, God's ordinances are attended to, the minister is caressed, and assisted in pecuniary matters; they do their duty, and hence they hope to go to heaven when they die. Poor deceived creatures! they neither know the guilt or the filth of sin; the righteousness and blood of Jesus is unwanted by them.

But what can be said to those who call themselves ministers of Christ, and are lulling souls to sleep with such pharisaical notions, constantly telling them it is their duty to do this, that, and the other, but concealing the fact from them that they are born under the law, and justly exposed to its curse as vile transgressors; and that unless they are born again, they can never enter into the kingdom of heaven. Ministers should never cease teaching their people the simple and sacred truths of the gospel; such as the Eternal Father's choice of a people to glorify his rich grace in their salvation—the redeeming acts of the adorable God Man Mediator, whose love was stronger than death, and as durable as eternity—the Holy Spirit's omnipotent power put forth graciously in the new creation, and revivication of all the people loved and ransomed.

It is not the province of a minister of the gospel, to elect, adopt, or enroll names in the Lamb's book of life, but it is their business to declare and explain the gracious acts of our heavenly Father, in electing sovereignly, in adopting graciously, and in enrolling names where there shall be no erasures. They are not called to regenerate; that is not their business; but to declare the necessity, its reality, and how it is effected by the Holy Ghost, and what are the evidences of a man having passed from death to life.

To justify the transgressor, and to pardon the criminal, is not the work of a preacher to achieve, but if he be a servant of Christ, he will open up those interesting subjects to the hearers, shewing them ministerially how Jesus has accomplished the sacred work, by his voluntary and vicarious sacrifice, and that Jesus is living in the heavens, to see to the application of the remedy, to all the purchased by his blood. The necessity of faith, hope, love, patience, and perseverance, is to be affirmed, but their production and continuance are of God. To distinguish between graces of the Spirit and counterfeits, will fall within the compass of a minister's employment; those are awfully deluded who have no higher views of the acts, than as mere natural performances, the effects of moral persuasion.

That faith with which salvation is connected, and which is the result of union to Jesus, flows from a living principle implanted in the soul of man, by the Spirit of God in regeneration. Repentance is the fruit of faith, and arises from a sense of guilt on one hand, and on the other hand, from a sense of pardoning mercy; so of every christian grace; if they do not spring from a living fountain within, from being created anew in Christ Jesus, the epithet "christian grace," would be false.

Ministers should study to be faithful in preaching God's Word, never shunning any part of the counsel of heaven, or how can they expect to have faithful hearers. If they hide the Word of God, or handle it deceitfully, keeping back the fundamental things of our holy religion, God hereby is dishonoured; carnal professors are contented and gratified; the saints are made sad; and the curse of God hangs over the head of all such time-serving, and flesh-pleasing, sycophants. From such dumb dogs the good Lord deliver his poor afflicted Zion; the signs around us evince that we have shadows for substance, and the professing church declares loudly that she loves to have it so.

In vain may we look for experimental godliness among those who are kept ignorant of these five points of doctrine—electing love, redemption by price, regenerating grace, justifying righteousness, and adopting favour. As these doctrines, with many others of a kindred nature, are made known in God's Book, they are unquestionably revealed for the church's edification. And happy is that minister and those people who enjoy those gracious verities; and honourably is that man employed, who is making an honest effort to give publicity to these heavenly truths. How oft has my soul been humbled, and drawn out in love and gratitude in the worship of God, when the minister is helped to declare the great transaction of the Three-One God in covenant; each Person engaged in various acts of divine power, and in offices of love, to save the sinner from merited punishment, and to prepare them for that glory afore prepared for them. Oh, what amazing grace! Let us review the subject a little, and see if these doctrines, with kindred ones revealed in the Scriptures, are not adapted to promote holiness and good works in them that receive them.

I. Election. It is a doctrine which the Scriptures declare, "There is a remnant according to the election of grace." Mankind discard the truth, load it with opprobrious names, and charge the Elector as unjust. The fact appears conspicuous, as the man reads his Bible, and his hatred to it tends to confirm the sentiment he rejects. But why is it so opposed? Because it lays the axe at the root of self-importance, human merit, and creature performances. Election injures none, but benefits myriads; vain man cavils at a truth which is essential to the salvation of every sinner who escapes the due desert of his transgressions. This blessed truth ministers much comfort to the soul whose election now, is a desire to be like Christ, see Christ, and be with him; God's choice of him has led him to choose Christ in return. My concern is, am I one of the Lord's chosen? He hath chosen his people to be holy and without blame, before him in love. Is it my desire to be delivered from the practice of iniquity, and to pursue a course of spiritually walking with God? If so, these desires spring from a principle of grace in the soul; and He that began this work, commenced it without my desires, and has carried it on without my desert; and will complete it as he eternally designed, and as I now crave it may. These sensibilities appertain alone to the child of God; they evidence his Sonship, and a sure pledge of his entering his Father's house above. Doubt not, therefore thy election, poor cast down, weather-beaten traveller; for though thy corruptions are strong, and thou frequently art groaning under a felt sense of sin and iniquity, bless the Lord that thou canst feel it, and that he hath not left thee to hardness and impertinence of heart, but that he has chosen such poor, worthless creatures, to glorify the riches of his grace in their salvation by Christ. Plead his promises, trust his faithfulness, and pray for an increase of experimental knowledge of divine things, "Knowing, brethren beloved, your election of God, for our gospel came not to you in word only, but in power, and in the Holy Ghost, and in much assurance." 1 Thess. i. 4, 5.

II. Redemption. Paul saith, "Christ hath redeemed us from the curse of the law, being made a curse for us." What a soul-vivifying truth to a sensible sinner, who feels he is justly condemned. We all sinned in our federal Head and Representative; Adam, our great ancestor, broke that covenant under which he was placed; do and live, transgress and die, were the conditions. The curse he entailed on all his posterity, and corruption we inherit as his natural descendants; and if God be the just and faithful Creator, that penalty must be inflicted on him who has sin found upon him. To be delivered, therefore, from the curse we incurred, is a matter of vast importance to a guilty criminal; none but Christ could redeem, and all who are not redeemed by the precious blood of Christ, will feel the just demerit of sin in endless punishment.

These truths are solemn; and while many are affirming that all mankind are redeemed, yet such assertions are falsified by God's Word, by common observation, by christian experience, and will be falsified at the day of judgment; for many shall go away into everlasting darkness. It is hard, says the friend of vice, and foe of grace, that man cannot obtain salvation do what they will. Repent, pray, and amendment of life, is their argument;—that it is all useless, they will not believe. If we do all we can, God will accept of it, and we shall be safe; is the blind man's creed. But all such arguments are worse than nothing—they are founded in falsehood; for sinners in their natural state do not desire deliverance from sin, for it is his element. Pray! he has as much heart for that as a full belly has for the honeycomb; man loves the ways of sin, though he objects to the wages being paid him when his work is completed. I admit that many choose in this day of general profession, to walk in a subjection to God's ordinances, and unite with the saints of God. Some so act, hypocritically; others, to satisfy their consciences; while satan is their prince, the world their element, and sin their delight.

None but the Lord's quickened family know what it is spiritually to be redeemed from the law as a covenant of works, from the wrath of God; as also from guilt, pollution, and condemnation, by the precious blood of Christ, as of a Lamb without blemish or spot. These things are being made known to all the purchased flock by the Holy Ghost, in the appointed season determined in infinite wisdom, long before Christ ransomed them by his blood which he shed for them, expressive of his infinite love to them.

The truth of our redemption is known to the soul, only as the fact is revealed by the Holy Ghost; at which season, the fact surprises, delights, and excites the soul's admiration, wonder, and gratitude; he then exclaims, "He loved me, and gave himself for me." Under such a discovery, humility is secured, self-loathing is produced, a holy longing for purity of heart and lip is coveted, and the redeeming blood of Jesus purges the conscience from dead works, and sets him apart from this present evil world. The soul struggles hard against corruptions, and longs to be made perfectly holy; yet it knows this will never be the case until it is delivered from this body of sin and death. Still it waits in faith and hope, knowing that shortly mortality shall be swallowed up of life. Then shall the poor tempted soul be put into the full possession of all the fruits of Christ's honourable, endless, and perfect redemption, pardon, peace, holiness, righteousness, and everlasting glory, in the presence of God and the Lamb. How precious is the redemption work of Jesus! how few they are who have any earnest desires to be interested in it! O Lord, I thank thee for what thou hast done for my soul.

III. Regeneration. How awfully defective must that man's ministry be, who knoweth not the nature of the new birth. What a misguided people must they be, who have over them a professed teacher, who himself knows not what divine teaching is. This cardinal doctrine is scarcely heard of from many pulpits, while from some it is sounded abroad; but the Almighty work is oftener denied by them unintentionally in these carnal appeals and exhortations to the ungodly, more so than than they are willing to admit. May my soul look closely into the doctrine of regeneration, that the Spirit who quickeneth whom he will may not be dishonoured by me. Let me, thy poor worm, whom thou hast taught to hang his hopes on Jesus, still be the subject of thy gracious operations, that all my acts of worship may be performed under thy energetic and genial influences, and rendered acceptable through the incense of a Saviour's sacrificial death.

My soul has oft been grieved to hear ministers spend their moments in a pulpit in little else than exhorting poor ungodly sinners to do a variety of things under the notion of it being their duty, instead of making known at once that by nature we are all under the curse of a broken law, and that we must fall eventually under the stroke of vindictive justice, unless God have mercy on us; that there is no deliverance but by the redeeming death of Christ; and no meetness for heavenly employment, religious acts, or godly sorrow for sin, except we are born again. Preachers who conceal the person and ministry of the Holy Ghost are only lulling self-sufficient professors to sleep in the cradle of carnal security. They think if they do as their minister directs them that God will have mercy upon them; and in our day preachers and people are jogging on in carnal security; they think you unkind, unsocial, and insulting if you make an effort to wake up their attention to their short doings, and Christ's perfect righteousness, sacrifice, and atonement.

I fear there are a vast number of our dissenting doctors, who in heart deny the necessity of a new creation being requisite, before an acceptable act can be performed by a fallen son or daughter of Adam, for if they knew their state by nature they would not fail to teach the necessity of the new birth, and aim at undeceiving their poor fellow sinners by exhibiting truth, exposing the delusive error of trusting in anything short of the services and death of the Lord Jesus Christ.

It is a fact, that a person may be outwardly righteous and possess many natural excellencies, and yet be a stranger to the regenerating grace of God. It is needful that a minister should explain what the new birth is by its effects, discriminating the Spirit's work on the soul, such as the hopes and fears, joys and sorrows, upliftings and down-castings, light and darkness. The Spirit's work is to break the rocky heart, give a just apprehension of deserved wrath, shew the soul the enormous debt due, give him to feel pennyless and hopeless in himself; then to open God's treasury, and shew the poor thing that Jesus is unsearchably rich, and that in him every blessing is laid up for the needy, guilty, helpless, and undone sinner. The Holy Ghost helps the poor soul to stretch out his withered hand and take hold of Jesus; the lame man is caused to throw away his crutches and leap for joy; the blind man sees blessedly, and dispenses with all his heretofore blind guides; the stammerer speaks plainly; and the deaf man hears thankfully. The new created's life, therefore, is unknown to a mere professor. Our life is a chequered one; oft anxious fears, then solid joy; "As sorrowful, yet always rejoicing; having all things, yet possessing nothing; he judgeth all things, yet he himself is judged of no man."

A mere nominal professor is pleased with being told what is his duty; he never feels concerned about what is to be believed, and what Christ has done, and is doing. I fear this is the habit of mind of most of the professing dissenters. A work of grace on the soul, most ministers, I fear, are strangers to; for how seldom do we hear from the pulpit, such expressions as "Born of God," "Born from above," "Born again, not of corruptible seed, but of incorruptible, by the Word of God which liveth and abideth for ever. Of his own will begat he us by the word of truth; and you hath he quickened who were dead in trespasses and in sins."

While I lament these things, yet I know the foundation stands sure. The Lord knows them that are his; the elect are safe; the ransomed will never be finally fettered; the renewed are the sealed to the day of perfect redemption. Our God is faithful. Blessed be God for the life-giving Spirit.

> "The Spirit, like some heavenly wind, blows on the sons of flesh,
> New models all the carnal mind, and forms the man afresh;
> Our quickened souls awake and rise from the long sleep of death,
> On heavenly things we fix our eyes, and praise employs our breath."

IV. Justification. How shall a man be just with God? is an important question; and had poor sinful men and holy angels sat in council on the possibility of a law-breaker ever being made a just man, from the day the query was propounded until now, they must have exclaimed, it's impossible. The act is God's from first to last; and here we see that what is impossible with men and angels, is possible with God.

This doctrine is a distinct branch of truth that enters into the vitality of godliness; it differs from pardon, sanctification, and effectual calling, but is inseparably connected with them all.

Hence the sinner who is redeemed by the blood of Christ, and renewed in the spirit of his mind, is a justified man; privileged, therefore, is that church who possesses a pastor who rightly distinguishes the words of truth under a feeling enjoyment of those mysterious verities that make glad some of the ruined household of Adam's posterity.

Our Three-One God is inflexibly just, immutably holy, and no unrighteous thing can abide in his presence. That we are by nature and practice unholy, requires no magnifying glass to exemplify. Having, therefore, no righteousness of our own production, we can never appear before God in anything of our own with acceptance. If, therefore, any sinner be just in God's sight, and such a man must before he can be justified, for he that justifieth the wicked, and he that condemneth the righteous, both are an abomination to Him who is the Justifier of the man that believeth in Jesus.

The matter of a sinner's justification, or that by which he is made just, is the Saviour's obedience unto death. The ground of it is the imputation of that obedience; blessed, therefore, is that man unto whom the Lord imputeth righteousness without works.

What an unspeakable favour to have an interest in Christ! What a blessed state and condition of mind to live in the knowledge of Christ, as the end of the law for righteousness to all that believe.

He that believeth is justified from all things, from which he could never be by the law of Moses. Christ's righteousness was wrought for, and imputed to, the church of God's choice; and the Holy Spirit teaches the same objects for whom Christ served, suffered, and now intercedes for the need of it, the preciousness of it, its adaptation; and ultimately the poor soul is led to put it on, and walk up and down in a garment he never made, deserved, or paid for.

The Lord Jesus Christ, the adorable God-Man Mediator, condescended to become incarnate to finish transgression, to make an end of sin, and to bring in an everlasting righteousness. He was made sin for them by imputation, not by infusion or imitation, that we should be made the righteousness of God in him. It is by divine will that Christ is made unto his people wisdom, righteousness, sanctification, and redemption, and in his righteousness, and his exclusively, shall all the seed of Israel be justified, and shall glory. "There is therefore now no condemnation to them that are in Christ Jesus." Who are they manifestatively? "Those who walk not after the flesh but after the Spirit." Here again we see that character and privileges enjoyed are associated. Self-righteous Pharisees and nominal saints may rave and rail against gospel mysteries all the days of their lives, (and there is ocular demonstration that they will, except God slay the enmity of their carnal hearts by the grace they trumpet against,) but it will be demonstrated clearly to all spiritual persons that the souls who are experimentally sprinkled by the blood of Christ, and sacredly worshipping in the righteousness of Christ, renouncing their own as a menstruous garment, that fruits of righteousness appear in them to the glory of God by Christ Jesus.

Good living and good practice are inseparably connected in God's household establishment. Well would it be for many if they waited until they had tasted God's grace before they had said things about it, which gives fearful evidence that they have lived without it. The best cure for the awful conclusions men are jumping at about the evils of doctrinal truths is tasting and seeing how gracious God is. These are sacred senses, seeing, tasting, and feeling, that God bestows on whom he will to the praise of the glory of his grace.

Election, redemption, regeneration, justification, are glorious doctrines, peculiar blessings, and precious privileges, unto which we will add one more.

V. Adoption. To adopt a people to himself is the display of his rich grace, and excites admiration, thanksgiving, and praise in the hearts of all to whom the Spirit witnesseth their adoption. "Behold," saith John, "what manner of love the Father hath bestowed on us that we should be called the sons of God." "And if children," saith Paul, "then heirs, heirs of God, and joint heirs with Christ." The saints of God are not only pardoned by the blood of Christ and vested with a title to life which will stand the scrutinising eye of justice itself, but they have God for their gracious Father, who has predestinated them unto the adoption of children by Jesus Christ, according to the good pleasure of his will; so that our relationship is rooted in Christ's sonship, so that while he remains the Son of God, so long will the relationship of all who are adopted in him abide. Now as our relationship is built in him, so our recovery from ruin, as the many sons that were chosen in him is effected by him, and as all spiritual blessings were treasured up in him for the benefit of his brethren, so all new Covenant blessings will be enjoyed in him, through him, and with him to all eternity.

The Eternal Spirit proceeds officially from the Father and the Son, influentially to make known the Father's love in adopting favour, and the Son's merit in ransoming blood and justifying righteousness. Thus the Holy Ghost witnesseth to the adopted family of their given interest in Christ, and their unforfeitable salvation by Christ. These are such blessings that a poor sinner could never have expected to have heard of. God's love-tale to sinners has such divine impressions stamped on it, that the believer wonders and adores.

Why, my dear brethren, should we sink with fear, or be dismayed at trials or difficulties, pains, poverty, or persecution, which are all transient, common, and needful? Let us look forward to our heavenly inheritance, unto which we are made heirs by the adopting grace of our covenant God and Father, whose faithfulness is engaged to perform all his gracious promises; whose power is put forth to accomplish all his wise councils, and whose veracity will be displayed in the fulfilment of all his unfrustrable predictions. "Fear not, little flock, it is your Father's good pleasure to give you the kingdom." So said he who is to be implicitly relied on.

What are all the honours and titles which are heaped on clay man (who will soon be food for worms, and, if grace prevent not, will be a brand of fire never to be quenched,) compared with the honour and privileges of that poor, unobserved being who turns aside to speak reverently to the King of kings, and is at seasons privileged to commune with him, as a man communes with another? Reverence is maintained at God's footstool, while the soul is admitted to great nearness through the rent vail of Emanuel's flesh. The Holy Ghost inhabiting a poor sinner's heart as his temple is because of his sonship; not to make him a son, but to give the temper and disposition of a son.

"It is because ye are sons," Paul affirms, "that God hath sent forth the Spirit of his Son into your hearts, crying, Abba, Father." Thus the privilege of adoption was secured to all the Father's children by their personal election in Christ before the world began.

O the matchless, measureless, love of our glorious Jehovah! in contriving and executing the great and gracious plan of securing and saving vile, base, good for nothing creatures! Christ has never been ashamed to own his guilty brethren, but he is ever ashamed of their conduct. He owns his Hepzibah, discharges her debt, cleanses her from all defilement, adorns her with a royal robe, and he will ultimately take her to court, befitting the high relationship she stands in towards God: through him I hope to be there, when he presents his Spouse faultless before the throne of infinite Majesty! May the Lord, the Spirit, bless the family with filial affection and child-like simplicity, that in all things God may be glorified in them, by them, and through them.

When these substantial truths are ministerially brought forth with kindred principles of the gospel, in an experimental way, then it is that my soul can frequently say, "it is good to be here;" and I think every believer in the Lord Jesus can say, at seasons, when waiting on God in his public worship, and these truths, with their blessed effects are set before them, that in waiting on the Lord, their spiritual strength is renewed. The daring assertions of many prove their awful state, when they affirm that the doctrines of grace have a licentious tendency. Every true-born child of God knows that they are doctrines according to godliness; and a steady contemplation of these things, and a faithful representation of them from the pulpit, will draw out the heart into a holy admiration of the grace of God, and a sacred veneration of the Lord God of his salvation: gratitude must spring up to God, our loving Ransomer, and cheerful obedience is yielded to Zion's exalted King. These things are made known in an influential manner to none but the Lord's new-born family. "The secret of the Lord is with them that fear him, and he will shew them his covenant."

Blessed is that minister who is thus taught and brought, by God the Holy Ghost, to teach and preach Jesus Christ; and happy is that people whose hearts the Lord hath opened to receive Christ, and all the rich doctrines of his Word, then his worship is their delight.

IV. I love the people of God, they have their faults, frailties, infirmities, and fears; but they are the excellent of the earth. We have no reason to be surprised at what appears amongst the excellent of the earth, in whom the Lord delights, when we reflect on the power, policy, practice, and unwearied efforts of the invisible and implacable enemy, together with the world's baits, gins, and traps, and their own native depravity; how oft does the real saint mourn over those things which he feels have a birth in thought and desire, but are not permitted to break forth in practice; outside cleanliness is not sufficient for the spiritual mind, he is grieved at what a mere professor is indifferent about, and he is pleased that there is a fountain opened for unclean thought's purgation, and atonement made for closet and sanctuary sins. All boasting perfectionists are deceivers; and they are verily given over to judicial blindness, altogether ignorant that God's law reaches to thoughts, looks, desires, and purposes. God's saints have to pray against their own thoughts, looks, longings, plans, and sayings. Oh! the awful delusion of that soul who has no daily faults to confess, no desires to be extinguished, and no petitions to present in character with them who had the valley before them. Cleanse thou me from secret faults! There is constant need that the man of God should appear at the mercy door in humility's garb, entreating for grace to be preserved from all those ungodly tempers and misconduct, which occasions so much strife and contention among the society of the justified, grieves the godly, dishonours the Lord, and oft is a dainty feast for the enemies of God, who exclaim, "Aha, Aha," and so would we have.

My cry is from a feeling sense of what I am in myself, and knowing that as in water, face answers to face, so does the heart of man to man. Heavenly Father, look mercifully upon the poor, weak, and exposed family, and bless them with keeping grace, renewing and reviving grace; cleanse us from all unrighteousness, and in greater abundance, pour down thy Holy Spirit as the spirit of wisdom, meekness, forbearance, and forgiveness, that we may love as brethren; be pitiful and courteous, and that we may shew to all around, that the grace of God, which bringeth salvation, has reached our hearts, it having taught and empowered us to deny ungodliness and worldly lusts, and to live soberly, righteously, and godly, in this present evil world. I do love the Lord's people, for there is in them some good thing to be seen towards the Lord God of Israel; God loves them, Father, Word, and Spirit. Our Father puts his name upon them; Christ impresses his image on them; and the Holy Ghost implants his graces in them. And the Lord says, that "these shall be mine in that day, when I make up my valuables or jewels;" all the world, in comparison of them, are as nothing; called dross, refuse, goats, tares, and stubble. With the Lord's people I love to associate, commune, and to seek council concerning spiritual matters. It is in company with Zion's children, in the solemn assemblies, that my soul feels at home with them. I hope we may live in a prayerful concern for each other's welfare; and to the general assembly and church of the first born. I am expecting to be gathered, when the Lord shall muster his ransomed in the heavenly

Jerusalem above. Ungodly men may point at them with the finger of scorn, and point at their failings derisively; they may stigmatize them as hypocrites and deceivers. But the Lord reads the heart while the Christian oft mourns over his conduct; it is his joy to muse on God's infinite perfections, as they blaze forth in the sinner's salvation, by the cross of Christ.

The day is fast approaching when the Lord will make his appearance to end the dispute between the world and the church; ye enemies of the Lord Christ, what will ye do in that solemn day? For, behold! the Lord cometh with ten thousand of her saints, to execute judgment upon all the ungodly, and to convince them of all the ungodly deeds which they have ungodly committed; and of all their hard speeches which ungodly sinners have spoken against him. Jude 15.

None but the Lamb's redeemed company will be able to stand with him upon the Mount Zion, in that day, clothed with robes of immortality, and crowned with eternal life.

> With them numbered may I be,
> Now—and in eternity.

W. B., *Drillman*.

We resided about two years in Norfolk Place, near the Grand Sluice, Boston; and removed on the 25th of May, 1825, to a small farm, in Gosbuton, Risegate. We frequently attended our old place again, at Pinchbeck, under the ministry of Mr. Thomas Robinson; still we kept our places, as members of the church, at Salem Chapel, Liquor Pond Street; coming over on ordinance days, and as oft as convenient.

About twelve months after leaving Boston, Mr. Hinmers, the pastor, left Boston. The church was then supplied with various ministers, many of the friends wanted a man sound in the faith; another party wished for a man of low principles, who would advocate a system of Fullerism; it occasioned shyness and distance among us. Two of the deacons used unfair means to obtain a man of the worse than half-and-half system, by stopping the friends on the Lord's-day, to consider the subject of sending for a person whom they thought free from those high sentiments which they abhorred. This was done, at a season, when they saw many of the high sentimental men were absent; and they at length suceeded in strengthening their cause, by fallacious arguments; and eventually, they declared that the place was built for the modern Calvinists; and if we were not contented, we might withdraw. What a grevious affair was here.

There was about thirty members, and others, who loved the doctrines of sovereign, free, rich, and distinguishing grace, as made known by Israel's Triune God, in covenant. And, because we could not fall in with the popular error of this day of great profession, namely, *profess* to believe in personal election, absolute redemption, effectual calling, and final perseverance of the saints : and yet, after all this *profession*, the minister must not preach *the gospel*, we are told of chance of salvation, a possible regeneration, a conditional salvation, grounded upon the creature's repentance, obedience and docility, representing the whole efficacy of the work of Christ to depend on the acts of the creature ; so pardon and justification, with similar blessings, are dependent on the creature's repentance, faith, and affection. I scarcely question whether these new fashion parsons and refined deacons, amongst the modern Calvinists, really believe that man is so vile, filthy, and base, as God declares he is; and as the quickened soul feels he is. Our present pulpit teems with descriptive tale of human ability. Man's reasoning powers and faculties are sufficient; and all that is needed is, let him use these according to his natural capabilities, and God will save if he will. But, resolve on becoming religious : this is so soft, smooth, and palatable to proud man, that he swallows the nostrum greedily, and pities the poor creature that feels and acknowledges his entire helplessness, and begs on the Lord to quicken his soul, for without him he can do nothing but undo himself. We need not wonder at the multitude taking up this flesh-pleasing and self-exalting religion, satan is leading in groups, men and women, down to the chambers of darkness, in this new-invented method of pleasing unregenerate sinners, and of distressing the Christ-needed and Christ-seeking sinner. It is one thing for the carnal heart to take up with a profession of religion, it is quite another for the man to be new-created, born again, to pass from death to life. Prophecy smooth things, is an an old desire of covenant nature. Search me, and try me, is the continual cry of the new nature. Religious goats want to be thought to be sheep: but the flock of Christ dread being deceived, and cannot be contented with being thought to be sheep, their satisfaction comes in by being led into green pastures, and laying down by the still waters, which flow from the throne of a sin-hating and sin-forgiving God, through Christ, the sin-bearer. The distinguishing doctrines of the gospel, are treated by the self-sufficient and self-called Christians, of the present day, as unimportant, and quite improper to be treated on by ministers of God: and those who feed on them and cannot endure the denial, concealment or misrepresentation of them, are denominated strait laced, bigoted, uncharitable, and unsocial. And, because we could not tamely submit to hear the misrepresentation of what they called gospel, we were told we might withdraw, so true is that scripture, " In the world ye shall have tribulation."

I complained, and affirmed with many others that we could not fall in with this yea and nay system, and for this reason —namely, the preserving grace of God; to this only do we attribute our steadfastness in the faith. We grieve to see the fashionable religion of the day spreading like a running leprosy, until the churches of the dissenters have but little more resemblance to the primitive churches of Christ than our national church.

How little is falling from the lips of our Dissenters that ascribes their salvation to God's free favour. "By the grace of God I am what I am," said an ancient dissenter, and a warm advocate to the interest of Emanuel, whom he once hated, maltreated, and abetted those whose hands were imbrued in the blood of the proto-martyr, for said Jesus, "Saul, Saul, why persecutest thou me." It is grace that brings us to the footstool of mercy; it is grace that heals the festering sore of sin; grace speaks pardon to the repenting sinner through the blood of atonement; and it is grace that prepared mansions for us in glory; and grace supplies us with suited strength all through this wilderness; at the close we shall sing that grace shall have the praise.

In the year 1829 one or two of the friends of Salem Chapel, without consulting the church, wrote for a Dr. P., of moderate principles, to appear amongst us, in the prospect of eventually becoming pastor of the church, and which eventually he did.

We complained of the steps taken, and after hearing this said doctor on the Sabbath day to no profit, I wrote the following letter to Mr. J. M., one of the deacons:—

Gosbuton, Sept. 28, 1829.

CHRISTIAN FRIEND,

From what transpired at our church-meeting yesterday it plainly appears that you and your brother officer, Mr. V., have committed yourselves, and have acted unbecoming the christian character; you are exercising an unlawful authority over the church, and acting with duplicity. On what authority does a deacon, or any other member, thrust a minister into the pulpit without consulting his fellow members? Is this walking in love and following after things wherewith one may edify another? You affirmed I was not a Calvinist. Be that as it may, I remain a Particular Baptist. This also you deny. Now unless I err greatly, it is you, with a small party of our brethren, who have swerved away from the Particular Baptist interest, and not me. For instance, I firmly believe the following biblical facts,—Personal and eternal election; special and eternal redemption; perfect justification in Christ, the church's Head, by righteousness wrought by him, and imputed to them; full, free, and everlasting pardon of all sins through his atoning blood, who appeared here as the Redeemer of his brethren, the church's certain regeneration, preservation, and glorification, to which they are predestinated as the adopted children of their heavenly Father, by Jesus Christ, according to the good pleasure of his will, and to them the Holy Ghost bears witness that they are the sons of God, and by him they cry "Abba Father." For this family an incorruptible inheritance is provided in heaven, and they are all equally heirs of that immortal heritage; they are all alike ransomed, justified, pardoned, and represented by Christ, and they all will be regenerated, sanctified, and preserved, and finally meet around his throne in glory to sing His worthy praises who died for them.

Now, brother M., can you clap your hand to your heart, and appeal to the Omniscient Jehovah, that you rejoice to hear these things proclaimed, explained, and dwelt upon by the preacher, together with that rich variety of Christian experience which a believing view of these truths produce, together with the manner the Lord deals with his people, in safely conducting them through this militant state? Or do you not rather prefer hearing grace huxtered, and a salvation intended for all men, if they will but accept of it? If this be the case with you, (and who can doubt it?) you are not a Particular Baptist. Cannot you see that the grace of God is free, full, and effectual; that its effects are sacred and visible, producing the most beneficial results on those characters in whom it is really displayed? Look at a Zaccheus, Mary Magdalene, the thief on the tree, a persecuting Saul, and those Gentile sinners converted at Corinth; and this doubtless is the character of all mankind until they are cleansed and sanctified by the Holy Ghost.

Can my brother bear with me while I open my mind a little further; for I have no secrets to keep back? You have been very officious in obtaining this Doctor, as you call him; had he not a fine opportunity yesterday morning to speak of these things? His text was Phil. i. 6. Had he not an opportunity to set forth the Spirit's agency on this good work, begun in his sovereignty, freeness and graciousness? But alas! scarcely a word was said about these things, as to the manner in which it was effected, nor did he describe the awful state and condition of the carnal mind, upon which the good work was wrought. Even his first head of the discourse, which was to shew the nature of it in its origin, consisted chiefly in pointing out its effects. He, as a Doctor, of course knows that all effects arise from some cause; why, I ask, did he keep the cause of salvation from the ears of his audience? Was he afraid the whole and sole agency of the Holy Spirit, in his life-giving operations in regenerating the vile and filthy sons and daughters of men would be too humiliating to his auditory? Alas, poor man, I think I shall not be too severe if I say he was actually endeavouring to exalt human nature in its present degraded state, trying to shew that by its exertions, care, and diligence, it might raise itself up, even to merit the applause of heaven, and that it might do a great deal towards extirpating moral evil out of the world! Witness his own words, when speaking of the goodness of some people, (who they were, we were not let into the secret of,) but in some instances he exclaimed, "They had altogether eradicated moral pollution and vileness from their minds." Again, says the D.D., "If men would but cherish this good work begun, what a different scene would appear upon the face of society—what universal love, harmony, and peace! We should soon have a heaven on earth!"

I cannot help thinking, whenever I hear so much trumpeting about what poor helpless guilty man can do, if he will but be stirring, that so far is the person who thus speaks from feeling the plague of his own heart, that he is a near kinsman to the ancient pharisee, who said, "God, I thank thee that I am not as other men; extortioners, adulterers," &c. Now if this preacher felt his own heart to be as hard as mine is at times, and the workings of depraved nature, in lustful desires, vain thoughts, and huge hosts of unwelcome visitors, with a bad temper, and a light spirit, to the annoyance of his peace, as I occasionally feel, he would be no longer harping about a heaven upon earth, through the devil's interment and man's loveliness. But he would be ready to cry out, "O, wretched man that I am! who shall deliver me from this body of death? for I see another law in my members, warring against the law of my mind, and bringing me into captivity to the law of sin, which is in my members." Every professor that does not feel this internal warfare between flesh and Spirit, are yet, I fear, in a state of unregeneracy, and are deceiving themselves with self-righteous opinions, and priding themselves in their own supposed goodness.

Thus for the musings of my mind; and having penned them, you are now presented with them; hope you may profit by them. As to what may take place, or how these unpleasant things may terminate, I know not. I beg for the Lord's guidance and counsel, who worketh all things after the counsel of his own will, and who will never suffer the discord and confusion of his creatures to nullify the purposes of his grace. To him be glory for ever. W. B., *Drillman*.

To the above I received no answer; but jeers and shy looks we had to endure, because we could not approve of this empty ministration; and we were dubbed with the name of hyper-Calvinists. Being thus situated, with barren ministration, a few hungry souls began to hunt for venison, such as our souls loved; and we began to attend at a small chapel in Hislem Alley, where a Mr. Lay preached, where we met with a man sound in the faith.

Here we heard the glorious doctrines of sovereign, free, and discriminating favour. I soon felt the difference between grace freely given, and grace offered; between a salvation to be perfected and secured by the sinner, and salvation finished on the cross; between a salvation attainable, loseable, forfeitable, and precarious, and one obtained by the sweat of blood, immutable, unforfeitable, and absolutely sure to all the seed of Christ.

I was soon decided what to do. Having tasted of the old wine of the kingdom, I was determined not to have my spiritual senses insulted, by hearing and beholding this new wine placed before me, as a substitute. My soul was hungry, and as a hungry labourer who has followed the plough for eight hours, prefers wholesome bread, and plain food, to game-shed dishes, and unsatisfying trifles, so my soul received the unadorned truths with zest, delight, and satisfaction.

That pulpit oration which buoys up the carnal mind, by exalting its capabilities to perform spiritual acts, and how nobly he is qualified to serve his Maker, love his God, and perform acts by which he ingratiates himself into God's favour; and if he becomes a member of a church, does his duty, prays for, and pays to, the upholding of the minister genteely, to heaven will go; this sort of preaching fosters the pride of man, pleases the self-sufficient professor, delights the carnal ear, multiplies professors, starves possessors of the grace of God, and supplies the publisher of these libels with a rich living, and will issue, if grace does not alter the course of preacher and hearers, with an awful fall into a fatal ditch.

What an awful condition is that man in, who professedly is engaged to know nothing among men, but Christ and him crucified; and yet, is perpetually concealing from his auditory the stupendous plan of grace; and, instead of laying the sinner low, and lifting Christ high, reverse the thing altogether. But, when God, the Holy Ghost, become a man's teacher, then he soon shews him hell is his desert. A corrupt nature he inherits, and a depraved heart; which, to trust he dares not, for the Lord has shewn him that such an act would prove his ruin; then sighs, cries, tears, fears, faults, foes, and woes, he is the subject of. His sensibilities of helplessness and wickedness, causes him to be importunate at God's door of mercy.

Nothing less than God's new-creating grace can teach man any real spiritual lesson; the jig-jog trot of customary profession, is as different from vital godliness as a leaden statue is from a living man. The present preachers who came forth from your dissenting academies, generally speaking, have no more vital experimental religion about them, than our Oxford and Cambridge students have. Men-made preachers are working out of our churches the glorious truths of the gospel: "Ichabod" must be written on many, very many pulpits, where the good old fashioned doctrines of the cross was once published by men whom God elected, anointed, called forth, and stood by, blessing their messages to poor lost sinners. In these pulpits, fashionable puppets are placed, it is made a theatre for worldly preferment. Professors are pleased, multitudes assemble; no wonder, since their eyes are blinded by a glare of splendid profession; satan is said to blind the eyes of them that believe not. Sometimes satan puts on sanctity to delude, it is but of small consequence to him whether poor souls walk on to perdition in a white or black coat. 'Tis God, by his sovereign grace, who opens the eyes to see and the ears to hear spiritually, and all his children shall be taught by him.

I now resolved on joining the despised few in the alley, not liking to flit sometimes to one place and then to another; so I wrote a letter to the church, in Liquorpond Street, under the ministry of Dr. P., stating my views of things, and the difference of our opinion, at the same time, resigning my membership. The following is its contents :—

Gosbuton, December 17th, 1829.
To the Baptist church assembling for worship, at Salem chapel, Liquorpond Street, Boston:

BRETHREN—

I was at Boston on Sabbath last, to hear the gospel, at Haslem Alley. It is right on my part to give you a reason for my conduct. It is well known that as a church we are greatly divided in our views of God's truth, and which I think, may be thus fairly set forth. The one believe that God from everlasting, immutably fixed his love on his people, having chosen them in Christ Jesus, before the foundation of the world. That our glorious Emanuel, the complex Head, Lord, and Saviour of his people, was a complex Person before he was an incarnate one; that our nature was brought forth in union with the Divine, in the Person of the Son of God, as the first-born of every creature; and that man's nature was raised up into personal existence, and possessed that glorious union which he now does, in that Personal subsistence as the God-man, possessing in his own Person, the nature of the offender and the nature of the offended; not two persons, but one glorious Person, the self-existent God, and the derived existence, Man, the ancient Lord Christ, Zion's only Representative and covenanting Lord, her ordained Head and enriched primitive Heir. That in the fulness of time he wrapped his Godhead in a veil of our inferior flesh; took a body prepared for him; was born of a virgin in Israel; entered upon the work given him to do; and which he voluntarily undertook to accomplish; in doing which work he manifested himself to be the Wonderful, the Child born, the Son given, the Mighty God; and having finished his work he ascended up where he was before;

and there he ever liveth as God-Man, the great and gracious High Priest, interceding for all his redeemed family, wherefore he is able to save unto the uttermost, all who come to God, by him. That the Holy Spirit is the efficient cause of divine life in the souls of the new-born, imparting light to the understanding; it is he that glorifies Christ, by taking of his things, and shewing them unto the quickened sinner, guiding them into all truth, testifying of Christ's Person, love, blood, and righteousness, bearing an internal witness, teaching them all things—ah, this inward witness and teaching is what but few, very few professors know anything about, neither do they want to know—but God's saints are made to taste the grace of the gospel. That the saints are chosen of God; they are given to Christ as his own sheep: redeemed by Christ, and quickened and made alive by his Spirit, and led into a saving apprehension of the truth as it is in Christ; and these are they who are coming up out of the wilderness, leaning upon their beloved Lord; these are they who rejoice in Christ Jesus, and have no confidence in the flesh. In a word, the Lord is their portion and their inheritance, their joy, strength, and song, in this the house of their pilgrimage; and he will assuredly and shortly bring them to his courts above. God will soon wipe away all tears from all his saints' faces! These are only a very few out of the many things that might be named, which we, as part of the church, believe, embrace, and delight in. The other part of you profess to believe most of these truths; but in fact is not the case; or, from what does the hatred to hear them preached spring from? Allow me to ask—is it not a shame for men, professing godliness, to pretend to believe in personal and eternal election, yet hate to hear the truth declared, and then, in the same breath in which you affirm the belief, you assert that all may be saved if they will. You believe that Christ has redeemed his people, by his blood, and yet all may escape the curse, if they choose! Monstrous! And some of you delight in saying, and in hearing your preachers say—All men may be saved, if they will but perform certain conditions, such as repent, believe, and obey. What inconsistencies here! Do you not know that faith, repentance, and remission of sins are free gifts of God's grace, the fruits of the Spirit, and flow from a new principle of life implanted within. As consistent would it be to tell a dead carcase that it might be taken to court if it would but rise and be active. Search the Scriptures, my friends; be not ashamed to confess the truth. How can you expect the blessing of the Lord, while you maintain such heterodox sentiments and flat contradictions? To profess to believe that God hath sovereignly chosen a people to glorify his own great name in their salvation, and yet affirm that God designs to save all the rest upon the conditions of faith and repentance, this is such sapless nonsense that it cannot be too severely censured.

But, on sober reflection, it is more becoming on my part to bow my knees at the footstool of mercy, and thank my eternal Father, redeeming Jesus, and enlightening Spirit, for the favour shewn to one so vile, helpless, and by nature ignorant, that I am delivered from the snares, trammels, and falsehoods which are so greedily swallowed by giddy professors. Yes; blessed be his name, he hath brought me to know the truth, love it, and rejoice in it.

Your confused notions about divine things, and your contradictory sentiments have led me to withdraw from your communion; to say nothing about your inconsistent conduct in obtaining and ordaining your present minister, contrary to the desires of a great part of the members. My wife coincides with me; and hence we no longer desire to be considered members of your church.

In taking our leave of you, our prayer is that the Lord would be pleased, if it is his holy will, to open your eyes to see, and your hearts to feel the value of those truths which are of everlasting importance, and which, at this time you pay little regard to.

W. Bowcock.

I received a reply to the foregoing letter from Dr. P., purporting to be written on the behalf of the church, in which our resignation was said to be accepted.

As there were some unhandsome reflections cast on me in the Doctor's epistle, I took up my pen again to address both the church and the minister, by a way of vindicating both my sentiments and expressions; the which letter I believe was never read to the church, as I suppose they who were its governors feared lest others should become disaffected to the yea and nay gospel, and the art and craft made use of by professors to push young men into the ministry and make a decent appearance in external profession, even where there is not evidence of a real work of grace on the heart.

To the Pastor and Church, at Salem Chapel, Liquorpond Street, Boston:

Friends—

I received your letter on Sabbath Day, January 24th, 1830; in which you lay heavy charges against me; it surprises and pains me; but innocent I plead. If there are things said in my letter that vexed you, my intention has been nullified. A justification of my conduct in withdrawing from your community became me; but if the expressions (in my letter) of thanks to the God of my salvation for his mercy in delivering me from the snares, trammels, and falsehoods which are greedily received by giddy professors, caused your anger to burn, this I can say, it should not have been written, had I have thought it would have so operated.

My reason for so expressing myself was—that the representation of salvation being partly by grace and partly by works, is such a God-dishonouring, Christ-denying, and soul-distressing a tale, that to be freed from taking satisfaction in it is a great blessing.

That God hath sovereignly predestinated his people to obtain salvation through the righteousness and atoning death of Christ, and that others have a chance of escape offered them, if they will but accept it—that there is a sufficiency in the death of Christ to save all men, and yet no man will be saved but on the ground of his faith, repentance, and obedience, is such a delusive, contradictory tale, that I could no longer submit to have my spiritual sensibilities annoyed by listening to. Surely there is a vast difference between these graces being set forth as conditions of salvation, and as being the blessings of salvation. Covenant blessings are one thing, covenant conditions are another. The conditions of salvation our covenant Head and Representative has fulfilled—the covenant blessings of salvation are freely and graciously bestowed on the heirs of the Kingdom, according to the arrangements of infinite wisdom.

The unsavoury testimony of urging persons to become pious, support missions, become Sunday-school teachers, and join churches, and then they may expect God will love them, bless them, and finally take them to heaven, is so delusive, that it grieves me to hear it. As to any knowledge of their own vile hearts, the evils of thoughts, words, and ways, and a cry for mercy, through a felt sense of wretchedness—this, as being absolutely needful to be felt before Christ can be appreciated, is wholly kept out of sight.

Our present uprising aspirants for pastoral respectability are a race of novices. Young men who appear to possess some gifts, are accosted by giddy professors, who persuade them to go to a *parson-manufactory*, where they are taught the rules of logic; and when they have acquired this art of reasoning, they will be able to preach methodically, acceptably, and usefully; and the spur to hasten him forward is—respectability, a great blessing to the church, and a good living, without hard and dirty work in the field, or in the manufactory. Are not these things transpiring in our midst frequently. This is the machinery by which churches are to have an efficient ministry, after the old-fashion preachers are got rid of. And I think it will be found true, amongst our dissenting churches, that when the old pastor is removed, there is but little chance of a better from these nurseries.

Alas! what a race of self-sufficient and self-conceited puppets are sent forth from these seminaries to supply vacated pulpits, or raise up new causes, in the hope of a good salary, a comfortable home, and making a respectable appearance in the world; and all this under the garb of religion; and indeed I believe, in most cases, it is only a mask, an outside shew; there is no heart-work.

Is not this self-righteousness and self-seeking? While I thus speak freely, it is not treating you with contempt, nor are these things merely fancy; for when a mere novice I was urged to go to an academy myself. Usefulness, respectability, and eventually settled down comfortably over a church, and many other enchantments were used; but the plough and harrow, the sowing and reaping, is the most honourable, unless God calls, qualifies, and sends forth. Even a member of your own church, not long since, was moved by these mercenary principles, as his communion with me, on the subject attested; and so far, altogether, from being in accordance with the apostle's advice to Timothy, that I wondered at his effrontery; so selfish, so stinkingly full of pride, wishing to become a gentleman; it really was detestable.

How many do we see occupying pulpits among the Particular Baptist Churches, who have emanated from Dissenters' colleges, that are men advocating those principles which were once advocated by our Baptist Brethren? The Lord's plan, by which faithful men have been sent into the vineyard, is now despised by professors generally! We have had the most useful ministers called to the work by God, from the sheepfold, the plough, the loom, the anvil, and the cobbler's stall! He hath fitted them to preach his truths with clearness, fulness, and success; and it has been by these feeble and despised instruments among the self-important, that God hath accomplished mighty feats, to the mortification of our collegiate gentry and to the vexation of nominal professors.

I most heartily thank my Lord, for graciously opening my eyes, and delivering me from receiving that yea and nay system which receives the applause of the professing public. Your accusations made against me are unfounded; that I am in error, sentimentally, and my temper wrong; imperfection in judgment, and in temper, I admit. But the sentiments I plead for, in the main, are truths God's word reveals; and God's Spirit hath endeared to me can admit of no doubt; and that those truths advocated by me do, and ever will, produce the best of practice. Besides, you assert that almost every principle which has to do with the sinner's justification, pardon, sanctification, preservation, and glorification, which I hold, you are of the same mind; then my surprise and pain is, that you do not preach them, and take delight in hearing them, and seeking fellowship with those who do. That which causes you to charge me with possessing a dogmatical spirit, is my determination, by God's grace, to contend earnestly for the truth; having felt its power, tasted its sweetness, and enjoyed its sacredness, I cannot but feel when trifles are substituted for solids, and shadows for substance.

Do, Dr., think of the glorious chain of salvation which exhibits the Father's everlasting love to his family, adopted in Christ, redeemed by Christ, and quickened by the Holy Ghost, called out of darkness into his marvellous light. Hence, possessing a life from Christ, they love him, fear him, call upon his name, rejoice in him, trusting their souls and their all to him; humbly adoring his dear name, and firmly believe they shall, through the riches of his grace, be with him in glory everlasting. While all formal, false, and fleshly professors, will be equitably sentenced to endless torment, with hypocrites and the openly profane.

Don't think, my friends, that I am ranking you with those to whom the Judge will say, "Depart from me, ye workers of iniquity!" My design is to distinguish between the precious and the vile, by a work of grace, wrought on the heart by God the Holy Ghost; for by nature there is no difference; for all have sinned and deserved condemnation. I hope the ever-blessed Lord will always keep me honest to declare his truth, though I incur the displeasure of the professors and profane, God is my all-sufficient and self-sufficient portion; and on him may we rely for every needful good. My prayer is, that our names may be found writtten in the Lamb's book of life.   Yours truly,
W. B., *Drillman.*

Thus terminated our connection with the Baptist church, worshipping in Salem chapel, Liquorpond Street.

We were speedily united to the church, assembling for worship in a small meeting, in Haslem Alley, under the pastoral care of Mr. Richard Lay. We found his ministry instructing and soul-reviving; having enjoyed much under his preaching, I was desirous that poor sinners around Gosbuton, where I resided, should hear the good news of salvation, I arranged for his coming there to blow the gospel trumpet; and as long as my stay was there, I regularly fetched him once a fortnight, and many gathered round to hear: his preaching excited the displeasure of the Methodists, and letters were written to him by a self-sufficient professor of the Wesleyan denomination, finding fault with his testimony of man's entire guiltiness, depravity, and helplessness, and that the salvation of a sinner, from first to last, is by sovereign, rich, and irresistible grace: this excited indignation in the bosom of Mr. Lay, and occasioned the manifestation of a wrong spirit in the pulpit: this caused a falling off in the attendance.

About this time my landlady died; we left the farm, and came to reside at Boston the second time; and as no one was disposed to fetch Mr. Lay, his labours terminated there. But I trust some have had ceaseless cause to bless the Lord for sending him there, for he certainly preached those wholesome doctrines revealed in God's Word, which are so calculated to encourage the tempted, tossed, and buffeted family of God. His ministry was sound, experimental, and practical, as many at Boston testified to, at the time; and for his first two years residence at Boston, his discourses were sound, savoury, cheering, experimental, and instructive.

Indeed, in those days his preaching honoured the Lord of our liberty, and yielded consolation to many. His efforts to expose error, led him into a state of mind that rendered his ministry barren, full of bitterness and strife, which drove away many of the Lord's seeking family, and pained greatly many of us who remained with him. Truth, he zealously contended for, shewed clearly the solemn consequences of error; therefore I waited hopefully for the Lord's appearance, begging him to turn our captivity, and refresh us by his dew-like influences; shedding abroad his love in our hearts, and put right what was wrong, and keep us right when we are right.

December, 1834.

On the 28th of April, 1834, I was requested by a member of an independent church at Boston, to look over a book, and give my opinion of its contents. The said work was the product of a George Wright, of Stamford, and entitled "Antinomianism examined, exposed, and subverted." After a careful perusal, I wrote as follows; delivering back the book, and the copy of what is here penned.

This Mr. Wright, is wrong at the starting point; the objects he assails as assembling for divine worship, and brands with the name of vile antinomians, turning the grace of our God into licentiousness. Can he point to a clan of men assembling together to worship God, thus speaking or acting? Probably his viciated palate would be satiated could he find such an assembly. That there are to be found mockers and scoffers at God's reigning grace, Stamford will witness to; preachers in abundance are to be found doing it; publishers also; professors in shoals. Pothouse prattlers do it, and so does the proud self-righteous pharisee; but the sensible sinner prizes those principles which exalts God's grace, and lays the impious sinner low. He thinks them who receives the salvation of our God without money and without price, are those who threaten to desolate the church. He would rest free from distraction on this matter from the objects he dreads, had he but tasted that grace which he despises.

The desolating principles, are those which he advances; Christ's death being designed for all men, and all may be saved if they will but believe, repent, and do their duty.

Election and predestination to eternal life, they still make to depend on human merit. Men and women are saved, not because the ransom price has been laid down and accepted, but because they believe and repent. If this author wishes to insinuate that the souls quickened by grace, and made to feel their own vileness, helplessness, and guilt, and are brought to rest their soul's eternal welfare on the atoning death, and justifying righteousness of Christ, rejecting every thing of their own as dross, dung, and disgrace, are antinomians—he is a libeller of God's sons and daughters, and he may rest assured the parent will avenge the wrongs of the offsprings.

However, if he be a man of God, I wish him further light, and let him not be alarmed, the church of Christ is safe; the blood-bought family are all secured; the heavenly inheritance is in reserve for them, and they will in due time occupy the mansion love prepared.

Remember, God hath not chosen his people to uncleanness, but unto holiness; his grace in effectual calling, delivers them from the former, and possesses them with the latter. The Father chose them before time began; Christ in the fulness of time redeemed them from the curse of the law, by being made a curse for them; and the Holy Ghost quickens them into life, to enjoy the blessings of peace by the blood of the Lamb, and to walk in communion with their sin-forgiving God, through faith in their sin-bearer. As to his arguments about man's duty and reprobation, they are futile and vain; none but living souls can enjoy spiritual truths, and spiritual life is God's free boon.

W. B., *Drillman*.

TO MARGARET A.

Accept of my best thanks for the perusal of Mrs. Pearson's letters; they abound with choice cordials for poor sin-sick souls. I bless the Lord Jesus who hath prepared and administers such precious dainties. What evidences he gives us of his sovereign power to save, his love to cheer, and his grace to sanctify, his poor afflicted saints, in the midst of pollution, defilement, and disgrace; we are under an everlasting obligation to him for his endurance with us. Alas! the pollution of my mind and the filthiness of my thoughts, sometimes causes me to go mourning before the Lord, and to hang down my head like a bull-rush; and I find this is a state to which all the Lord's own children are constrained at seasons to acknowledge they are in.

There are but few of the household of faith, who are so highly favoured with such clear views of truth and gracious access to the Lord, as was our late sister. Her's was not only a faith which gives credit to the truth of a Saviour's personal glories, love, grace, merit, and mercy; but it was a use-making of Christ, a laying hold of Christ in the complexity of his adorable Person, as God-Man, Zion's Representative and Saviour. She lived in communion with him in the perfection of his work, in the fulness and freeness of his great salvation; and though storms and tempests arose, knowing whom she believed, she rode steadily in the vessel, having confidence in her skilful and Almighty Pilot, who could hush the tempest, and quiet the billows at a word; and now she is safely housed in the haven of rest.

"There sin no more assails, there sorrows cease,
And all the host of heaven doth rest in peace."

There are three or four excellencies very observable in her epistles, which distinguish her as guided most blessedly by the Holy Ghost. Her exalted views of the glorious Person, characters, offices, and relations of the Son of God, his Head-ship and Surety undertakings. Also a deep sense of her guiltiness, depravity, and helplessness, with a conviction of God's justice in the sentence passed upon her as a fallen creature. Great humility is evinced on the account of her pollution, and God's mercy towards her; a holy longing after close fellowship with her Lord, is very conspicuous; and an anxious desire for conformity to her beloved Lord Jesus in righteousness of demeanour, and holiness of temper, which is to be fully enjoyed in the upper church state. In an assured confidence that such would be her happy state, when the tabernacle was taken down, which confidence was possessed through faith in the atoning blood, and perpetual, personal, and prevalent, intercession of the Great High Priest over the house of God. On these immoveable, premises, Christ's love, blood, righteousness, intercession, and reign, her faith was fixed as upon the immoveable Rock.

Happy souls, that are thus favoured to live on high; whose place of defence is the munition of rocks. Blessed be our covenant-keeping God, for such holy mysteries which make glad the heavy heart—thanks eternal to our wonder-working Comforter, who is opening up the gracious heart of Jesus to poor sinners, teaching them unhesitatingly to say, "I will trust in him at all times." Well might David say to all Zionites, "Trust in him at all times, ye people, pour out your hearts before him: God is a Refuge for us."

It will rejoice my heart to see my young friend treading in the footsteps of Christ's flock, and following after those, who, through faith and patience, are now inheriting the promises.

W. B., *Drillman*.

Mr. Lay continued his ministry in Haslem Alley, until August, 1835, when he sent in his resignation, the church accepting of the same; and on the 14th of February, 1836, he preached his last sermon, and ceased being our pastor; and we had supplies occasionally, but as a church, the Lord assisted us greatly, and we held our meetings regularly three times on the Sabbath; we congregated, read the Scriptures, and earnestly sought the Lord's direction. On Thursday evenings also, we met for the same purpose; and oft we found the Lord to be with us, causing his favour to distil like dew. Thus we were helped forward up to August, 1837, when arrrangements were made with Mr. Felton, of March, to become our pastor. He entered on his stated labours Old Michaelmas Day, 1837. May the Lord bless him, and make his services useful to promote unity, peace, and concord amongst us, and glorify the name of his Master in lip and life.

About this time, a Mr. M., with whom I once stood in church fellowship, at Salem Chapel, Liquorpond Street, Boston, requested a correspondence with me in writing, upon the points of difference there was between us; and in a friendly and profitable manner: to this I cheerfully acquiesced. He wrote his first letter, August, 27th, 1837, to which I replied as follows.

Boston, August 30th, 1837.

DEAR BROTHER M:—

As such I can truly address you; for we are both descendants of our fallen progenitor, and are alike involved in guilt. We were born in sin, and have gone astray from the womb, and are consequently exposed to the curse of God's righteous law. But it is one thing to acknowledge the fact, another to feel the important truth; whether you approve of the distinction, I do not know, but I fear you are easily satisfied with verbal acknowledgements, and outward appearances. I can heartily adopt the language of the poet with yourself, and sing gratefully,

"O, to grace, how great a debtor," &c.

I admire the plan of heaven in saving sinners, and with hopeful anticipation am looking forward to the sacred meeting, when all the ransomed family will unite in ascribing unceasing praises unto Him that hath loved us, and washed us from our sins in his blood.

You say "My design is to write upon a controversial subject, and the Lord's guidance I implore;" to which petition my soul saith amen. And may the great Head of the church favour me with light, liberty, and love, in my communications.

You say that your views of truth in early days, were the same as mine are now. Here you are affirming untruth, as you assert in early days, you thought it inconsistent for a God-fearing man to pray for his posterity to be brought into an enjoyment of salvation, because he did not know he was one of the elect. Such a principle I never did advocate; and a man of such views no one need wonder at any utterance he may make. It never did grieve me as it did thee, to hear a man ask in humble submission to the will of God, to bless his family with grace, to serve the Lord Christ. As it respects my own sensibilities as a man of prayer, when earnestly pleading at my Father's mercy seat for many blessings, especially that the Lord would build up Zion, by quickening dead sinners into life, I at seasons feel perfectly satisfied that if my requests are not answered in my time, and according as I wish, yet they will be answered in his own time, and to the full intent of his own sovereign good pleasure. The election of grace, are chosen to obtain salvation through our Lord Jesus Christ. Here is solid ground for faith to rest on. Does not my brother see the glory and stability of this truth on which faith lives and acts? Paul saith, "We know that we shall receive the things that we ask of him, because we ask according to his will." And a certain fact it is, that we ask under the guidance of the Holy Ghost, when we rest satisfied and contented with God's own method, and his own time, in communicating the blessings promised.

Hence, if I ask the Lord humbly, for the sake of Jesus, and for the glory of his own name, to convert and save my natural offspring, and at the same time feel assured that the Lord will do it, if he or she be a chosen and ransomed vessel of mercy; also equally certain it is that my prayers will not alter God's plans, but that if his purposes are to punish for fault in the person of the transgressor, that his justice will be glorified, and my petitions will not thereby be nullified; for the prayer of faith is always resolved into "Thy will be done." And for persons who are in nature's darkness, the supplication under the Spirit's guidance is, "If it be thy will, save those who are near and dear to me, from nature's darkness." But if under natural excitement and philanthrophy, an individual rants in his expressions, believing that it is only for us to be importunate with God, and with sinners, and then the borders of Zion will be sure to be extended; exhortations to sinners who are dead in sin, grounded on the ability of the exhorted to act spiritually, is the bane of the present day. God's acts of salvation are regulated by his sovereign will; immutable grace shines in it, and omnipotent power is displayed in the impartation of life to the dead; then comes in the use of God's ordinances to instruct, clothe, cleanse and feed the new born. God inspires man with the breath of life, then man respires toward God. The reversing of these things by public teachers, pains me, dishonours God, and is a shame to them.

I wish to exercise bowels of compassion, but I have not charity enough to believe that men who so misrepresent heavenly verities, have passed out of nature into grace. Do you, my brother? If you do, you will, as there is reason to fear you do, embrace those in your arms as dear creatures, who wage war with their Creator's grace. I confess to you, I cannot feel any more union to the man who would deny or conceal the sovereign system of mercy triumphing over man's apostacy, through the gracious interposition of our one glorious Mediator, than with an infidel. Salvation is not a dubious matter, but an unfrustrable deliverance, willed in heaven, wrought on earth, and consummated in the world of glorified spirits in all the predestinated familiy experience; to the endless praise of its glorious Author, Father, Word and Spirit.

God's salvation a contingent matter! hanging upon the decision of a worm, yea of a monster! Lord, I exclaim, "What is sinful man that thou art mindful of him; and so mindful of a remnant of rebels that thou hast blessed them with all spiritual blessings in heavenly places in Christ, according as he hath chosen us in him, that we should be holy and without blame before him in love;" and all to the praise of the glory of his grace. If you repent, God will save you, is a libel on God's grace; a delusion to poor self-sufficient mortals; it is the opiate that carnal professors are taking greedily, swallowing thoughtlessly; but its effects are as deleterious and as visible in the professed churches of Christ, as the effects of the drug opium which is now taken by thousands, is visible by their countenances.

The great difference between the world and the church is, the one is delighted with God's grace in election, redemption, justification, pardon, and sanctification. The other is vexed with these acts. The one finds his entertainment in looking at the person, love, blood, grace, merit and mercy of Jesus; the other finds his mortification when these things are distinctly and continually exhibited. The one finds a repast, while Christ is presented before him in his offices, characters, and relationships; the opposite is produced on the bosom of a carnal professor. As to the Holy Ghost's personality, ministry, and glory in salvation's work, it is either denied verbally or tacitly; alas! we may say of the present race of men-made preachers, when we have heard them, we do not know by their ministry, that there is any Holy Ghost or any salvation to be received; it is virtually save yourselves, and then Jesus will be your helper. O my brother, beware: I have never yet met with one that I remember, whose eyes the Lord hath opened to see their wretched and helpless state, as law breakers, and their interest in the finished work of Emanuel, but have always lamented over that legal spirit by which they were held in bondage for a season, for it is the natural bent of the human mind to become a self-saviour, and on this ground it is that the God-dishonouring doctrines of Arminianism afford such satisfaction to the multitude, while the liberated man of God blesses and praises the God of his salvation, for having brought him to live on Christ and him crucified; Christ now dwells in that man's heart by faith; they now joy in God by whom they now receive the Atonement; now his incarnation, obedience, death, resurrection, ascension, intercession, and reign, are viewed, as acts of a head, representative, and Saviour; and that an interest in any one thing that he has accomplished, is inseparably connected with all he effected, and will perfect as the saving Lord of Zion. In such teaching, the Lord the quickener and glorifier of Christ appears glorious in his official work and immense love to the enlightened sinner.

Now my brother, I feel for you, while I see you so anxious in amalgamating the present natural worldly system of profession, with God's spiritual inheritance, and the Lord's unearthly system of sovereign grace. May the Lord Jesus himself help you to consider and compare the heavenly mysteries recorded in his

Word, which are hinted at in this letter, with the graceless, sapless, and tasteless harangues which are fallen from the unhallowed lips of our refined modern divines, which you know consists chiefly in exhorting dead sinners to perform spiritual acts, that they have now an opportunity of making their salvation certain, and that if they miss this excellent opportunity, God will be just in punishing them; and the poor preacher cheers himself with the cordial, that now he is free from their blood. Alas! the preacher's business now-a-days, is not to preach what is the faith; but you *must* believe, and while he thus exhorts poor sinners to believe, should there happen to be one who is mercifully helped to believe the good news of a salvation complete in Jesus, and sing of a conquest complete, a righteousness replete, and an atonement fully made by Jesus, when he died, — that man is marked as a speckled bud, and not a few shots are levelled at him from the rostrum, when the unsavoury proclaimer is calling upon all, now at this time you have an opportunity of making your peace with God; and the humble follower of the Lamb, who has entered into peace through faith, in the Peace-maker, is shot at by a side pop. High sentimented men are dangerous characters, confidence is presumption, hyper-calvinism, awful; be sure you keep from them as from a deadly serpent. All that is requisite for membership in most of our Baptist causes is, be moral, repent, be baptized, and join the church; then God will love you, we will receive you, and it will be all well with you at last. I have heard sermons where there has been neither food nor physic, neither robe nor rod, neither law or gospel, and many have been so satiated, that I have asked myself these important questions:

"How stands the case, my soul, with thee?
For heaven is thy credentials clear?
Is Jesu's blood thy only plea?
Is he, thy great Forerunner there?"

In these solemn moments, when such weighty interrogatives are propounded, my soul speaks in the affirmative, being fully persuaded that the same Lord Jesus who shed his precious blood to atone for my sins, now lives in the heavens as my personal, prevalent, and perpetual intercessor, and that by the efficacy of his intercession, which arises from the virtue of his sacrifice, the Holy Spirit descends and testifies the same to my conscience. And I believe God's method of salvation is uniform, that the eternal comforter will take of the things of Christ's, and his only, and bring joy and peace through the knowledge of this Almighty HE. O the frothy things which are daily presented in our churches to amuse mortals, instead of shew bread being set on the tables to feed hungry souls. Jehovah's family are loved immutably, they are purchased by the precious blood of Christ, out of the hands of punitive justice, and will all of them assuredly be rescued out of the hands of satan, by him who is our spiritual

Cyrus; not by price or reward, but by an energy irresistible, and will all in God's time, be quickened into spiritual life, and lead on safely through the wilderness to the heavenly Canaan. In our passage-way home, as saints of God, a humble life of faith on the triune God of Israel, is a safe path; short doings, daily falls, blots and inconsistencies mark us, and oft cause mourning before the Lord, when cries are excited for deliverance, "Restore unto me the joys of thy salvation," are sensibilities God's quickened people are the subjects of, as really so as they are of the want of food and fuel.

Now my friend, are you alive to such experience? Is sin thy burden? Is Christ the burden-bearer endeared? Is self renounced and Christ embraced? I confess with shamefacedness and humility, that my heart departures are many, my sins are great, and my corruptions my pest. A daily pardon, daily cleansing, daily help, daily deliverances, and daily bread, I am constrained to seek at my Lord's hands, and in whose inconceivable grace I find a redress for all my grievances. But what can I say to you friend M.? You wish me to unite with those men who treat God's eternal choice of his people with contempt. His pardoning their daily iniquities and healing their daily diseases with a sneer. I appeal to your own soul, whether you have not had it again and again declared that the doctrine of election and God's everlasting love to his people are doctrines which lead to careless, loose, and licentious living? Then how can you treat such men as the servants of our most holy Jehovah, who in consequence of his electing love to his people before the world began, hath blessed them with life to feel their lost estate, light to see their wretchedness, and hath put a cry into their hearts, "God be merciful to me a sinner?" In your next, tell me if you do not now hear, and have not often heard, these truths of God's Word trumpeted against.

Now I think you cannot charge me with uncharitableness, when I say practically as well as verbally, "O my soul, come not thou into their secret; unto their assembly, mine honour be not thou united." Whatever may be your opinion of such preachers, I frankly confess, my opinion is that they are altogether in the dark about spiritual subjects. As to the Holy Spirit's blessing the labours of these men, in calling dead sinners to life, that will admit of great doubt; these preachers excite the natural passions, and persuade many to join in their ranks, and many have I known who have dated their conversion from some revival rants, which profession has lasted little longer than the sound of the ranter has reverberated on the ear; but such conversions are not from error to truth, from sin to sanctity, but from one error to another. The doctrines of grace they hate; the heritage of God they despise, they love a salvation lingering on human contingencies, and speak naughty words against the just, whom the

Lord delights in; but will not God avenge his own elect, that cry day and night unto him? I tell you he will avenge them speedily.

I remain your well-wisher,

W. BOWCOCK.

TO THE SAME.

Boston, 6th Oct. 1837.

BROTHER M.

When you proposed writing, your request was, let all angry words and unprofitable arguments be avoided, and let our communications aim at each other's edification, while we declare our views on divine subjects. Now you have written me two long letters, in neither of which have you declared what you do and do not believe. I fear you have some other object in view, and not real Christian edification. Either you are seeking to draw from me some concessions, whereby you might expose my apparent inconsistency, or else excite me to evince a bitter censoriousness whereby I should betray a spirit at variance with the Gospel of Christ; my prayer is that the Lord may preserve me from both; in the absence of a natural education, a verbal error or errors may easily be accounted for, and with a hasty temper that is my daily plague, the latter, I may be easily drawn into unless the Lord preserve.

You say my prayers are limited to the elect; you suppose I believe you wilfully remain blind on this matter; read over my former epistle, for more explicit I cannot be. You appear to have your scruples in your conscience about the doctrine of election, though a deacon of a Particular Baptist church honestly demands your renunciation of such an office; why not go over to the camps of the generals? I asked you plain questions, and, instead of shewing me how those men can be worthy of the name of the servants of the most high God who pour contempt on the doctrines of sovereign grace, you immediately depict the characters of those whom the Lord, by his blessed Spirit, has brought out of nature's darkness into Gospel light and liberty, triumphing in a free-grace salvation. Why, my friend, you never knew such an heterogeneous monster as this—a man enjoying salvation by grace, and yet pouring contempt on the grace that saves him. You have supposed what is impossible, and left the queries unanswered.

As to the felt necessities of a drowning man driving him to his deliverer, this is an inadvertency of expression, though it may accord very well with your in and out, say and unsaying system of divinity. It is impossible. That man is not drowning who has wings to fly to a deliverer. But all God's people were actually in a drowning state, and would, if left to themselves, have sunk to the bottomless pit: but the gracious, mighty, and glorious Deliverer who came out of Zion, came for the express purpose of turning away ungodliness from every spiritual Jacob. He does not offer and propose help, but he rescues their souls from merited destruction; hence hear him saying, "Mine own arm brought salvation; and as to the people there was none with me." It was his love to their persons, as composing his church—his body—that he came here to deliver them from satan, sin, death, hell, and the grave. He gave his life for their lives, his soul for their souls; he made his soul an offering for sin, that their souls should, and bodies should, be dedicated a living sacrifice to God, acceptable through him. None but the new created know the secret of the Lord. Mere professors may talk about it parrot-like, but they are living without it.

As to your string of questions, they are beneath a living soul's notice—they are as barren as the heath. Lead the soul from Christ, and you must quench the sacred fire of devotion in any man's bosom who would attempt to follow such a querist. Communion with the dear Redeemer in his personal glory, sacred offices, endearing relationships, interesting characters, and finished work is no speculative affair, and would sweep off the premises as with a besom of destruction, those empty quibbles that would pine an hungry soul to death when answers were given.

In the will of God the blood and obedience of Christ, and the official work of the eternal Comforter, are all harmoniously conspiring to effect the church's honourable, endless, and perfect deliverance, and all will issue in the ceaseless praises of the triune God of salvation.

I will just observe two or three things upon one of your questions, namely, "Do you not grieve the Spirit when you think lightly of Christ's commission—Go ye into all the world, and preach the gospel to every creature; and lo! I am with you always, even to the end of the world." I should dishonour Christ, disgrace myself as his follower, and grieve the Spirit Jehovah, by whom I am sealed, were I guilty of thinking lightly of his command, or doubt the fulfilment of his promise. What! because I stand aloof from the missionary societies, am I to be branded with being an enemy to his mandates? Shew me a society that are electing men of sound experience, gospel lovers, whose determination is to preach Christ and him crucified, and are resolved on sending out none but such characters, to that society I would give my aid in prayer and pocket. But alas! to the shame of those men who are very active in missionary enterprize, the sterling truths of the gospel are opposed, and the men elected to preach in foreign climes, are individuals who preach almost every thing except that which Christ commissions his missionary men to proclaim. Are not the preachers of sentimental and experimental godliness counted by the travelling missionary gentlemen as enthusiasts and antinomians, enemies to good works and piety? Charging me with grieving the Spirit and opposing Christ's mandate, falls harmlessly on my head; for it has been my prayer for years that God would send out his truth far and near; also my effort to aid his sent servants in propagating his gospel has been uniform; but to aid those who are leagued together for the disseminating anti-scriptural doctrines, my conscience would condemn me. Your questions are all on circumstantials and not substantials. Nothing could be gathered in discussing them but what would starve a hungry soul; not a word in your two epistles that would impart instruction to a sin-sick soul, or a word of direction to the weary mind, whereby he might be guided to the sin-atoning Lamb.

I decline your invitation to discuss those subjects so completely graceless, and consequently useless to a helpless sinner like myself, and will aim to profit by your advice, namely, abide by the Scriptures in all our arguments, or rather, I would say, in all our investigation of spiritual subjects, for on those I purpose only to dwell. How concise is God's Word in declaring our lost and ruined condition by the fall, and that salvation was purposed, arranged, and adjusted in infinite wisdom by the eternal Three-One Jehovah before sin had its birthday; that all spiritual life and blessedness was secured in Christ for all his family before his seed was brought forth into open existence, as really as all natural life and its consequences were settled in Adam for all his posterity, before his descendants walked into the theatre of action. Spiritual blessings were designed for the Lord's chosen family, and no power shall prevent their actual possession of the good things provided for them. Rom. ii. 7; John x. 28; xvii. 12. Do you believe it? if not, it yet remains an immutable and glorious verity.

The rich blessings God's family are predestinated to possess through Christ are pardon, justification, sanctification, repentance, faith, hope, and ultimate promotion. They are a distinguished people, and a distinguishable clan, set apart by the free favour of heaven, and segregated from among men in the day of God's power, by an influence they did not desire, and they are kept by favour momentarily, they never could deserve, since these quickened souls have been led earnestly to desire the renewings of the Spirit, and the replenishing of their spiritual powers.

He whose holy mandates I wish ever to regard, and whose heavenly testimony I wish we may both revere, saith, "The Holy Ghost, whom the world cannot receive, neither knoweth him, but ye know him, for he dwelleth with you, and shall be in you, and he shall glorify me, for he shall take of mine, and shall shew them unto you, and he shall guide you into all truth." Now in a spiritual apprehension of these truths the soul is led to bless God who hath thus graciously taught them, and how much more God-honouring it must be, and soul-satiating, to abide by his truth and assemble with his illuminated family, who are worshipping God in the Spirit, rejoicing in Christ Jesus, having no confidence in the flesh, however few or despised they may be, than to mix up with carnal, worldly professors, who are talking about the saving of all the world; and one question stirs their ire, namely, how an unholy sinner can be justified in the sight of a just and holy God.

O the misguided zeal and fallacious talk of the untutored professor, who is going to accomplish what God never designed, and means not ordained for. Jehovah's means of mercy will ever effect the merciful end for which he appointed them. Election, redemption, and renovation will be all of the same extent, which will be gloriously exemplified at the last day, to the confusion of the opposers of election, the deniers of absolute redemption, and the ridiculers of irresistible energy in the soul's new creation.

To preach God's gospel is to manifest declaratively the person, love, and grace of Christ shining forth in his life, sufferings, death, and dominion; to exhibit through him Jehovah's immutable hatred to crime, and infinite, ceaseless, and causeless love to the guilty criminal. Such subjects are as tasteless to the general herd of professors as the white of an egg. It is while truth is preached character is manifested. The one despises God's method of saving a sinner; another finds his salvation in the subject; and it is to him the power of God in his soul's experience; for to him the subject brings hope, satisfaction, great encouragement, and attachment.

In this the children of God are manifested, and the children of the devil—"Whosoever doeth not righteousness is not of God." It will be impossible for you, my friend, to prove that to be a righteous work to unite with those who reject the righteousness of God, and are labouring to establish creature righteousness. O my brother, come out from among them (unless you are one of them) and be ye separate, and touch not the unclean and unhallowed things; and leave off your catechetical questions, whether it be the duty of all men to obey the law of God perfectly; talk to your fellow travellers to Zion, if to that city you are bound, about Zion's Deliverer who came here with a living copy in his heart, and never blotted it in the acts he performed, but has gone to the end of it for righteousness to every one that believeth. May the living in Jerusalem be more anxious to shew forth his praises who had compassion on them in their low estate, and saved them for his mercy's sake. Let us walk in close communion with his people, hoping, as we profess to do, to dwell with them eternally.

Your's for Jesu's sake, W. BOWCOCK.

TO THE SAME.

Boston, Nov. 11, 1837.

BROTHER M——.

In my last epistle I told you that your question about a dead sinner performing a spiritual act was such a empty, unmeaning, and contradictory idea, that the discussing it would be useless. I should as soon think it would prove useful to answer the querist who might start the question, Can the body, when the soul has fled, perform an intellectual action? The practice of those preachers who are calling dead sinners to perform acts which requires God's new creating energy first to be put forth, ere they can so act, is no better than the conduct of those degraded individuals who gather round the corpse, as is the case at the Irish wakes, and shout to the dead, "O why did ye die? Awake; come and take of the good things, which are all ready for you, if you will but rise. Wake, wake, come, come, and do partake." But this I leave. The subject of salvation is too sacred for a sober-minded christian to be diluted with an offer for the dead to live if he will. It is life given to us in Christ, life conveyed by Christ, and life enjoyed in communion and fellowship with Christ.

I strove to follow your advice by keeping to the Scriptures, I wish you had pursued a similiar course. I tried to wake up your attention to some of the blessed subjects of salvation, but you have passed by them as if they were uninteresting themes to you. One would be ready to think you had no spiritual appetite, but that your vitiated appetite could find food on that dry subject; the sinner's duty to act spiritually before life is imparted graciously; that he will be condemned for not believing, and that he ought to be punished eternally because he repents not, which repentance the Scriptures tell me Christ is exalted to give, together with remission sin. Your system of divinity, God is no more the author of than he is the author of the alkoran. Your answers to your own questions are vague, God-dishonouring and soul-perplexing; your last epistle is a complete jargon; surely, friend, you do not go about preaching after this manner, and call it the gospel of Christ; if you do, you will assuredly smart for it if you are a man of God. Certain I am that such preaching will have a tendency of making them sad whom God would have ministerially made glad. I pray God to bring you into his stripping room, that you may feel the the want of Christ's robe, and be led to cry out with Peter, "Lord! save, or I perish!" then you leave all those who assume a profession, from human persuasion, and will feelingly unite with those who ascribe all the glory of their salvation to the blood of the Lamb, triumphing in a free grace deliverance. At present you seemed amused with questions of no profit, instead of taking delight in the matchless, measureless, and dateless love of a Triune God; from your letters, I expect your occasional ministration is not tinctured much with the sovereign love of God to his people, the mediatorial work of Christ for his sinning brethren, or the soul-renovating work of the Holy Ghost on the hearts of these people, who are loved and will never be left, who are ransomed and will never be repudiated.

I will now ask you three questions; and as a deacon of a Particular Baptist church, and as a professed preacher of righteousness, let me have a plain answer, for you possess capabilities that I pretend not to have.

First—Do you believe that God designed that all the family of mankind should be saved by the sacrificial death of Christ?

Secondly—Do you believe that any one of the fallen sons of Adam will ever enjoy the benefits of the sacrifice of Christ; by any other influences than that of the irresistible and unfrustrable operations of the Holy Ghost?

Thirdly—What is it that justifies in the sight of God a legally condemned criminal?

May the Lord help you to consider these things for yourself, not for the sake of argument, but for your own satiation, as a professed follower of Christ, and then, I believe, you will be constrained to say, "Once have I spoken: yea, twice; but I will proceed no further." I pray God, if it be his Sovereign will, to bring you forth to worship him with his own quickened family.

W. BOWCOCK.

N.B.—If you have no higher views of the mysteries of redemption than that it removes every obstacle on the part of God, so that he can be just in forgiving every sinner, why call yourself a Particular Baptist? Is this particular redemption? You, as much as in you lay, destroy the whole system of sovereign grace. Such were not Paul's views. (See Eph. i.) Neither does our dear Lord teach any thing of the kind; and, as to your belief that endless punishment cannot be maintained unless universal sufficiency be admitted of the meritorious death of Christ, what an hateful idea. Christ's interposition, or non-interposition on the behalf of a sinner, rules not the duration of punishment to a guilty criminal. What you have introduced such a thought for I know not; unless it is that you hold up endless punishment before the poor guilty soul, to frighten him into sanctity by it. I am truly thankful that I am not an hearer of your's, and I am aggrieved that you do not know how to speak in harmony with what Christ saith, "I give unto my sheep, eternal life; and they shall never perish, neither shall any pluck them out of my hands."

TO THE SAME.

Boston, 30th December, 1837.

MY FRIEND—

You have committed yourself most egregiously in saying you have answered my questions; for, instead of a yea or nay to the question, of its being the design of the Lord to save all the fallen sons of Adam, by the sacrifice of Christ, your whole cry is, unbelief is a rejection of the truth of God — sin is opposition to the will of God; and what answer is this; or what has these observato do with Christ's appearing here, to put away sin by his own vicarious death, or the end of heaven designed in laying on him the iniquity of us all. Such proceedings as yours is trifling with substantial realties, and evinces a dislike to the glorious truths of the gospel. You must think me untutored in divine things if you supposed I could receive your asseverations as a concise answer to my interrogations. Why not speak plainly and say it was or was not the design of Eternal Majesty to save all men by Jesus Christ. Why leave the question and affirm Christ's death is sufficient atonement for all, and then presently affirm that it only suffices for some men, and that it is their faith makes it suffice for them. This is not divinty, but blasphemy! What! the act of the sinner renders effectual the atoning death of Christ; and if men would but believe, then Christ's death would be satisfactory for them! Christ has atoned or he has not, the atonement is revealed as made, or revealed to be made; under the law it was the latter—under the gospel the former; and by faith, through the law of ceremonies, the spiritual worshippers were looking for him who is come to make the atonement. And now, the spiritual worshippers, under the gospel dispensation, are looking to him who has made reconciliation; and now the act of the believer is receiving the atonement made, and joying in God through the Lord Jesus Christ, by whom the atonement was made; let us maintain that as sufficient which has, does, and ever will be found efficient.

I say, friend, beware! lest you find yourself enveloped in a vortex of confusion, in the night, when your soul shall be required of you! Your sentiments are rotten at the core: your doctrines devised for conciliating purposes, are enimical to the welfare of Zion; they eclipse the glorious grace of God—read God's own declarations. He came to liberate the captives, to open blind epes, unstop deaf ears, throw open prison doors, to heal broken hearts, and bless the people with unloseable life: and yet, you presumptuously say, none can overturn that sophistry which you call arguments, defending your doctrines. Certain I am that they are not doctrines according to godliness; for his majesty, justice, grace, or mercy, are not exhibited by these principles you advocate; and if grace was not a different thing from what you cariacature it, not one sinner would be saved. Read the Old and New Testament language, and see what majesty and mercy are thereby discovered. "I will say to the north give up; to the south keep not back; bring my sons from afar, and my daughters from the ends of the earth. I am come to seek and to save that which was lost; I will bring the blind by a way which they know not: I will take away the stone out of their heart and will give them an heart of flesh. A new heart also, will I give them, and cause them to walk in my ways, and I will be their God, and they shall be my people. These things will I do unto them, and will not forsake them." Now, my friend, this is good news; here the

Lord graciously declares what he will do for helpless, guilty sinners: these things gladden the hearts of some, and grieve the minds some. How does thy and my heart despond? You appear to be on the side of those who insist on man's making the first move towards God, and then he will meet them to encourage them forward. Conditions are propounded in man's creed for sinners to perform, in order to be saved, that are as impossible to be performed by them as the creation of all things out of nothing; but natural men love to have plenty to do in religious matters, though they leave the things undone perpetually; and when work-mongers hear it affirmed that Christ has done enough and suffered enough, to save the vilest of the vile who come to him, their spleen and enmity rises against this sovereign method of God's saving his own in, and by Christ's, obedience and blood exclusively. And that class of professors, you seem much pleased with, who are best pleased with the least being said of God's rich grace in election, redemption, and vocation. It is a proof to me, that your heart is not stedfast in God's covenant. Again I say, beware! Depend upon it, every species of Arminianism is Anti-Christ, and every preacher and hearer that denies God's choice of, and opposes God's sovereign and gracious operations on the hearts of his rebellious family, is an enemy to God; and you know what is the final and endless state of all such.

Do not think I speak in anger, or out of any ill feeling towards persons. Let me beg of you to read attentively and think seriously over the words recorded by him who is appointed the Judge of quick and dead. Matt. vii. 21, and following verses; Psalm xcii. 9. And I pray you don't act any longer with duplicity, filling a sheet of paper with words tending to eclipse the glory of God's grace in regeneration and effectual calling. Speak openly as conscience dictates and truth directs, and then see and say, is salvation by works, or grace? And let me hear something sacred from you, instead of affirming that salvation does not depend on Christ dying for me, but upon my acceptance of it; the taking upon himself the profession of Christianity is the securing cause of salvation; for this has been the substance of your epistles. Your desire for me to embrace those whom I consider the enemies of God's truth will never be complied with; and to assist such, is to me aiding and abetting traitors against Christ, encouraging men who are fostering hypocrites and formal professors. From such, my soul, turn thou away.

You request me to write over again, for your use, two of my former letters. Is it not that some inconsistent Particular Baptist may see if he cannot propound to me some queries? I decline, acceding to such a request; for you have declined answering my plain questions, and all I have received from you is anti-gospel. May the Lord preserve you from duplicity.

Your's   W. Bowcock.

A few months after Mr. Felton's arrival amongst us, he accepted an invitation to become our pastor; several were added to the church the first three years he abode amongst us. He continued ministering amongst us until July 3rd, 1842, on which day he delivered his last lecture, and departed for Deptford, and my prayers were up unto the Lord on his behalf.

On the 10th of July, the pulpit was supplied by a perfect stranger to us, from Surrey, who preached in the morning from Isaiah xliv. 22, with much acceptance. His visit was for four Sabbaths, but he prolonged it two Sabbaths more at the request of the church. There was a great desire expressed for his coming amongst us. After several communications on the subject with him after his return into Surrey, arrangements were made for his removal to Boston on six months probation, and on January 8th, 1843, he preached amongst us, having removed with his companion into our midst. His stedfastness in the truths of the gospel is admirable; the savour attending his ministry most salutary, and his movements, firm, steady, and commendable. There are some amongst us inclined to arminianism, others to Fullerism, and not a few, customary professors. Here the man of God has to declare the truth unhesitatingly, which he does fearlessly, and many of us have to say that a sweet unction attends his testimony, which is filled with the love, blood, righteousness, and glory of Immanuel. Arminians are galled; Fullerites murmur, and the professors often find fault with such a separating ministry. Many things perplex me as an officer of the church; for there are those among us who complain of the want of love and unity, while they themselves are actively engaged in sowing discord to the grief of our supply; and oft I fear will be the cause of our wished for minister, declining any further engagement amongst us.

Herein lies my satisfaction. The Lord of Zion watches all our ways, words, and thoughts: his eyes are over the righteous, and his ears are open to their prayers; but the face of the Lord is against them that do evil. To his fatherly care and guidance I desire to commit my soul, my friends, my foes; my esteemed brother, who is now ministering unto us the bread of life; yea, all my concerns to him: I desire to surrender, exclaiming with one of old, "Thou shalt guide me with thy counsel, and afterwards receive me to glory."

Christ's church has often been in a storm, but he never abandoned her, but ever acts the part of a skilful Pilot. Clouds, darkness, and enemies, have oft made her afraid; but Jehovah the everlasting God hath always appeared in his own good time. Let us look back as a church on the past twelve months, and may we not say, he has stilled the tempest, and sent us an undershepherd who hath ministerially led us into green pastures and caused his distracted flock to lay down beside the still waters, and restored peace in our borders. Let us remember that the right hand of the Lord is exalted, the right hand of the Lord doeth valantly. Bless his holy name for ever and for ever. After hearing a Mr. De Fraine from Lutterworth, who supplied for three weeks, in June 1844, our minister having written to him to supply during his absence, his message was savoury, and rendered helpful to many; on one occasion, he was speaking of Christ's presenting all his saints to his Father, without spot, wrinkle, or any such thing, and very blessed observations he made. A Christian friend inquired of me, how we are to understand that passage, 2 Cor. v. 10, "For we must all appear before the judgment seat of Christ, that every one may receive the things done in his body, according to that he hath done, whether it be good or bad." The following thoughts occurred to me:

Man has fallen, and by a just sentence, every man is held over by law to punishment; but it is also a fact, "That as by one man, came sin, judgment came upon all his posterity to condemnation: even so by the righteousness of one, the free gift came upon all his posterity unto justification of life. For as by one man's disobedience many were made sinners, so by the obedience of one shall many be made righteous."

There are, therefore, two distinct heads, Adam and Christ; the one brought ruin, disgace, and depravity on his family; the other brings pardon, righteousness, and purity to his. We are all alike ruined in our universal head, Adam; the election have a perfect salvation by their Head and Saviour. The whole race of mankind are described by two characters, the believer and unbeliever; in the flesh and in the Spirit, under the dominion of sin, or under the reign of grace. Now, we must look to the scriptures to prove these facts, and may the Lord help us to examine ourselves as we proceed, that we may trace out the class to which we belong, seeing that we must all appear before the judgment seat of Christ, and all must receive according to the deeds done in the body, and that we are all alike guilty before God; it must follow, that if all are not alike condemned, a gracious interposition must appear; this is the subject matter of the gospel dispensation; and most truly may it be said to be good news. The forming the soul anew is marvellous mercy: let us try to trace out the work of the blessed Spirit, in quickening, calling, and sanctifying, thus forming the righteous characters; and let us never forget that this arises from the sovereign love of God, bearing in mind that the ungodly, who are left to fill up the measure of their sin, are uninjured by the gracious acts of God towards the vessels of mercy, who are pre-ordained to obtain salvation through our Lord Jesus Christ.

First, God hath an elect people according to his own foreknowledge, to whom he purposed, and promised, and settled, eternal life, to, in, and with, Christ Jesus, before the world begun. God hath from the beginning chosen you to salvation, through the sanctification of the Spirit and belief of the truth: knowing, brethren, your election of God.

II. This remnant according to the election of grace, though dead in trespasses and sin, and by nature children of wrath, as others; yet, in due time, are quickened together with Christ, having forgiven them all tresspasses—having predestinated us unto the adoption of children by Jesus Christ according to the good pleasure of his will, and all to the praise of his glorious grace; being born again, not of corruptible seed, but of incorruptible, by the word of God, which liveth and abideth for ever.

III. These people are also sanctified by God the Father, preserved in Christ Jesus, and called: (Jude i.) called to be saints. Rom. i. 7. "He hath called us with an holy calling, not according to our works, but according to his own purposes and grace; which was given us in Christ Jesus before the world began." 2 Tim. i. 9.

Now for some clear demonstration of who these chosen, called, and sanctified people are, who shall stand with holy boldness and sacred confidence in the solemn day when all are to mustered, to receive at the Lord's hands, according to the deeds done in the body. The writer and the reader will then appear, and all will be awake to their own matters, and not another's, at that solemn meeting and parting.

Without a gracious and glorious Mediator to look to in the Person of Christ, my righteous Judge, what a fearful and hopeless prospect would my poor immortal soul have before me.

Now, on the Holy Ghost's quickening a sinner from death to life, new sensibilities are produced; the poor sinner feels wretched, miserable, and completely undone: an accusing conscience, a holy law, and a just sentence, denounced against the law breaker, fills him with dismay; the terrors and fears cause him to tremble, and a "what must I do to be saved," arises from his inmost soul, with a glance upward, bordering on despair; his petitions are short, earnest, and pithy. "Save me! help me! God be merciful to me!" Light is let in on the understanding, and now sin is discovered to be exceeding sinful: self is a loathsome, diseased, and contaminated mass of putrid matter. Now, hear him cry, "Cleanse me! wash me! purge me!" Behold him now a vindicator of God's holy law, and a subscriber to the sentence denounced against himself as a law-breaker; and not unfrequently does the trembling criminal fear that God will pour on him justly the wrath he deserves. This knowledge prepares the man for a joyful reception of the mystery of the mediatorial character of Christ. How welcome to such an one is the doctrine of forgiveness, through the atoning death of Christ and the imperishable obedience of the Son of God, by which the sinner is justified to the honour of law, the glory of grace, and to the praise of God's great name. When the Lord brings down he will build up—those whom he empties he will fill; stripping goes before clothing, imprisonment before enlargement, and condemnation before justification. What surprise fills the soul, when out of much obscurity he begins to discern a glimpse of him who is the hope of Israel and the Saviour thereof, in time of trouble. What a springing up of hope and expectation arises, when the spiritual ear is arrested with the news of Christ as a sin-bearer, soul-purifier, satan-vanquisher, death's destroyer, and grave's victor. After much soul-conflict, sometimes hope, with many fears, lifts up its head like a cork in the water, and a small, still voice, whispers "peace, through the blood of the Lamb!" and Jesus speaks unheard by the congregating crowd to the troubled conscience, "Thy sins are forgiven thee!" This so echoes through the soul. at seasons, that no diabolical temptation however painful, nor any flesh-pleasing system of do, and live, can bewitch or drive him from this hope of the gospel, which he finds now to be as an anchor to his soul, both sure and steadfast, entering into that which is within the vail. The work of grace in the heart, began in the day of God's power, is carried out effectually, and forms the character unto that pattern to which the soul was chosen by electing favour, namely, the image of the first-born. Now, this will put most of the professing world to a stand, except a few who are awfully blinded, and suppose they are perfect in the flesh; but the new-born heir of heaven will not only be brought to say "how can this be," but he will be brought on his knees to confess himself corrupt, unclean, impure, and defiled by thoughts, words and ways, himself nothing but a lump of loathsomeness; and had God swept me as a lump from these earthly premises, and consigned me a place with sinning angels, his justice would have been glorified, and my conscience would have subscribed to the equity of the procedure. How can sinful man be just with God? is an important interrogation. Who can bring a clean thing out of an unclean thing? That which to man, is utterly impossible, is possible, ah! and is accomplished by infinite wisdom, unsearchable goodness, and measureless mercy, through the interposition of a Day's-man, God-man, Glory-man. Thus, saith the Lord, "When I passed by thee and saw thee polluted in thine own blood, I said unto thee, live! then washed I thee with water, and I anointed thee with oil, and thy time was a time love; and thou wast beautiful through my comeliness, which I had put upon thee, saith the Lord God." Ezek. i. 6. This causes the poor soul to sing with the Prophet, "I will greatly rejoice in the Lord; my soul shall be joyful in my God, for he hath clothed me with the garments of salvation. He hath covered me with the robe of righteousness as a Bridegroom decketh himself with ornaments, and as a bride adorneth herself with her jewels." Isaiah lxi. 10. Now, he that wrought us for the self same thing, is God, who hath given unto us the earnest of his Spirit; and this blessed earnest of the heavenly inheritance holds the soul up in the midst of rolling billows and howling tempests. Faith being fixed on Jesus, the grand and glorious centre of salvation, beholds a permanency and certainty in his acts of justifying, redeeming, and sanctifying, that brings comforts under crosses, peace in conflicts, and joy in sorrows. The eternal Spirit of grace and supplication, will continue to aid the beggar at mercy's door, to cry for pardon, purity, light, protection, and sustentation; and Christ will be lived upon as that bread which satisfies, sanctifies, and appetizes. Thus, the child of God will go on from day to day, mourning its own vileness, seeking communion with God, relying on the obedience and blood of the Lamb of God, waiting for his dismissal from this body of sin and death in a hopeful anticipation of being with, seeing of, and being like him, in whom Paul laboured to give a representation of a sinner being perfected.

At the day when worlds are congregated, the church will appear arrayed in that wedding robe, which will cause her to stand unashamed and unconfounded, then shall she enter into the joy of the Lord. We read in Jude 14, of the Lord's coming with ten thousand of his saints to execute judgment upon all, and to convince all that are ungodly among them, saints are safe in every storm: and in the morning of the resurrection there will be an orderly process; Christ, who is the first fruit, will awake his first at his coming. Every man is to rise in his own order, as the tree falls it lies until that solemn epoch. The order of the wicked are classified in this world; what an unspeakable mercy, to be plucked as a brand from this dry stubble! There is the clan of deluded idolaters, mental, and bodily, or gross; there is the openly profane, profligate, lying, cheating, coveteous class; there are the God-denying, Christ-deriding, and persecuting tribe. Then the last, but not the least in number or guiltiness, is the self righteous, customary, and empty professors, who are building their hopes on repentance, obedience, improvement of gifts, and renounce the atonement of Jesus as being of itself that which secures the soul from endless ruin, and that affirm all the dolorous sufferings and death of Christ to be inefficient to save; unless they, by their puny acts, put the finishing stroke to the business. Let me listen to my Lord, who always spake truth, but never spake a sentence so fraught with soul-animating importance as just when he yielded up his life a sacrifice to put away sin—"It is finished!" Now, all these classes will stand at the last day, in their order, at the left hand of the Judge. While the righteous, made so by an act of grace, will stand at the right hand of the Judge, and ascribe their honourable justification to the free favour of God, through the doings and dyings of the Lamb.

So we shall appear at the judgment seat, but every one in his order, to receive according to the deeds done in the body. And though the acquitted were condemned by a holy law, yet in time they have been washed, taught, and acquitted by, in, with, and through Christ. And now, on the day of the great assize, their open justification will be made known to all their enemies; then God will give their enemies to see and know that he hath loved them: while his just indignation will be poured out on none but enemies, as the following scriptures declare: "When the Lord Jesus shall be revealed from heaven, with his mighty angels, in flaming fire, taking vengeance on them that know not God." He shall at the same time come to be glorified in his saints, and to be admired in all them that believe in that day. 2 Thess. i. 7, 10. The Lord knoweth how to deliver the godly out of temptation, and to reserve the unjust unto the day of judgment to be punished. 2 Peter ii. 9. Christ's wheat are the children of the wicked one. "I will say to the reapers gather ye first the tares, and bind them in bundles to burn them; but gather the wheat into my barn." (Matt. xiii. 30.) For the Son of Man shall send forth his angels, and they shall gather out of his kingdom all things that offend and them which do iniquity, and cast them into a furnace of fire, there shall be wailing and gnashing of teeth." Then shall the righteous shine forth as the sun, in the kingdom of their Father. (Matt. xii. 41, 43.) "When the Son of Man shall come in his glory, and all his angels with him; then shall he sit upon the throne of his glory, and before him shall be gathered all nations; and he shall separate them one from another, as a shepherd divideth his sheep from the goats, and he shall set the sheep on his right hand, but the goats on the left, (every one you see in his own order.) Then shall the King say unto them on his left hand, Come, ye blessed of my Father, inherit the kingdom prepared for you from the foundation of the world. Then shall he say also unto them on the left hand, Depart! ye cursed, into everlasting fire, prepared for the devil and his angels! And these shall go away into everlasting punishment, but the righteous into life eternal." Matt. xxv. 31, 46.

May the Lord help me and my few christian friends now, while we are in the body, to arise in our thoughts to Jesus and love him.

> "How he sits God-like, and the saints around him,
>   Thron'd, yet adoring!
> O may I stand there when he comes triumphant,
>   Dooming the nations, then ascend to glory!
> While hosannas, all along the passage,
>   Shout the Redeemer!"

July 3rd, 1844.

It pleased the all-wise Disposer of every event, to visit me with a heavy affliction, by a small tumour on my under lip; for some few years it continued painful, constantly forming a tender skin over it, becoming nearly healed, and then breaking forth with a small discharge. I at length consulted the surgeon, Dr. Snaith; and in the month of June, 1844, he cut a piece out nearly an inch wide; and, through great mercy, it soon healed and all went on favourably.

At this time our minister, who was on probation, acceeded to our unanimous call to take the pastoral charge. This was a great relief to my mind; and has been a cause of much soul-satisfaction to me and many others; the Lord continue him amongst us, and make him a lasting blessing to the church; and may we, as a church, uphold his hands by prayer, attention, kindness, and liberality.

In the month of November, 1845, I took cold, and a severe pain settled in my bottom jaw-bone. Many things were recommended to me as a sure cure. After using externally some oils, I by the advice of my pastor, who was then about journeying to London, travelled with him. And in London I consulted Dr. Keys and Dr. Callaway, of Guy's Hospital; they said but little, and advised me to come home, live moderately well, and keep myself quiet. The pain increased, and much anxiety pervaded my mind, lest it should prove an immoveable disease; the pain became excruciating; a round bright lump appeared; it soon turned into a running tumor; and at length was pronounced to be what I and many of my friends feared it was—a cancer. It is now near two years since; and it keeps spreading slowly around my jaw-bone and inside the mouth, and the pains occasionally are most intense and very trying indeed. Whether it be sent by my heavenly Father for my removal from this state of trial to the world of triumph, time will determine; however, I wish to bear this humble testimony to the honour of my God, that he has been with me according to his promise, and that as my day, so has been my strength; the gracious Lord hath so favoured me with his presence and opened up his covenant love to my mind, that I have "rejoiced in the hope of the glory of God." Such has been my communion and fellowship with Jesus in the mystery of his saving acts, at seasons, that the things of this life have appeared to me what they really are, in comparison with the mysteries of grace—toys, trifles, and bubbles.

My christian friends, and such to me are the excellent of the earth, are all most kind, feeling, sympathetic, and a spirit of prayer is evidenced in the assembly of saints on my behalf, as also in their social prayers with each other; importunate they are with the Lord that his grace may be displayed in supporting, consoling, and bearing my spirits up under my present inconceivable bodily pains; and truly the Lord doth hear and answer their petitions in my soul's experience—but my pains are past description. Among many friends, who have shewn their interest on my behalf, I have to record the sympathy and kindness shewn me by that dear man of God, John Stevens, of Meard's Court, London, who wrote me a letter, and I think one of the last letters he ever wrote to a christian brother. At the end of my narrative is a copy of it. (p. 162.) I found it to be a word in season: it was full of christian tenderness and consolation; the advice and encouragement given is blessedly calculated to lift the soul up, and cause it patiently to endure the pain and suffering of the body. He bears such an honourable testimony to the unchangeable love and faithfulness of the Lord Jesus Christ in all his ways to every saint, as their Surety, Redeemer, Sympathizer, and Succourer.

I felt a desire to write a few lines in return to this honoured messenger of mercy, to testify my gratitude to him for the good feeling evinced, and to testify that Christ is precious to my soul, under this heavy affliction; though I feel quite inadequate to make use of such words as would set forth the worth and value of that dear Lord Jesus Christ, who once groaned beneath my damnable crimes, when he paid into the hands of Divine Justice its equitable demand, honouring that holy law for me, which I had violated, liberated my captive soul from all the trammels, snares, and temptations of satan, and brought me most blessedly to put my trust beneath the shadow of his wings. What a blessed reality there is in God's salvation! How secure are all the heirs of grace—all the children of God!—babes, young men, and fathers.

The following is a copy of what I wrote to that minister of the New Testament, John Stevens:

Liquorpond Street, Boston, October 2nd, 1847.
DEAR AND HONOURED SIR—

I received your kind and sympathetic letter with thankfulness. (See p. 162.) The first sentence arrested my attention and excited admiration and gratitude; to think that I, a poor illiterate sinful creature, should be justly entitled to be acknowledged a ransomed brother! Is it true, thought I, that I am ransomed by the precious blood of Christ, as of a Lamb without blemish and without spot? Why, it really is. To deny it would be sin. Truly, my soul is most grateful to him that bought me by his own most precious blood; and unceasing praise would I give to my covenant God that he hath been pleased to make the fact known to my poor soul. It is that, and all the great blessings connected with Christ's vicarious death, that causes me to lift up my head, under this heavy affliction, with a sweet anticipation that when these storms of life are past, I shall then enter the peaceful harbour, see my adorable Pilot, love him as he deserves and I desire—in the "beauties of holiness;" and praise him without defection or cessation. O! blessed, blessed be his holy name, who hath brought me, once a poor, ignorant, vile, farm-yard youth, out of darkness, into his marvellous light, and taught me, who was as ignorant as an Hottentot, to see that the price of my ransom is the precious blood of Christ, my adorable Surety, Mediator, and Saviour, from whom comes my pardon, justification, sanctification, with all the blessings of a full, free, and glorious salvation.

My heavenly Father, seeing my rudeness, untowardness, and stubbornness, in hankering after the flesh-pleasing things of this life, hath taken up his rod, he hath put me into the furnace, he lays his rod upon me sharply; his hand hath done it, my position is to adore! I richly deserve it; bless his holy name, he gives me to see it is a fatherly chastisement; it's not to punish, but to prune; not to destroy, but to rectify. Had the Lord dealt with me as a judge, I must have sunk for ever in the dismal abodes of endless ruin!! But as Jesus voluntarily became my Surety, the punishment fell on him, and the pardon reaches me. As you observe, my sufferings are all restricted to this body, and shall terminate with it; they are ending sufferings, and the glory which shall be revealed hereafter buoys up my feeble mind, and makes me long to fly away and be at rest. To escape pain is desirable, but to be delivered from sin and be made perfect in character and bliss, is what my soul thirsts for. O! the beatific vision of God and the Lamb! What beauty and glory streaming forth on all the blessed society of ransomed, sanctified, saved sinners. It makes me long to

"Drop dull mortality behind,
And fly beyond the grave."

And yet, for all this, when I am favoured with freedom from pain—would you think it sir?—I feel a cleaving to the earth and things of time still. How amazing that a heaven-born and heaven-bound soul, who yesterday was groaning and crying for deliverance from a body of sin and death, should to-day feel an inclination to tarry longer on the premises, where before the next sun sets, I shall again be all in confusion and distress, racked almost to pieces, by acute pain in my face and chin. Ah! I find the fleshly appetite takes a great deal to subdue it. Still, however, notwithstanding all my ups and downs, I feel the words of the apostle afford me consolation—"For we know—(O! this knowledge is worth more than worlds!)—that if our earthly house of this tabernacle were dissolved, we have a building of God, an house not made with hands, eternal in the heavens; for in this we do groan, being burdened; so that we would rather be absent from the body, and present with the Lord."

It is not very likely that you and I shall see each other again in this mortal state, but we can recognise each other as brethren in the same pathway to our Father's kingdom, exercised with various pains, afflictions and sorrows; we can remember each other at the throne of grace; and our dear Lord having loved us and bought us with his own most precious blood, he will be our God and guide, even unto death. You feel yourself getting towards the end of your journey. Age and infirmities are our monitors. I apprehend my race will soon be ended; this great affliction—these sore pains will ere long dissolve this tabernacle; but our God is faithful, his supporting hand is all-sufficient, and his grace gladdens the heart under gloomy dispensations. Sovereignty, you observe, is written on all God's ways, yet no injustice is seen. O, may he help us to adore him reverently, keep us waiting at his footstool prayerfully and hopefully, even unto the end. We have not much longer to wait, ere he will receive our immortal souls, blessing us with a capacity to take in larger draughts of bliss from the fulness of Christ, with all the ransomed, than what we are here capable of doing.

To his holy name be everlasting honours given. He lives in the heavens, having obtained eternal redemption for us.

I remain, most affectionately, your brother in Jesus,

W. BOWCOCK.

Having written the above letter, intelligence reached me of the state of Mr. Stevens's health, who it was announced, was not likely to be raised from his bed of sickness; soon after which, we had the official announcement from our pastor that he was called from this world of imperfect service, to his eternal home, where labour ends, and service is perfect. This took place on Wednesday, October 6th, 1847, in the 71st year of his age. So the above letter was not sent.

It may be truly said of Mr. John Stevens, that he was a laborious, able, and faithful minister of the New Testament; he was a highly favoured man of God; his gifts, abilities, and parts were far superior to any minister I ever heard. Multitudes can bear testimony, in this part of the Lord's vineyard, to the clear powerful, and concise manner of his stating the truths of the everlasting gospel. It was not his practice to trifle with the moments of his hearers, by rehearsing anecdotes and unmeaning tales, but to bring before his hearers the glorious doctrines of grace, shewing their influence on the heart, when renewed by faith, and demonstrating their effects on the walk and conversation; he was favoured to possess that useful gift, as a public speaker which few have, that is, to say much in few words; hence there was a fulness in sentences which dropped from his lips, that you seldom meet with in lengthy paragraphs from most; the Lord endowed him with peculiar speaking gifts—such a flow of ideas—and a happy mode of conveying them, by a blessed choice of words, that you seemed to be carried along in the subject with interestedness of mind; and so far from being wearied under lengthened discourses, I have heard many, as I have also myself stated our regret that time forbid him to prosecute his subject further.

The great subject of his ministry was Jesus Christ and him crucified; his glorious Person, as the God-Man; the perfection of his sacrifice; the perpetuity of his priesthood; the glory of his righteousness; and the completeness of the church in him, as her head, and by him, as her Mediator. These subjects filled his ministry.

My soul hath been feasted, while I have heard him exalting Christ as freeing his people from condemnation, by his atoning blood and justifying obedience; the same Lord sitting at the Father's right hand, interceding and swaying his righteous sceptre, as King in Zion, ruling, guiding, and managing all the affairs of his kingdom for the ultimate good of his blood-bought family, and to his own eternal praise; the sovereignty of God in the choice of his people; the love of Jesus breaking forth to them, through his official work on their behalf, and the grace of the Holy Spirit displaying itself towards the same persons, in the regeneration, verification, and illumination, were among the many good things which that earthen vessel was filled with, and used frequently to give out unsparingly; but now the cistern is broken at the bowl, and that God who raised him up, crowned his labours with much success while he spake. And now, being dead, he speaketh to us by his pen; and God will bless his labours, causing the fruits of righteousness to appear in the lives and conversation of many to whom he ministered by his lips, and now ministers by his works, who being now dead, yet speaketh.

May the Lord grant that the precious truths which I have heard from his lips, may be blessed to my soul; and may my memory be sanctified to retain the truths, and may a savour of them pervade my bosom all my days.

February, 1848.—It is now more than two years since my jaw began to be very painful, and frequently it has been excruciating. Bless the Lord he has been my support and my stay; he hath comforted me with many sweet assurances of his Fatherly love, and given me to believe that this affliction is not sent as a punishment, but as a chastisement, and that his love and wisdom designed it for my correction and instruction, and I earnestly pray that it may be sanctified to my immortal soul. I acknowledge that I have gone astray like a wandering sheep, he has mercifully gathered me up and brought me into green pastures, and caused me to lie down beside the still waters; I do feel thankful that he is often refreshing my soul in public and private, and he is causing faith, hope, and love to abound, satiating my soul with marrow and fatness. Blessed be his dear name, he keeps me day by day from murmuring and repining, although the pains are become almost incessant. Oft the way appears dark and dreary, the time long; satan is busy with me, trying to bring me into despair, by lifting up my criminality as being too great for Jesu's blood to remove; and that it is my wretchedness that brings God's judgments on my head, and that if the Lord loved me, and Jesus died for me, he would not thus sorely visit. Yet the Lord shines again, yea and again, and gives me such heart-cheering and soul-animating promises, that causes me to lift up my soul with joy. Oft the Lord says to me, "Fear not, for I am with thee, I have redeemed thee, I have called thee by thy name, thou art mine. When thou passest through the waters, I will be with thee; and through the rivers, they shall not overflow thee; when thou walkest through the fire, thou shall not be burnt, neither shall the flames kindle upon thee. For I am the Lord thy God, the Holy One of Israel, thy Saviour." Isa. xliii. 1—3. Questions arise in my mind, how came he to be my Saviour? Who intreated him to save my soul, when sunk in sin, guilt, and misery? Did I? Alas! I was altogether a child of wrath, even as others, and should have remained so, had he not loved me, pitied me, bled for me, and given me life unasked for by me. O the untellable love of Christ, which moved him to the great work of saving poor sinners, ere Adam was formed, or angels made. What grace reigned in the bosom of Deity, towards a wretch like me, that I was to be one of those for whom Christ would bleed and die, and in due time I should be made partaker of that precious faith which makes Christ more precious to the soul than all the wealth of worlds. What an inestimable blessing is that faith which leads the soul to Christ for pardon, sanctification and justification. But how is my redemption accomplished? By Jesus paying down the ransom price into the hand of Divine Justice, so that justice is satisfied, the law magnified, and Jehovah, Father, Son and Holy Ghost is eternally glorified, and my poor worthless soul saved honourably for ever.

When was all this achieved? When he bare our sins in his own body on the tree; when he was made a curse for us, then we were redeemed from the curse of an irreparable sentence annexed to the law as a broken covenant; when Jesus died, he removed our sins from himself and his Church as far as the east is from the west. He did it voluntarily; he did it nearly eighteen hundred years before I was born; therefore it was not because I entreated him to do it, or that I could ever deserve that he should do it.

Why did he do it? That he might be glorified in the salvation of his people who shall dwell with him for ever, completed in character, and consummated in bliss, ascribing all the praise of their ultimate perfection to the Lamb in the middle of the throne, who loved them and washed them from their sins in his own blood, therefore are they before the throne. Salvation from wrath incurred, is not by an act of power, but price, justice, love, holiness, grace, mercy and truth, all are harmonized through the substitutionary death of Christ in the release of the offender. O what a honourable redemption; what a glorious salvation. My soul rejoices in the manifestation of it, and especially that I should have an interest in it, and an interestedness of mind about it, while myriads are pouring contempt on it. The thought again and again arises, how do you know that you are a child of God, and that you are ransomed with so great a price, that you are adopted into the royal family of heaven? These are important queries, and thus I solve them to myself.

Jesus loved his people from everlasting; "He was rich, and he became poor; he laid aside his glory which he had with the Father, before the world began; in the fulness of time, he was made under the law, that he might redeem them that was under the law; he was made sin for us who knew none, that we might be made the righteousness of God in him; he bare our sins in his own body on the tree, he was holy, harmless, and undefiled, yet it pleased the Lord to bruise him, by his own offering he hath put away sin for ever, and by his perfect righteousness, he justifies many." Since Jesus in the day of his incarnation thus effected these mighty wonders, and is now gone up where he was before, and there as the great and gracious Intercessor before his Father's throne, pleads the cause and sympathizes with his suffering saints, sending his Holy Spirit down into the hearts of sinners, teaching them to cry Abba Father; shedding abroad his love in the heart, and bearing testimony to the personal glory and perfect work of Christ; leading the poor undone soul to Jesus; blessing him with life to feel his own vileness, and light to see Jesus as a suited Saviour; opening the lips to cry for pardon in a Saviour's name, pleading the sacrificial death as the basis of its hope for pardon at the hand of a sin-hating and sin-avenging God. The all gracious Redeemer encourages the soul with some sweet assurances of his love, and graciously says in effect, "Thy sins are all forgiven thee, go in peace." Now my soul can through grace, say that he hath thus taught me to look to him as a sin-bearer, and law-fulfiller, and that by his stripes my soul has enjoyed healing over and over again; and will the blessed Jesus after having of his own free favour, paid down to justice the price of his own precious blood for my redemption, and given me a sweet sense of it in my soul by his Holy Spirit, can he, will he give me up after all? No he will not. He'll never, no never, no never forsake. I desire to mark interestedly, and to honour God while I do mark the influence these things have on my own mind, "Most painfully do I find a law in my members warring against the law of my mind, and bringing me into captivity to the law of sin, which is in my members, so that I cannot do the things that I would." Rom vii. Yet I bless the name of my

Redeemer Lord, for what he hath spoken by the mouth of his servant, and for making me a witness to his faithfulness to the truth, "Sin shall not have dominion over you, for you are not under the law, but under grace." Rom. vi. 14. So that sin works in my thoughts, words and acts, depressing my poor mind; yet it does not reign and domineer as a ruling tyrant, but Christ my gracious prince helps me to triumph over sin, satan and the world, by his precious blood, righteousness and spirit. My only hope which is a good one, is built on him, my expectations are from him, and in him, and in him I am looking to be found living and dying, for the Lord will not forsake them that seek him, them that put their trust in him. Psalm ix. 10. Blessed be the Lord, so far from taking a delight in sin, because I am not under the law, but under grace, the directly opposite is produced, I hate sin, and I abhor myself on the account of it, and long to be delivered from the very being of it. And I have this assurance, through faith in my glorious Jesus, that shortly my perfect emancipation from its being and effects will be my happy portion. Blessed Jesus, I do earnestly long for thy arrival, when this earthly house shall be dissolved and I sink into the arms of death: then shall my redeemed soul, sanctified, and made holy, fly to thy embrace in those pure mansions where happy spirits be.

February 22.—While musing on my bed last night, full of trouble and sorrow, though my pains were mercifully abated for a season: Well, there is but one more obstruction in the way to my Father's kingdom, that is the grim monster death, the king of terrors, and the terror of kings; but it will soon be removed when the appointed time comes by the captain of my salvation. Death lost its sting when Jesus died, and therefore is a vanquished foe. The Lord Redeemer will not leave one of his flock to travel that dark valley alone; his kingly authority and pastoral office will then be displayed to the soul delight of his flock! In the days of his flesh those sweet lips exclaimed, "Fear not, it is your Father's good pleasure to give you the kingdom." Then fear not my soul, if the death of his saints are precious in his sight, we may rest assured he will not leave them. Again, he will not leave my poor soul in the trying hour, (though I have sinned against him) "For he hath begotten me again unto a lively hope, upon an immoveable foundation, the resurrection of Jesus Christ from the dead;" so that he died to put away our sins, so he rose again to justify our souls for ever, and the saints' heavenly inheritance, is reserved for them, and they for it; it is incorruptible, undefiled and unwasting. I put in my humble claim for the possession of these great blessings, on the foundation of grace, and feel persuaded that he who hath called me into the fellowship of his Son, will keep me by his own Almighty power through faith, unto the full possession of this inheritance, this salvation. Fear not my soul to pass this dark valley; Christ will be with thee, and all is light, holiness and bliss beyond it. 1 Pet. i. 2, 3. The apostle saith, "Our light afflictions which are but for a moment, worketh for us a far more exceeding and eternal weight of glory." And can we suppose Christ will leave the souls of his saints at death and not bring them to possess this glory? O dear, no! for we know "That if our earthly house of this tabernacle were dissolved, we have a building of God, an house not made with hands, eternal in the heavens;" and as sure as this heavenly house is prepared for the souls of the redeemed, so sure shall they be brought to inhabit it, for in this we groan being burdened, but there praising without groaning. While here in this body, we are absent from the Lord, but we are confident that we shall be present with the Lord on the day of our dissolution. No, the Lord will not leave me in the dark valley.

March 4th.—The Lord Jesus himself says, "Let not your heart be troubled; ye believe in God, believe also in me. In my Father's house are many mansions; if it were not so I would have told you. I go to prepare a place for you, and I will come again and receive you to myself, that where I am there you may be also." Bless his holy name, he will not falsify his word, but will surely bring my soul safe through the conflict of death to dwell in that celestial mansion where perfection of holiness shines eternally. Ah! but your sins have been so double dyed; your faults so glaring in the eye of infinite holiness; your guilt so great; you may well fear! Yea, how dare you presume to expect that you will be brought safely through the jaws of death. Under these solemn thoughts my soul hangs on the word and promise of a faithful God. "Come now, and let us reason together, saith the Lord. Though your sins be as scarlet, they shall be as white as snow; though they be red like crimson they shall be as wool." Here Jehovah himself invites my poor soul to come, and assures it that such cleansing shall be effected as to wash out the deepest dyed stains, and that the soul shall be made white as snow, clad in such robes as will be an honour to appear before holy angels and redeemed saints before the throne. Bring forth the best robe, and put it on this returning prodigal. "And they shall walk with me in white," says the dear Saviour, "for they are worthy." Rev. iii. 4. Again he says, "I, even I, am he that blotteth out thy transgressions for mine own sake, and will not remember thy sins. Therefore, O Israel, fear not, for I have redeemed thee; I have called thee by thy name; thou art mine." Again, "O Israel, thou shalt not be forgotten of me."

With such gracious invitations and precious promises of pardon, purification, and acceptance I will venture through grace to come as a poor, lost, helpless, defiled, worthless sinner, and cast myself at the footstool of sovereign mercy; nor shall satan with all his accusations, nor all the sins which I know are enough to sink me to hell which have been committed by me, drive me from the blood-besprinkled throne; and though the Lord may be pleased to hide his face and I may be troubled, yet he says, "I will come and see you again, and will receive you to myself, that where I am there ye may be also." And though my heavenly Father may lay upon me his rod, which is the case, and sharply I feel it, yet he is righteous. I acknowledge I have wandered grievously from him, and the rod is as needful for me as the food. He hath brought me back with confession, supplication, and thanksgiving. I hope and pray that God will continue to sanctify this affliction to my good, that I may honour him as an adopted son, for it is only children that receive correction in this afflictive manner. Bastards are allowed to run on in error and disobedience, and are finally punished.

What proof we have of the Lord's fatherly tenderness and care towards his people in the furnace of affliction, recorded in Psalm l. 14, 15, "Offer unto God thanksgiving, and pay thy vows unto the Most High, and call upon me in the day of trouble I will deliver thee, and thou shalt glorify me." What a gracious admonition attended with a double promise! Not only an assurance of an exit out of the furnace of affliction, but a promise of grace, strength, and ability to glorify the Lord in it, by it, and out of it.

Now this is just what I want to do. I would be continually calling upon him, and hourly blessing and praising him; but alas! alas! what interruptions; what vain and foolish thoughts rush suddenly into my mind, even while I am supplicating for mercy, and imploring the Lord for fresh manifestations of his pardoning love to my soul; how oft am I grieved to find my thoughts drawn off from the Lord in a moment; thus intercourse with heaven is interrupted, and the object of my delight and adoration lost sight of. Verily, if he was not the God of patience I must have been banished from his presence long since for my fickleness and folly. What amazing grace have I to celebrate; he remembereth my frame; he knoweth what a dusty thing I am. "I will deliver thee, and thou shalt glorify me." Amen, amen.

O blessed be the Lord who fixed his love on me from everlasting, and adopted me into his family. Hence it is that he hath made known unto me all these things, so that the hope of seeing his face in righteousness, and dwelling in his presence, makes me at times to sing for gladness of heart even in this furnace of affliction. Yea, I appeal unto my covenant God. I love him because he first loved me; I love him because he hath blotted out all my transgressions, and blessed me with a knowledge of it; I love him because he hath heard the voice of my supplications, therefore will I call upon him as long as I live; I love him because he hath promised sin shall not have dominion over me; I feel sin and satan daily striving to distress me, and I am grieved at my own poor, vain, and bad heart, but, bless the Lord, sin has not dominion. I do believe his holy word of promise, and I love him because he hath promised great things to me, and that he will never leave nor forsake me. "I will praise thee, O Lord, with my whole heart; I will shew forth all thy marvellous works; I will be glad and rejoice in thee; I will sing praise to thy name, O thou Most High. Blessed be the name of the Lord, for his right hand and his holy arm hath gotten him the victory," and in his name and in his righteousness I hope to shout victory too, over sin, over satan, over death, and the grave. Amen.—*Dated March* 4, 1848.

This was the last effort made by our departed brother to express himself in writing. For some considerable time prior to this his articulation was very defective in consequence of the mouth, and especially the tongue and throat being so diseased. A few weeks before he departed this life, but little communion could be had with him, but the company and conversation of saints afforded him pleasure, and, by his feeble voice and disfigured countenance, intimations were given his friends that the rehearsal in his ears of the glory of Emanuel, and of his gracious acts in the salvation of his people was the only subject he wished to hear of, and which blessed theme yielded him solid and substantial joy; and though he was incapacitated to converse on the subject, it was his great mercy God continued him a receiving vessel, perfectly satiated from his fulness who is the Father's storehouse, where all spiritual blessings are deposited for the poor, lost, guilty creature. Much delight it afforded the deceased in reflecting on the free manner of Christ's imparting every suited blessing to the repenting, returning sinner, together with the love of his heart, the nearness of his relationship, the importance of his offices, the sweetness of his characters, and the tenderness of his conduct. Oft he enjoyed a repast on this sacrificial Lamb, when he gave those around him to understand that his animal appetite was such that he could greedily take solid food had he but the power of so doing; but such was his situation for weeks before his death that liquids could scarcely be received by him sufficient to sustain life. Oh, how oft in this bodily malady he adored the God of his salvation that he had not a Saviour to hunt for, but that Jesus had sought him, and brought him to behold a salvation perfectly suited to him, endearing the same to his heart. Conversation on the voluntary and vicarious acts of Christ oft attracted his attention, and excited admiration at those times when nature seemed exhausted with pain. Christ in the womb, in the tomb, and on the throne—a Priest to sacrifice, intercede, and bless, truly refreshed his soul while closeted in a tabernacle that was a wreck, and such an one that no creature could behold without painful emotions.

His case was laid on the hearts of his fellow members; a spirit of prayer on his behalf was most evident; and certainly the Lord graciously answered their petitions in ministering many cordials to him during the heavy affliction. Many petitions were presented on his behalf at his bedside by the which he was often led into sweet communion with his heavenly Father, many times expressing his thanks to friends, and praise to the prayer-hearing God, who remembered him in his low estate. An earnest solicitation about the welfare of the cause at Ebenezer was manifested to the last, many anxious desires for its peace and prosperity was expressed.

After he was deprived of attending the public worship he evinced much anxiety to know what had been the subject matter of the ministration on the Lord's-day, regretting his loss of the privilege of waiting on the Lord in his public gates, at the same time looking forward hopefully for his dismissal from the vale of tears, exclaiming gratefully, "I know that if this earthly house of my tabernacle were dissolved I have a building of God, a house not made with hands, eternal in the heavens. In this I do groan, earnestly desiring to be clothed upon with my house which is from heaven."

Not a friend who was privy to his state and circumstance but was anxious to hear of his removal from this militant state, where he had mercifully been taught to know how an equitably condemned criminal could be honourably justified, pardoned, and promoted, and was graciously led into communion with his justifying Lord.

In his removal the church sustained a great loss, for in him was combined (what is seldom to be met with in one individual,) —a laborious deacon, a most acceptable leader of the praises of God, a methodical secretary, a valuable treasurer, and a sympathising visitor of the poor. One thing which rendered him capable of attending to many of these things was his retirement from business. He was an untiring servant of the church. The doors of the house of God were never open and he absent or late in his seat, and oft he exclaimed, it was good to be here.

The last visit he paid to the house of God was to commemorate the death of his redeeming Lord, at which time the reception of the elements occasioned him much pain, and his appearance excited sympathy, sorrow, and tears from some.

A few weeks before the Lord removed him, he enquired at the close of the Sabbath about the text which had been spoken on, and some of the ideas delivered. The text was quoted, and some of the observations advanced and recited. With much expression of countenance he, with great difficulty, requested those words might be a text for his funeral sermon, providing any notice was taken of his decease, which request was very soon complied with by his pastor.

It pleased the Lord on the 4th of May, just two months from the date of his last written statements of the Lord's gracious dealings with him, to release him from his pains, and administer unto him an abundant entrance unto the mansion love ordained; having continued unto him his mental powers, and favoured him to the last with a steadfast faith in Him who was dead and is alive again, and lives for evermore, in whose hands are the keys of death and hell, power to subdue and punish his foes, power and grace to protect and enrich his friends. Well might John fear not when the Exalted One spake as he did. Blessed be the Lord Christ, his promises are public property for the whole household of believers to use! Lord, increase our faith.

On the following Monday he was interred in the burial ground belonging to Ebenezer Chapel, in a spot of ground he had many years before selected for his remains to be deposited, hoping there to rest, with many of his brethren, until the morning of the resurrection.

According to his request an effort was made to elucidate the Scripture selected; together with a few observations on the passage as expressive of his own experimental sensibilities on the Sabbath evening following. The words selected were Rev. i. 5, 6,—"Unto him that loved us, and washed us from our sins in his own blood, and hath made us kings and priests unto God and his Father, to him be glory and dominion for ever and ever. Amen."

The leading thoughts presented to a crowded congregation on the passage were of the following nature:

The love of Christ; the manifestation of it; the sacred advantages conferred upon us; the doxology in which his redeemed are employed; an application of the words as most expressive of the deceased's feelings towards the Lord Christ, who voluntarily became poor, that he might graciously be enriched; none could evince more of an abhorrence against every idea that would exalt the creature and debase the Saviour than the departed; most heartily he could unite with the church in her repulsive expressions—"Not unto us, not unto us;" as also with Paul "God forbid that I should glory, save in the cross of our Lord Jesus Christ." It was on the head of Christ Jesus the Lord that he declaratively put the crown; and he with us as a church, has and does, in the language of our text, ascribe to the Lord Jesus Christ endless praises, universal authority, and perpetuity of dominion.

APPENDIX.

The following is the letter referred to on page 150. It is the latest letter written by Mr. Stevens, of Meard's Court, London, (dated, September 10th, 1847, just twenty-six days before his dismissal from the church militant,) which has appeared in print.

September 10th, 1847.

My Esteemed Brother Bowcock—

It is your mercy to know that your sorrows and pains are fast hastening away, being redeemed unto God by the blood of his own dear Son; your sufferings are all restricted to your natural body, and will terminate with it; for with the worm that never dieth—the fire that shall never be quenched, you have nothing to do, since Jesus has already saved you from the wrath to come; this he effected by a great ransom, and herein you may read his great love, and join with the apostle in saying, "He loved me, and gave himself for me." He that bought your person with so great a price, will follow up his purchase by his sovereign power; nor will he permit any calamities to befall you but which shall consist with his having loved and ransomed you to life everlasting. The afflictions of the saved are wonderfully numerous and inconceivably diversified. O, the depths of the wisdom and knowledge of God! how unsearchable are his judgments, and his ways past finding out!" When his providence confounds us, we have his precepts to direct us, and his promises to enrich us. We are objects of his care when we are not the subjects of his comforts. If he assign uncommon trials, he will also afford us proportionate aid; else it would not be true, that "as thy day thy strength shall be." Why such peculiar trials were ordained for some, while others remain free from them, is beyond our knowledge; sovereignty is written on all God's ways, yet no injustice is seen; this is seen in electing some, and rejecting others; we see the same features in his afflicting some and sparing others. What charge of injustice could fallen man establish, if the whole world were an hospital, and health and soundness could no where be found? All the covenant right we had in our father Adam was lost at once when he ate the forbidden fruit; it is by divine sufferance that men continue on earth at all! What a scene would present itself to notice, if every man was cancerated! How greatly is misery moderated to what it might be; his mercies, even "his tender mercies are over all his works;" Psa. cxlv. 9; and he is good to all. Acts xiv. 15—17.

I was glad to learn, by brother Potter's letter, that you were favoured with gracious aid, and mercifully upheld in your heavy affliction. Steady faith in Christ is the principle by which the suffering saints have made their way through seas of tribulation, and obtained their wished for end; the spiritual and endless cure of the soul is a potent support in bearing the pains and frailties, agitations and distresses of the body; Jesus Christ once dwelt in a natural body; he knows its weaknesses and liabilities; you will do well to make frequent applications to him for help in every time of need. Thus did Paul, when painfully tried by a visitation, the effect of which resembled the anguish of a thorn in the flesh. May his grace be found sufficient for you, and his strength exemplified and commended through your great weakness. The well-taught christian can glory in his infirmities, when he learns that the power of Christ is magnified in his endurances.

Now, my brother, I say farewell in Jesus, and may the rich unction of his name rest upon you, and your faith therein be strong and stedfast to the last. Thus breathes

Your willing servant in the gospel,

JOHN STEVENS.

I continue much tried in breathing, and sometimes think I must desist from public speaking; but I hope to work as long as I live. I am glad my debts are paid, my sins pardoned, and my life insured. He died for our offences; he rose again for our justification.

TO THE EDITORS OF "THE GOSPEL STANDARD."

June 20*th*, 1838.

MY BRETHREN—

As a friend to truth, I have taken and read the *Gospel Standard* from its first appearance, and at times have had sweet fellowship with some of your correspondents. I hope you will not think me in my address to you vain or dictatorial; but certain observations found in the June number (similar pieces have appeared in previous numbers,) constrain me to ask a few plain questions; and while I offer a few thoughts on the piece above referred to, I pray that it may prove profitable to all your correspondents.

I am as far as either "J. K." or "A Traveller" can be from wishing to bolster up a fleshly profession. Alas, we have too much double dealing and smooth talking amongst even some of whom we hope they are right in the main; but that dear Lord who hath quickened their souls, will bring them under his rod of correction, and afford them lasting instruction, teaching them to depart from all false ways.

The acrimony and bitterness evinced by the two correspondents referred to, savours much of the leaven of self, and I fear pride is lurking under what these writers call honesty. I ask, what necessity is there for a whole piece on the doctrine of Reprobation? What can induce a good man to be dilating upon the portion of the damned? Would "J. K." not be better employed in setting forth the soul travail of all who are oppressed, and to point out the way in which the Holy Ghost trains up a sinner to feel the need of salvation and to live by faith on the finished work of Immanuel? Allow me to ask "J. K." what satisfaction will it yield to the soul, or what consolation will it afford on a dying bed to look back on all this censoriousness in writing, month after month, in the *Standard?* O, my friend! rather let your pen and tongue be employed in setting forth his praises who hath "called you out of darkness into his marvellous light." Look over the apostle's declaration, and think soberly thereon—"Who hath made thee to differ—and what hast thou that thou hast not received?" I was once in the sink of sin—then in the muddy water of a false profession, seeking to establish a righteousness of my own, being ignorant of the righteousness of Christ, Zion's King. But now the Lord hath manifested himself in mercy to my soul, and taught me to see and believe that the salvation of the whole family of Zion, from first to last, originated with, and shall be completed by Jehovah, Father, Son, and Holy Ghost, according to his infinite wisdom and covenant love, developed on Calvary in the sufferings of Zion's Surety, and manifested to the soul, when the blessed Spirit quickens the dead sinner into life, shews him his wretchedness and helplessness, and leads him to the Lord Jesus, and blesses him with a living faith, so that he renounces self, and commits his soul into the hands of Christ, with a "Lord! save, or I perish!"

With regard to your Correspondent who signs "A Traveller," finding fault with the ministers around him so incessantly, I fear there is a great deal of religious, or, as it might more properly be said, irreligious cant. Certainly if "A Traveller" continues writing, and preaching as he has written, he will be of no use to a broken hearted sinner, who, under soul travail, is longing to obtain rest. How much better and more becoming it would be if the young man were to study to approve himself before God as "a workman that needeth not to be ashamed, rightly dividing the word of truth;" then we should hear no more of his regret that he is not favoured to live near such men as "J. K.," whose severity and unchristian-like writings in the *Gospel Standard* has caused many a living child to heave forth a sigh while reading them, and to say that such like epistles are of no use to me, and I frankly confess they are of no use to my soul, and I thank the Lord of my life that such writings disturb not the peace of my mind, for I know that "Our God is a Rock—his work is perfect." The Lord will perfect that which concerneth me.

When I reflect upon the Lord's dealings with his people in this wilderness state, how they are scattered up and down like flocks on the mountains and in the valleys, two or three here, and four or five there, longing to feed in green pastures, and to lie down by the still waters, I look upon the *Gospel Standard*, as among the most valuable monthly periodicals, and if conducted with a single eye to honour and exalt the great Redeemer in his person and work, debasing the sinner, aiding the enquirer, encouraging the fearful, saying unto the poor feeble traveller, go forward, it might indeed prove a great blessing to the church of the Lord Jesus. Such pieces for instance, as that inserted on page 42, February number, 1836. I do not know who is the author, but suppose it to be Mr. Gadsby. If I know any thing of a work of grace, and the exercises of faith, hope, and love, contending with unbelief, depravity and enmity, such productions are calculated to help forward the exercised household.

Will you pardon me, Messrs. Editors, when I ask you as in the sight of God, who will avenge his own elect, how it is, and how you can clear yourselves in his sight, while you admit such heterogeneous perplexing irony and bitterness, as are displayed in the pieces of "J. K." and "A Traveller?" Can you conscientiously say that you think such pieces, tend to promote the glory of Christ in his Church? And may I be permitted to ask the writers alluded to, how matters stand between Christ and their own souls, when indulging in such invectives against their fellow-men? Consider, I beseech you, friends; you were each of you in the same state of darkness and ignorance, and had the Lord left you as he has them, you must have stumbled on until you had fell into the pit of distruction!

May it be the anxious desire of both Editors, writers and readers of the *Standard* in future, to honour our Lord by exhibiting the great work he hath accomplished for us and in us, thereby a distinction will be maintained and evinced between the sheep and the goats, the precious and the vile. Our God will always honour those who honour him; he will carry on his own work in the hearts of his people, and he will bless his people with peace. Then let us not perplex and grieve saints, under a pretence of exposing the hypocrite.

May the Lord bless you, Messrs. Editors, with wisdom and prudence in conducting the *Gospel Standard*, and may it prove a blessing to many in Zion.

W. B., *Drillman.*

Lincolnshire.

The foregoing letter sent in the simplicity of my mind and in love, was noticed by the Editors of the *Standard* with bitter irony, sarcastic remarks, and erroneous conclusions were deduced. These things occasioned me to write the following epistle requesting the appearance of both letters in the *Standard*.

But not being of *Standard* value when weighed by the scales of the adjusting Editors, they were deposited among the waste papers, or consigned to the flames as not negotiable.

AH! MESSRS. EDITORS,—the paragraph which has appeared in the *Standard* as a complete extinguisher to the Lincolnshire

Drillman, as you intended, is altogether wide of the mark. You have quite mistook the man, his employment, and his character, for instead of being a raw recruit as you affirm, his locks are becoming silvery, and instead of pushing himself up to a paltry post of honour in the British army as you again suppose, he has been brought up in the laborious employment of cultivating the land.

But I suppose you have more to do with parsons, pens, and religious disputations, than with that hard labour appointed to man, in consequence of his transgression; still had you taken the trouble to look into an English Dictionary, you would have seen that the term Drill is not confined to the coxcomb employment of a Sergeant with three stripes on his sleeve and a cockade on his hat, as you fancied was the case with me; but that it is a machine used to deposit the seed in the ground, after it has been properly prepared by the plough and harrow, but I can make an allowance for you, gentlemen, in all this.

The reason of my previously writing to you was, that in consequence of myself and a few country friends having enjoyed many pieces which has appeared in your columns; that if "J. K." after having exposed false professors and hypocrites, would record the Lord's gracious dealings with his own soul, and point out the narrow path that leads to life, or describe the exercises of soul, and shew what living faith is, as the piece referred to in my former letter, viz., page 42, February number, 1836: our souls would be much more instructed, edified and encouraged while we are wading through waters of woe, arising from the flesh and the devil.

But it appears because I have charged "J. K." with irony and bitterness, the editors are offended, and I must endure their lashes. "J. K." well knows, however, whether he will confess it or not, that although some are pleased with his pieces, there are many of the Lord's quickened family regret he makes use of such unjustifiable language.

Your remark as to my deserving many stripes on my back, more than strokes on my arm, is partly correct, for I confess unhesitatingly that my deserts would bring down the cause, but then the Lord the righteous Judge does not render unto the children of his love according to their deserts, because he himself has born our griefs and carried our sorrows, and with his stripes we are healed.

You say positively, the Drillman has never been in the valley of decision, here Mr. Editors you speak without your book; perhaps I had been brought there before you knew yourself to be guilty, filthy, and helpless; the fact is you have looked over the letter with a jaundiced eye, or you would not have classed the Lincolnshire Drillman with the enemy's soldiers!!!

It is true I was in and among such a company as "J. K." calls dead Calvinists, but when that God who leads the blind by a way they know not, imparted life to my soul and opened my eyes, then I complained and my spirit was overwhelmed, I communed with my own heart, and my spirit made diligent search. The Lord also brought me up out of an horrible pit, even the pit of nature's corruption, and out of the miry clay of a false profession, stripped me bare, washed and clothed me, and set my feet upon the Rock, Christ Jesus. Shall I not say, "He hath established my goings, and put a new song into my mouth?" But I do not wish to intrude upon your time, and as you have formed such an unfavourable opinion of the Lincolnshire Drillman for speaking as I have about "J. K." (at the same time, I look upon him as one of the King of Zion's watchmen, but a severe one,) I can hardly expect you will receive anything from the Drillman, but with the greatest suspicion, otherwise I might send to the *Standard* some account of the Lord's dealings and manifested grace and mercy to a once poor plough-boy, afterwards a Drillman, and now a retired man from the turmoil of business.

However, it becomes you to be careful, for many false prophets are gone out into the world; but in expressing an opinion to a watchman of Zion, and that opinion not being permitted to meet the watchman's eye through the same medium as his piece reaches the eyes of God's people, and then to be publicly branded as an enemy, such a practice displays little more wisdom or prudence I apprehend, than "J. K.'s" flogging the dead Calvinists for not being living souls! What would "J. K." think of that man who would go into the churchyard, open the sepulchres and begin to use the most cutting and awful language of condemnation to the dead bodies, because they did not speak and act as living men? O it is the living, the living shall praise the Lord; and he says, "Let the dead bury the dead, but go thou and preach the kingdom of God." I knew a minister who got into this tract of preaching not many years since, and when he was asked why he continued so severe, he said, he did so "to caution God's children, and expose the hypocrite." However, as there was no food in whipping and flogging for hungry souls to feed upon, no best robe to clothe the naked sinner, but little instruction for the inquiring soul, so no rest to the weary and heavy laden, the consequence was the ungodly and the daring hypocrites began to laugh and triumph, the seeking soul was disappointed, God's saints lamented, the minister himself grew angry and contentious, and was ultimately obliged to leave the place. Perhaps "J. K." is not so old as the raw Drillman, but he will learn in time that although physic and the rod are highly necessary in the family, yet it is wholesome food and sound instruction matures the children of Zion up to good citizens and good soldiers, and, through the blessed Spirit's teaching, they can both fight his battle and do his work; they shall most assuredly be crowned with victory at last over his and their enemies.

Now I hope, Messrs. Editors, you will publish these observations in the *Standard*, that "J. K." may peruse them, and if he drubs me he drubs me; but who can tell, perhaps, in looking over his pieces again on Reprobation and the bramble branch, where his favourite epithets appear so repeated—bastard Calvinists, dead and rotten Calvinists, more than a dozen times, he may begin to see the impropriety of such pieces, and he may think more soberly, and pray more fervently to his heavenly Father to reconcile his mind to his Lord's sovereign will and pleasure. Depend on it that an angry contentious spirit cherished will be connected with soul-sterility and dissatisfaction, even with the Lord himself, for permitting so many bastard Calvinists to overspread the land, (though we in Lincolnshire have more of the arminian tribe about us,) and what then? "J. K." should remember that this is not a time of outward persecution by fire and faggot, but a time of false profession; but the Lord will save all his ransomed family, and deliver them from all the snares of satan. "I give unto my sheep eternal life, and they shall never perish." I feel quite satisfied with these words of my Lord and Master.

I am sure he is doing all things right, and that I am safe in his hands, and not all that mortals can say will ever alter the state of my soul in his sight; blessed be his holy name, he is my rock, my refuge, my defence, yea my Lord, my life, and my everlasting dwelling place. Do not be alarmed, "J. K." nor give way to perturbation of mind; the popular parsons and gaudy professors spread over the world, they shall do God's spiritual church no real harm. I wish all God's sent servants may be preserved from committing themselves by pronouncing judgment and condemnation upon these wandering stars; leave that to the righteous Judge of all the earth, and aim ye sent ministers to feed Christ's sheep and lambs.

I subscribe myself in the best of bonds,

Your's in the Covenant of Grace,

THE DRILLMAN.

Lincolnshire, Nov. 8, 1838.

FINIS.

www.ingramcontent.com/pod-product-compliance
Lightning Source LLC
LaVergne TN
LVHW061310060426
835507LV00019B/2093